THE MODERN LIBRARY
of the World's Best Books

LEO TOLSTOY

Selected Essays

The publisher will be pleased to send, upon request,
an illustrated folder listing each volume in
THE MODERN LIBRARY

LEO
TOLSTOY
Selected Essays

Translated by Aylmer Maude

Selected *and* Introduced *by*

ERNEST J. SIMMONS

The Modern Library
New York

THE MODERN LIBRARY
is published by
RANDOM HOUSE, INC.
BENNETT CERF   DONALD S. KLOPFER

Manufactured in the United States of America

INTRODUCTION

I

When Leo Tolstoy and his three brothers were children they used to play a game which had been started by the eleven-year-old Nikolai. He possessed a wonderful secret that would make all men happy, he told them, and he had written it on a little green stick which he had buried at a certain spot by the edge of the road in the Zakaz forest near their house at Yasnaya Polyana. By performing special tasks his younger brothers would one day learn the secret. Huddled together in a shelter made of boxes and chairs covered with shawls, the children would talk fervently about the mysterious secret written on the green stick. When it became generally known, they decided, it would bring about a Golden Age on earth. There would be no more sickness, no human misery, no anger, and all would love one another.

Tolstoy never forgot this childhood game which may be said to mark the beginning of his lifelong quest for the secret of earthly happiness. That is, the search did not begin, as is commonly supposed, at the time of his intense spiritual experience at the age of fifty. Throughout his early years and during the period of writing *War and Peace* and *Anna Karenina*, his diary, letters, and even his fiction contain abundant evidence of a preoccupation with religious and moral problems. To cite just one of numerous examples, at the age of twenty-seven he entered in his diary: "Yesterday a conversation about divinity and faith suggested to me a great, a stupendous idea to the realization of which I feel capable of dedicating my whole life. This is the idea—the founding of a new religion corresponding to the development of mankind: the religion of Christ, but purged of all dogma and mystery, a practical religion, not promising future bliss but realizing bliss on earth. I understand that to bring this idea to fulfillment the conscientious labor of generations towards this end will be necessary."

There can be no question, however, that shortly after finishing *Anna Karenina* in 1877, Tolstoy experienced a shattering moral and spiritual crisis which brought him to the verge of suicide. *Confession,* one of the noblest utterances of man, is the chronicle of his doubts and merciless self-examination. He admitted that he had everything to live for—a loving wife, family, wealth, fame, and good health. Yet life seemed stupid, a spiteful joke that someone had played on him. Why should he go on living, he asked himself? Did life have any meaning which inevitable death did not destroy?

In a prolonged effort to resolve his doubts, Tolstoy devoted the next ten years to an exhaustive study of the works of renowned thinkers and the great religions of the world, especially Christianity. In general he came to the conclusion that the teachings of the Christian churches consisted of meaningless verbiage and incredible statements which afforded no satisfactory direction to man. But in the thoughts of Christ, corrected as he felt they should be if they were to retain their original substance, he discovered an answer to his question about the meaning of life. To put his conclusion in very simple form: the purpose of life on earth is to serve not our lower animal nature, but the power to which our higher nature recognizes its kinship. There is a power in each of us, he asserted, enabling us to discern what is good, and we are in touch with that power. Our reason and conscience flow from it, and the purpose of our conscious life is to do its will, that is, to do good. This is the purpose of life which Tolstoy finally accepted.

In the Gospels, specifically in the Sermon on the Mount, Tolstoy sought light on the practical application of this purpose in daily living. From the commandments he extracted five which, he maintained, were the true utterances of Christ. Set down in brief form they are: Do not be angry; do not lust; do not bind yourself by oaths; resist not him who is evil; be good to the just and the unjust. All of Tolstoy's future teaching, as well as his own behavior, were guided by these commandments.

Tolstoy's new convictions drove him into a comprehensive examination of the whole organization of modern society. His findings astonished many, and convinced others that he was somewhat insane and government authorities that he was a dangerous threat to established order. To his own satisfaction at least, Tolstoy proved that modern religious faith as preached by the churches amounted to a belief in what one knew to be untrue. The Russian Church replied by excommunicating him. Next the institutions of government came under his lash. The result was their theoretic destruction. For a man who will take no oaths, that is, will not submit his will to another, who will not resist evil by force, and who loves all nations and peoples equally and will not punish the just or the unjust, such a man obviously can take no part in war, be patriotic, or hold property, since force is necessary to protect it.

In essence, during the last thirty years of his life Tolstoy labored mightily toward the realization on earth of the kingdom of God, which for him meant the kingdom of truth and good. He did not demand that men be truthful and do good in order to achieve a personal immortality, but because this was the fullest expression of their own personalities and the only way that peace and happiness could be achieved. He saw in the simple tillers of the soil, the hewers of wood, and the drawers of water a deeper understanding of the meaning of life, of goodness, and of truth. Organized government was for him a vast conspiracy against man, designed to exploit his labor, corrupt his soul, and murder him in the violence of war. He fully realized that the end he sought belonged to a distant millennium, but this did not prevent him from devoting all his extraordinary intellectual and artistic powers to denouncing nearly every aspect of modern society which he considered a violation of the natural rights of man.

II

It is difficult for us today to believe that Tolstoy was at one time regarded as the conscience of humanity, the greatest single moral force in the world during the last years of the nineteenth century. This internationally famous author of fiction who had suddenly become an advocate of a new way of life, probing fearlessly into vital moral, social, political, and artistic problems of his time, won thousands of adherents who set up organizations to carry out his beliefs, although he discouraged any "church" in his name, learned to detest Tolstoyans, and once sadly confessed that the spirit of stupidity as well as the spirit of God lived in every man. Lenin proclaimed him "the mirror of the Russian revolution," and the fearful government of the tsars, unwilling to risk universal indignation by making a martyr of him, contented itself with jailing his followers and forbidding the publication of his "treasonable" books and pamphlets.

Actually Tolstoy's writings on these matters were extensive, including at least a half-dozen full-length books, numerous brochures and articles, and scores of lengthy letters which in effect were essays on special problems raised by correspondents. And all this writing went on and much more of a purely creative kind while he was fantastically busy with many civic and family concerns, receiving endless visitors from all over the world, and hardly ever free from governmental harassment and persecution. Few of his works on nonliterary themes were permitted publication in Russia, though many were widely circulated in clandestine hectographed and mimeographed copies. The bulk of them were sent out of the country and published abroad which resulted in printing errors and mutilated texts. Not until the authoritative Centenary Edition, edited by Aylmer Maude, whose admirable translations are used in the present collection, did English readers obtain a reasonably complete and correct understanding of the development of Tolstoy's philosophy of life.

However one may regard Tolstoy's often highly original views, the various problems he wrote about have a striking relevance to burning issues today: The Modernist movement in religion, war, peace and peace conferences, disarmament, nonviolence, underprivileged people, colonialism, civil liberties and civil disobedience, capital punishment, governmental coercion, alcoholism, the perils of smoking, and mass art. Perhaps we have something to learn from his abrasive ideas and uncompromising stands on such matters. At least one thing we may learn is the little progress that has been made over the last sixty or more years in solving these problems; on the resolution of some of them the future of our civilization depends. However, a few of his solutions, which were ridiculed as hopeless Tolstoyan ideals in his own day, have ceased to be regarded as idealistic when realized in our day. Thus Gandhi, who listed himself as a humble follower of Tolstoy, was influenced by his teaching in mounting the nonviolent civil-disobedience campaign which contributed so much to winning Indian independence. And these same methods are proving their worth in the American Negro struggle against a denial of civil rights. Though Tolstoy's beliefs, derived primarily from the teachings of Christianity, have so often been dismissed as of no consequence precisely by the Christian West, they are much alive in the non-Christian East, especially in India, where the mass movement Sarvodaya aims at the creation of a social order based on the Tolstoyan principle of love inspired by nonresistance or nonviolence.

The manifest importance of Tolstoy's views today has inspired this effort to present them within the relatively short compass of a single volume, in which an attempt is made to emphasize the sequential development of his thinking on major religious, moral, social, and political problems. Some of these subjects have been treated at great length in Tolstoy's books—*Confession, On Life, The Kingdom of God Is Within You, What I Believe,* and *What Then Must We Do?* Of course, no student of his thought should neglect these famous works. But a careful selection of his shorter pieces provides an opportunity to offer a more comprehensive impression of the total range of his thought than any one of these separate volumes does, and chronologically the shorter pieces have the advantage of representing the final form his views took on some of these subjects.

It is probably true that if Tolstoy had not first published his celebrated novels, the numerous didactic works that followed would not have received the widespread attention they did. In sheer writing skill, however, most of them can stand on their own merits. That is, it would be a mistake to imagine that they lack elements of the rich art and vision of life of the master novelist. For the remarkable persuasiveness of the best of these moral and religious writings depends in large measure on Tolstoy's matter-of-fact imagination and that quality of his fiction which reveals a natural concern for the universal activities of humanity. The ruthless realism and brilliant descriptive powers of his fiction are frequently carried over into this nonfiction, and his agonizing search in it for the moral law that will determine the course of his own life is really a continuation of the intense artistic preoccupation with the moral laws that guide the lives of the great characters of his novels.

The selections in the present volume are arranged under three broad headings in order to provide a schema for convenient thematic reference and also to bring out the scope and development of Tolstoy's views on the subject matter indicated in each of the divisions. In the first, on religion, the "Preface" to his unfinished *Christian Teaching*, an attempt to state his religious perception in systematic form, recapitulates in a concise manner the doubts and difficulties Tolstoy experienced in arriving at his beliefs. In a sense it is a kind of later summary of the detailed account in *Confession* and hence provides an effective brief introduction to his whole treatment of religion.

In *Religion and Morality* Tolstoy examines several religions in an effort to answer the frequent query of what religion is and whether morality can exist independently of it. He concludes that the relation which man establishes between his individual personality and the infinite universe or its Source is religion and that it cannot exist apart from morality which is an outgrowth of this relation and the ever-present guide to life.

Tolstoy's rationalism, his emphasis on the primacy of reason in any concern with faith, is stressed in the succinct treatment of *Reason and Religion*. There he underscores the point by his characteristic insistence that every man should do his own thinking and not let others do it for him.

The *Reply to the Synod's Edict of Excommunication* is a dignified and impressive rejoinder to the Russian Orthodox Church's exclusion of Tolstoy from its membership. His fundamental differences with the Church had been a matter of public knowledge for a long time before this official separation, but he avails himself of the opportunity to restate his views on the Church and to point out in forceful language why he believes that it is the chief obstacle to those who seek a reasonable understanding of religion.

At about the same time (1902) Tolstoy completed a long essay, *What Is Religion, and Wherein Lies Its Essence?* Within its scope this work is perhaps his most conclusive, best-tempered, and persuasive treatment of the subject. He approaches it historically and reaches a definition of true religion as the relation which man, in terms of reason and knowledge, establishes with the infinite life surrounding him, and it binds him to that infinity and determines his conduct. The real essence of Christianity, he declares, is allied with the essence of all other major religions, whereas faith is neither hope nor credulity, but a special state of the soul that obliges man to do certain things.

The second grouping is on peace, a subject that commanded a great deal of Tolstoy's attention during the last years of his life. Here not only his central doctrine of non-violence is involved, but also his conviction that the amazing advances of science would be used more and more to develop frightful instruments of war to kill millions of people more expeditiously. His vigorous efforts to unmask the social, political, and economic forces that cause war and prevent peace are often most effective, but the remedies he offers appear to defy the logic of civilization's progress, although it must be realized that Tolstoy seriously questioned the validity of what is generally accepted as "modern progress."

The extensive essay, *Christianity and Patriotism,* is one of the finest of these efforts and at the same time an excellent example of his polemical skills. He begins with a shrewd and often amusing account, based on newspaper reports, of the outpouring of fraternal admiration and patriotism that gripped Russia and France on the occasion of the exchange of visits in 1893 of their respective fleets to Kronstadt and Toulon. Then Tolstoy debunks all this manufactured enthusiasm as something contrived by the two governments to enlist public support in case war breaks out between France and Germany. He indicts patriotism as a false sentiment and demonstrates that it and war have nothing in common with the true interests of the masses or with the precepts of Christianity.

"Patriotism and Government" is a shorter and more angry article, prompted by the cynicism of the peaceful professions of the great powers at the very time they are planning further strife. To deliver mankind from the ever increasing evils of growing armaments and war, Tolstoy argues, neither congresses nor conferences nor courts of arbitration will do; simply destroy those instruments of violence called governments from which humanity's greatest evils flow. To eliminate the violence of governments only one thing is needed: people should be made to realize that the feeling of patriotism, which supports violence, is a bad feeling, and, above all, is immoral. It can be eradicated, he points out, only when men are educated through Christ's teaching that it is wrong to kill. And he prophetically anticipates more terrible wars—the First World War began fourteen years later—unless universal disarmament can be achieved.

Tolstoy accepted an invitation to participate in the Eighteenth International Congress for Peace at Stockholm in August 1909, although earlier he had repeatedly refused to attend such gatherings. He now felt it his duty to use this opportunity to present his views at a world forum, and he eagerly set to work on his speech. It appears that the organizers of the Congress were more surprised than pleased by his acceptance. They had not expected this feeble old man of eighty to attend and had merely wished to use his name and receive his moral support. Their surprise turned into embarrassment when the news leaked out to the world press that Tolstoy would challenge the Congress to be honest for once and demand the abolition of all armies as the only sincere and effective way to obtain world peace. Because of health and family complications, it was unlikely that he would have attended anyway, but the Congress leaders suddenly announced that the meeting would be postponed until next year owing to a workers' strike—some newspapers flatly declared that the real reason was the fear that Tolstoy would actually appear and deliver his speech. They had cause to fear, for his "Address to the Swedish Peace Congress" is one of Tolstoy's strongest denunciations of war and of the governments that perpetuate it.

The five commandments which Tolstoy had distilled from the Gospels to guide his daily conduct and his devotion to the Christian ideal as he understood it—a renunciation of one's self in order to serve God and one's neighbor—made of his conscience a watchdog to detect the slightest intrusion of heretical thoughts or actions. In these terms he not only tried honestly to reform his own behavior, but also, through his writings, the moral, social, and political abuses of society. A selection of such works makes up the final grouping of this volume.

At the age of sixty, for example, Tolstoy finally renounced meat, alcohol, and tobacco. The next year he wrote his article, "Why Do Men Stupefy Themselves?" in which he roundly condemned drinking and smoking as habits employed by mankind to still the voice of conscience. The peasants of Yasnaya Polyana were among his first converts; they reluctantly surrendered their tobacco pouches and took the pledge not to drink and then broke it by stealth. Though Tolstoy's absolutism in these matters is discouraging, it is interesting to observe, because of his nonresistant views, that he does rule out the use of force or laws to obtain his ends, compulsions that are advanced and sometimes unsuccessfully employed to eradicate these habits in our own day.

"The First Step" is really a moral essay on right living and points out the wisdom of moving toward virtue by taking the first step up the ladder on which all other steps depend. The simple way of life which Tolstoy had begun to lead after his spiritual revelation he now advocates as the rational and

Christian way for people—taking care of all one's needs one-self and not depending on the labor of others. The final part of the essay is a powerful argument for vegetarianism. Here the novelist's art is employed in the nightmarishly realistic description of the slaughterhouse and its dumb victims, the material for which he gathered at first hand.

The third selection in this grouping is the only one in the collection drawn from a full-length book—the final chapter of *The Kingdom of God Is Within You.* It has been chosen not only because it has a unity of its own and deals with moral problems belonging to this final group of writings, but also because it is an artistic gem comparable to Tolstoy's other wonderful autobiographical works—*Confession* and *What Then Must We Do?* The core of the piece is the vividly real-istic narrative of the rich landowner who pilfers peasant wood-land and is protected in his action by the authorities. This be-comes a text for examining society's acts of violence and why men commit them. Tolstoy sees the main cause in social hy-pocrisy—the tendency of man to avoid Christian truth and hypocritically justify his evil deeds.

A moral question is again dealt with in "'Thou Shalt Not Kill,'" inspired by an anarchist's assassination of King Hum-bert of Italy. Here Tolstoy's tone becomes somewhat shrill, and his customary moral earnestness gives way to harsh criti-cism of the mighty rulers of the earth who cause the deaths of countless people without risking the indignation that swept Europe over the murder of a single king. But in the end Tolstoy draws the moral that it is just as evil for private in-dividuals to kill kings as it is for kings to send thousands of their subjects to death in wars.

In *What's To Be Done?* Tolstoy attempts to answer the question put by young radicals caught up in the turmoil of the 1905 Revolution. Since the government and the revolu-tionists who opposed it were both committed to violence, Tol-stoy's answer is that all should accept God's law to love one another, but that in any case they should not kill or attack each other's liberty.

None of Tolstoy's many articles and pamphlets on contemporary issues won for him such international *réclame* as *I Cannot Be Silent.* The emotional intensity and high serious- ness of the piece were no doubt influenced by a long series of police prosecutions of his followers for publishing, possess- ing, lending, or distributing his antigovernment writings. If these acts were crimes, he felt equally guilty, and the fact that he was not also punished tormented his conscience. Then, too, the rising incidence of executions of revolutionists and terrorists caused him much anguish. He wrote a friend: "My God, my God, these executions, prisons, jails, these exiles! And they imagine that they will improve something or other." Then came the newspaper report of the hanging of twenty peasants (actually twelve) for attacking a landowner. This was more than Tolstoy could bear and he wrote his famous article, an effort that gave him a feeling of great moral relief. Tolstoy's superb literary talent and his knowledge of human psychology and sense of drama contribute to this impressive and anguished outcry against man's inhumanity. He struck a note that won response from all thinking people. The crimes of the revolutionists, he points out, are terrible, but they do not compare with the criminality and stupidity of the organ- ized legalized violence of the government. The delusion is the same in both, he added, and the excuse is that an evil deed committed for the benefit of many ceases to be immoral. Since the government claims these executions are done for the general welfare, Tolstoy declares, then he as one of the people cannot escape the feeling that he is a participator in these horrible deeds. In the end he defies the government, promis- ing to circulate his article by every means in his power, in the hope that either these inhuman punishments may cease or that he may be sent to prison and thus be relieved of the burden of conscience that the executions are committed on his behalf. Better still, he declares, let them "put on me, as on those twelve or twenty peasants, a shroud and a cap and push me also off a bench, so that by my own weight I may tighten the well-soaped noose round my old throat."

III

It is possible that the universal deterrence of fear, which contributes to anxiety over the state of the world today, is reviving an interest in Tolstoy's conviction that the tendency to replace moral and spiritual values with technical progress is one of the main calamities of modern life. Western critics after his death usually made a sharp distinction between Tolstoy the supreme literary artist and the Tolstoy who, after his religious crisis, turned his back on art and became the cranky preacher of an uncompromising and impractical moral philosophy, a kind of latter-day prophet tiresomely warning the world that, if his prescriptions for its social ills were not heeded, the very existence of civilization would be threatened. At most they give him credit for diagnosing correctly certain of the ills of society, but they accuse him of offering incantations as cures, especially in the sense that he carried his remedies to extremes. And they point particularly to his major doctrine of nonresistance, which for Tolstoy meant that no physical force must be used to compel any man to do what he does not want to do or to make him desist from doing what he likes.

In reality, though Tolstoy was adamant about the theory and ends of his beliefs, he was anything but dogmatic concerning the means of achieving them. He fully realized that the goal he set was often perfection, and though he might be uncompromising about it as a goal, he never really expected men to achieve it. Striving for perfection became the end and the highest good in his eyes. "We search for mind, powers, goodness, perfection in all this," he wrote in his diary, "but perfection is not given to man in anything."

In general, the dualism of Tolstoy's moral and intellectual development has come to be more thoroughly understood by modern students of his thought. In his tireless search for truth, he sought for absolutes in a world of incomplete knowledge and imperfect men. His unwillingness to compromise about ends and his compulsive need to arrive at the ultimate rational explanation often led him to push theory to the limits of absurdity. Yet any systematic study of his thought reveals its relation to the concepts of nineteenth-century liberalism. He believed that the whole history of the last two thousand years has been shaped essentially by the moral development of people and the demoralization of governments. Tolstoy placed his faith in the moral development of the people as a final answer to what he regarded as the universal oppression of the many by the few. For him, the progressive movement toward a classless and stateless condition of mankind depended—contrary to the economic determinism and class struggle of Marxism—upon the growing moral perfection of each individual through observance of the supreme law of love and the consequent repudiation of every form of violence. Considered opinion today tends to place Tolstoy, despite the extremes to which he carried his rationalism, among the leading thinkers of the nineteenth century.

Tolstoy's supreme law of love, which had dimly entered his consciousness in the childhood game about the little green stick, symbolically presided over his death at the age of eighty-two. For he had asked to be buried—and so he was—in that very spot by the side of the road in the Zakaz woods where his brother Nikolai had hidden the little green stick on which was written the wonderful secret that would banish every human misery and evil and would teach all men under the wide dome of heaven to love one another.*

ERNEST J. SIMMONS

* All explanatory footnotes in the selections signed by A. M. are by Aylmer Maude; the rest, signed L. T., are by Leo Tolstoy.

CONTENTS

Introduction   **v**

On Religion

Preface to *The Christian Teaching*   3
Religion and Morality   7
Reason and Religion   33
A Reply to the Synod's Edict of Excommunication   38
What Is Religion, and Wherein Lies Its Essence?   48

On Peace

Christianity and Patriotism   97
Patriotism and Government   155
Address to the Swedish Peace Congress in 1909   178

On Moral, Political, and Social Subjects

Why Do Men Stupefy Themselves?   185
The First Step   204
Conclusion: *The Kingdom of God Is Within You*   242
'Thou Shalt Not Kill'   323
What's To Be Done?   330
I Cannot Be Silent   339

ON
RELIGION

PREFACE TO
THE CHRISTIAN TEACHING

I lived to the age of fifty thinking that the life a man lives from his birth till his death constitutes his whole existence, and that therefore his aim should be to secure happiness for this mortal life. I tried to secure that happiness, but the longer I lived the more evident it became that such happiness does not and cannot exist. The happiness I sought did not come to me, and what I did attain immediately ceased to be happiness as soon as I had attained it. My unhappiness became greater and greater and the inevitability of death more and more apparent, and I understood that in this meaningless and unhappy life nothing awaited me but sufferings, sickness, old age, and destruction. I asked myself: Why is this so? and received no reply. And I came to despair.

What some men said to me and what I myself sometimes tried to believe, namely, that one should not desire happiness for oneself alone but for others—those near to us and all men—did not satisfy me: first because I could not sincerely desire happiness for other people in the way that I did for myself, and secondly and chiefly because those others were doomed to unhappiness and death just as I was, and so all my efforts for their happiness would be in vain.

I came to despair. But I thought that my despair might be the result of my being an exceptional man, and that other men know why they live, and therefore do not despair.

I began to observe other men, but the others did not know why they were living any more than I did. They tried by the bustle of life to stifle this ignorance; some assured themselves and others that they believed in the different religions that had been instilled into them from childhood—but to believe in what they believed in was impossible, it was too stupid. Yes, and many of them, it seemed to me, only pretended to believe, while in the depth of their souls they did not do so.

I could no longer continue to absorb myself in the bustle of life: no bustle could hide the question that continually presented itself to me, and I was unable to begin to believe afresh in the faith taught me in childhood, which had dropped away from me of itself when my mind had matured. The more I studied, the more I was convinced that truth could not be there—but only hypocrisy and the mercenary aims of those who cheated the people, and the feeble-mindedness, obstinacy and fear, of those who were cheated.

Not to speak of the inner contradictions of that teaching, of its meanness and cruelty in acknowledging a God who punished men with eternal torments,[1] the chief hindrance to my believing it was that I knew that besides this Orthodox Christian teaching which asserts that it alone has the truth, there was also another, a Catholic; a third, Lutheran; and a fourth, the Reformed Church—and all had different Christian teachings while each declared that it alone had the truth. I also knew that in addition to these Christian teachings there are non-Christian religious teachings—Buddhism, Brahmanism, Mohammedanism, Confucianism, and others, which in a quite similar way consider that they alone are true and that all the other teachings are delusions.

I could not return to the faith of my childhood, nor could I believe in any of the faiths professed by other nations, for in all of them there were the same contradictions, absurdities, miracles, denials of all other faiths, and above all the same dishonest demand for blind confidence in their teaching.

So I became convinced that I should not find an answer to my question and the alleviation of my sufferings among the

---

[1] All these contradictions, absurdities, and cruelties, have been set out by me in detail in *A Criticism of Dogmatic Theology*, in which all the Church dogmas of the Orthodox theology are examined thesis by thesis.—L. T.

existing faiths, and my despair was so great that I contemplated suicide.

But then I came upon my salvation. And this salvation resulted from the fact that from childhood I had retained a dim idea that the Gospels contain a reply to my question. In their teaching—despite the perversions to which it is subjected by the doctrine of the Christian Church—I scented the truth. And I made a last attempt to solve the problem. Putting aside all interpretations, I began to read and study the Gospels and penetrate into their meaning. And the more I penetrated into their meaning the more something new manifested itself to me, quite unlike the teaching of the Christian Church, but which answered my question. And at last that reply became perfectly plain.

And that reply was not merely plain but indubitable, first because it fully coincided with the demands of my heart and my reason, and secondly because when I understood it I saw that it was not my exclusive explanation of the Gospel, as might at first appear, nor was it even an exclusive revelation of Christ's, but that it was the same reply to life's question that has been given more or less clearly by all the best representatives of humanity both before and since the Gospels— beginning with Moses, Isaiah, Confucius, the ancient Greeks, Buddha, Socrates, and down to Pascal, Spinoza, Fichte, Feuerbach, and those others—often unnoticed and undistinguished men—who without accepting any creed on faith, have sincerely thought and spoken of the meaning of life. So that in the knowledge of truth that I gathered from the Gospels, not only was I not alone, but I was in the company of all the best men of former and present times. And I became assured of this truth and was reassured, and have joyfully lived twenty years of my life since then and am now joyfully approaching my death.

And now I wish to pass on to others that reply as to the meaning of my life, which has given me such full tranquillity and joy.

By my age and the state of my health I am standing with one foot in the grave, and so human considerations have for me no importance. Even if they had, I am well aware that this exposition of my faith would not conduce to my welfare or enhance people's good opinion of me, but on the contrary could only disturb and grieve both unbelievers who demand of me works of art and not discussions of faith, and also the believers who are perturbed by everything I write about religion and scold me for it. Moreover, this writing will in all probability not become known to people till after my death.[2]

Therefore in what I am doing I am prompted not by avarice, desire for fame, or any worldly consideration, but only by fear of failing to fulfil what He who sent me into this world desires of me, and to Whom from hour to hour I await my return.

And so I ask all who may read this to read and understand what I have written, setting aside, as I have done, all worldly considerations, and keeping in view only that eternal source of truth and goodness by Whose will we have come into this world—from which, as corporal beings, we shall very soon disappear—and that they should without haste or irritation consider and understand what I have set down; and if they disagree, should correct me not with contempt and hatred but with compassion and love, and if they agree, should remember that if I speak the truth it is not mine but God's, and that it is only accidentally that a part of it has passed through me just as it passes through each of us when we become conscious of truth and transmit it.

---

[2] This remark was made in view of the fact that the publication of what Tolstóy wrote on religion was forbidden in Russia.—A. M. [First published in 1898, though written considerably earlier.]

RELIGION AND MORALITY[1]

You ask me: (1) What I understand by the word *religion*, and, (2) Is it possible to have a morality independent of *religion* in the sense in which I understand that word?

I will do my best to answer these most important and excellently-put questions.

Three different meanings are commonly given to the word *religion*.

The first is, that religion is a special and true revelation given by God to man, and is a worship of God in accord with that revelation. This meaning is given to religion by people who believe in one or other of the existing religions and who consequently consider *that* particular religion to be the only true one.

The second meaning is, that religion is a collection of certain superstitious beliefs, as well as a superstitious form of worship accordant with such beliefs. This is the meaning given to religion by unbelievers in general, or by men who do not accept the particular religion they are defining.

The third meaning is, that religion is a collection of propositions and laws devised by wise men and needed to console the common people, to restrain their passions, and to make the masses manageable. This meaning is given to religion by those who are indifferent to religion as religion but consider it a useful instrument for Governments.

Religion according to the first definition is a sure and certain truth which it is desirable and even necessary for human welfare to promulgate by all possible means.

---

[1] A reply to questions put to Tolstoy by a German Ethical Society.

According to the second definition, religion is a collection of superstitions from which it is desirable and even necessary for human welfare that man should be emancipated by all possible means.

According to the third definition, religion is a certain useful appliance, not necessary for men of high culture but indispensable for the consolation and control of the common people, and which must therefore be maintained.

The first is like the definition a man might give of music, who said that music is a particular tune—the one he knows best and is fondest of,—and that it ought to be taught to as many people as possible.

The second is like a definition given by a man who does not understand and consequently dislikes music, and who says that music is the production of sounds with one's throat or mouth, or by applying one's hands to certain instruments, and that it is a useless and even harmful occupation from which people ought to be weaned as quickly as possible.

The third is like the definition of music by a man who says it is a thing useful for the purpose of teaching dancing, and also for marching, and that it should be maintained for those purposes.

The diversity and incompleteness of all these definitions arise from the fact that they fail to grasp the essential character of music, and only define some of its traits from the definer's point of view. The same is true of the three definitions given of religion.

According to the first of them religion is something in which the definer rightly believes.

According to the second, it is something in which, according to the definer's observation, other people mistakenly believe.

According to the third, it is something the definer thinks it desirable to get other people to believe in.

In all three cases the thing defined is not the real essence of religion, but something people believe in or consider to be religion.

The first definition substitutes for the conception of religion a faith held by the definer; the second definition substitutes a faith held by other people, something they take to be religion; while the third definition substitutes people's faith in something supplied to them as religion.

But what is faith? And why do people hold the faith they do hold? What is faith, and how did it arise?

Among the great mass of the cultured crowd of to-day it is considered a settled question that the essence of every religion consists in superstitious fear, aroused by the uncomprehended phenomena of Nature, and in the personification and deification of these natural forces and the worship of them.

This opinion is credulously accepted without criticism by the cultured crowd of to-day, and not only is not refuted by the scientists, but among them it generally finds its strongest supporters. If voices are now and then raised (such as that of Max Müller and others) attributing to religion another origin and meaning, they pass almost unheard and unnoticed among the common and unanimous acknowledgement of religion in general as a manifestation of ignorance and superstition. Not long ago, at the beginning of the nineteenth century, the most advanced men—if (like the Encyclopaedists of the later part of the eighteenth century) they rejected Catholicism, Protestantism, and Russo-Greek Orthodoxy—never denied that religion in general has been, and is, an indispensable condition of life for every man. Not to mention the Deists (such as Bernardin de Saint-Pierre, Diderot, and Rousseau), Voltaire erected a monument to God, and Robespierre instituted a fête of the Supreme Being. But in our time—thanks to the frivolous and superficial teaching of Auguste Comte (who, like most Frenchmen, really believed Christianity to be the same thing as Catholicism and saw in Catholicism the complete realization of Christianity)—it has been decided and taken for granted by the cultured crowd (always eager and prompt to accept the lowest view) that religion is only one special, long-outlived phase in the development of humanity, and a hindrance to its further progress. It is taken for granted that humanity has passed through two stages, the religious and the metaphysical, and has now entered on a third and highest one—

the scientific—and that all religious manifestations among men are mere survivals of humanity's spiritual organ, which, like the fifth toe-nail of the horse, has long lost all meaning or importance.

It is taken for granted that the essence of religion lies in fear evoked by the unknown forces of Nature, in belief in imaginary beings and in worship of them, as in ancient times Democritus supposed and as the latest philosophers and historians of religion assert.

But apart from the consideration that belief in invisible, supernatural beings, or in one such being, does not always proceed from fear of the unknown forces of nature—as we see in the case of hundreds of the most advanced and highly-educated men of former times (Socrates, Descartes, Newton) as well as of our own day, whose recognition of the existence of a supreme, supernatural being certainly did not proceed from fear of the unknown forces of Nature—the assertion that religion arose from men's superstitious fear of the mysterious forces of Nature really affords no answer to the main question, 'What was it in men that gave them the conception of unseen, supernatural beings?'

If men feared thunder and lightning, they feared them as thunder and lightning; but why should they invent some invisible, supernatural being, Jupiter, who lives somewhere or other and sometimes throws arrows at people?

Men struck by the sight of death would fear death; but why should they invent souls of the dead with whom they entered into imaginary intercourse? From thunder men might hide. Fear of death might make them try to escape death. But if they invented an eternal and powerful being on whom they supposed themselves to depend, and if they invented live souls for dead people, they did this not simply from fear but for some other reasons. And in those reasons, evidently, lay the essence of the thing we call religion.

Moreover every man who has ever, even in childhood, experienced religious feeling, knows by personal experience that it was evoked in him, not by external, terrifying, material phenomena, but by an inner consciousness which had nothing

to do with fear of the unknown forces of Nature—a consciousness of his own insignificance, loneliness, and guilt. And therefore, both by external observation and by personal experience,
man may know that religion is not the worship of gods, evoked
by superstitious fear of the invisible forces of Nature, proper
to men only at a certain period of their development, but
is something quite independent either of fear or of their
degree of education—a something that cannot be destroyed
by any development of culture. For man's consciousness of his
finiteness amid an infinite universe, and of his sinfulness (i.e.,
of his not having done all he might and should have done)
has always existed and will exist as long as man remains man.

Indeed everyone on emerging from the animal conditions of
infancy and earliest childhood when he lives guided only by
the demands of his animal nature—everyone on awakening
to rational consciousness cannot but notice that all around
him lives, renewing itself undestroyed, and infallibly conforming to one definite, eternal law: and that he alone, recognizing
himself as a being separate from the rest of the universe, is
sentenced to die, to disappear into infinite space and endless
time, and to suffer a tormenting consciousness of responsibility for his actions—i.e., the consciousness that having acted
badly he could have done better. And understanding this, no
reasonable man can help pausing to ask himself, 'What is the
meaning of my momentary, uncertain, and unstable existence
amid this eternal, firmly defined and unending universe?' Entering on truly human life a man cannot evade that question.

That question faces every man, and in one way or other every man answers it. And in the reply to that question lies the
essence of every religion. The essence of religion consists
solely in the answer to the question, 'Why do I live, and what
is my relation to the infinite universe[2] around me?'

All the metaphysics of religion, all the doctrines about dei-
ties and about the origin of the world, and all external worship—which are usually supposed to be religion—are but

___

[2] 'Universe' is used here and elsewhere in its primary significance,
embracing the totality of existing things, spiritual or material.—
A. M.

indications (differing according to geographical, ethnographical, and historical circumstances) of the existence of religion. There is no religion from the most elevated to the coarsest that has not at its root this establishing of man's relation to the surrounding universe or to its first cause. There is no religious rite however coarse, nor any cult however refined, that has not this at its root. Every religious teaching is the expression which the founder of that religion has given of the relation he considered himself (and consequently all other people also) to occupy as a man towards the universe and its origin and first cause.

The expressions of these relations are very numerous, corresponding to the different ethnographical and historical conditions of the founders of these religions and the nations that adopted them. Moreover all these expressions are variously interpreted and perverted by the followers of teachers who were usually hundreds, and sometimes thousands, of years ahead of the comprehension of the masses. And so these relations of man to the universe—i.e. to religion—appear to be very numerous, though in reality there are only three fundamental relations in which men stand towards the universe and its author. They are: (1) The primitive, personal relation; (2) the pagan, social or family-State relation; (3) the Christian or divine relation.

Strictly speaking, there are only two fundamental relations in which man can stand towards the world: the *Personal*, which sees the meaning of life in personal well-being, obtained separately or in union with other individuals; and the *Christian*, which sees the meaning of life to consist in service of him who sent man into the world. The second of the three divisions mentioned in the first classification—the social—is really only an extension of the first.

The first of these perceptions, the oldest—now found among people on the lowest plane of moral development—consists in man considering himself to be a self-motivated being, living in the world to obtain the greatest possible personal happiness regardless of the suffering such attainment may cause to others.

From this very primitive relation to the world (a relation in which every infant lives on first entering the world; in which humanity lived during the first, pagan, period of its development, and in which many of the morally-coarsest individuals and savage tribes still live) flowed the ancient pagan religions as well as the lowest forms of the later religions: Buddhism,[3] Taoism, Mohammedanism, and Christianity, in their perverted forms. From this relation to the world comes also modern Spiritualism, which has at its root a desire for the preservation and well-being of one's personality. All the pagan cults: divinations, the deification of beings who enjoy themselves like man, Saints who intercede for man, all sacrifices and prayers offered for man's earthly welfare and for deliverance from calamities—come from this conception of life.

The second form of the pagan relation of man to the world, the social, which he adopts at the next stage of development —a relation natural chiefly to adults—consists in seeing the meaning of life not in the welfare of one separate individual, but in the welfare of a group of individuals: a family, clan, nation, empire, or even of all humanity (as in the Positivist's attempt to found a religion).

In this relation of man to the world the meaning of life is transferred from the individual to a family, clan, nation, or empire—to a certain association of individuals whose welfare is considered to be the aim of existence. From this view come all religions of the patriarchal and social type: the Chinese and Japanese religions, the Jewish religion of a 'chosen people', the Roman State-religion, our Church and State religion (improperly called Christian but degraded to this level by Augustine), and the proposed Positivist religion of Humanity.

---

[3] Buddhism, though demanding from its followers the renunciation of world blessings and even of life itself, is based on the same relation of a self-motivated personality (predestined to personal well-being) to the surrounding universe, but with this difference—that simple paganism considers man to have a right to happiness, while Buddhism considers that the world ought to disappear because it produces suffering to the personality. Buddhism is negative paganism.—L. T.

All the ceremonies of ancestor-worship in China and Japan; the worship of Emperors in Rome; the multitudinous Jewish ceremonials aiming at the preservation of an agreement between the chosen people and God; all family, social, and Church-Christian prayers for the welfare of the State or for success in war—rest on that understanding of man's relation to the universe.

The third conception of this relation, the Christian—of which all old men are involuntarily conscious and into which, in my opinion, humanity is now entering—consists in the meaning of life no longer appearing to lie in the attainment of personal aims or the aims of any association of individuals, but solely in serving that Will which has produced man and the entire universe not for man's aims but for its own.

From this relation to the world comes the highest religious teaching known to us, germs of which existed already among the Pythagoreans, Therapeutae, Essenes, and among the Egyptians, Persians, Brahmins, Buddhists, and Taoists, in their best representatives, but which received its complete and final expression only in Christianity in its true and unperverted meaning. All the ritual of those ancient religions that proceeded from this understanding of life, and in our time all the external forms of worship among the Unitarians, Universalists, Quakers, Serbian Nazarenes, Russian Dukhobórs, and all the so-called rationalistic sects: their sermons, hymns, conferences and books, are religious manifestations of this relation of man to the universe.

All possible religions of whatever kind can, by the nature of the case, be classed according to these three ways of regarding the universe.

Every man who has emerged from the animal state inevitably adopts the first, or the second, or the third, of these relations, and that is what constitutes each man's true religion no matter to what faith he may nominally belong.

Every man necessarily conceives some relation between himself and the universe, for an intelligent being cannot live in the universe that surrounds him without having some relation to it. And since man has as yet devised but three relations

that we know of to the universe—it follows that every man
inevitably holds one of these three, and whether he wishes to
or not, belongs to one of the three fundamental religions
among which the human race is divided.

Therefore the assertion, very common among the cultured
crowd of Christendom, that they have risen to such a height
of development that they no longer need or possess any religion, only amounts to this—that repudiating the Christian religion which is the only one natural to our time, they hold
to the lower, social, family, State religion, or to the primitive
pagan religion, without being aware of the fact. A man without a religion—i.e., without any relation to the universe—is as
impossible as a man without a heart. He may not know he has
a religion, just as a man may not know he has a heart, but he
can no more exist without a religion than without a heart.

Religion is the relation in which a man acknowledges himself to stand towards the infinite universe around him or towards its source and first cause, and a rational man must have
some relation to them.

But you will perhaps say that to define man's relation to
the universe is not the affair of religion but of philosophy, or
of science in general if one includes philosophy as part of science. I do not think so. On the contrary I think that the supposition that science in its widest sense, including philosophy
as part of it, can define man's relation to the universe is quite
erroneous, and that this supposition is the chief cause of the
confusion concerning religion, science, and morality, which
prevails among the cultured classes of our society.

Science, including philosophy, cannot define man's relation
to the infinite universe or its source were it only for this reason
—that before any philosophy or science could arise, *that* must
already have existed without which no activity of thought or
relation of any kind between man and the universe, is possible.

a man cannot by any possible motion discover in which
he ought to move, and yet every movement is nec-
med in some direction, so also it is impossible by
philosophy or science to discover the direction
forts should be performed, and yet all mental

effort is necessarily performed in some direction that has been predetermined for it. And it is religion that always indicates this direction for all mental work. All known philosophers, from Plato to Schopenhauer, have always and inevitably followed a direction given them by religion. The philosophy of Plato and his followers was a pagan philosophy which examined the means of obtaining the greatest possible well-being for separate individuals and for an association of individuals in a State. The Church-Christian philosophy of the Middle Ages, proceeding from a similar pagan conception of life, investigated ways of obtaining salvation for the individual— that is, ways of obtaining the greatest personal welfare in a future life, and only in its theocratic attempts did it treat of arrangements for the welfare of society.

Modern philosophy, both Hegel's and Comte's, has at its root the State-social religious conception of life. The pessimistic philosophy of Schopenhauer and Hartmann, wishing to free itself from Judaeo-religious cosmology, involuntarily adopted the religious basis of Buddhism.

Philosophy always has been, and always will be, simply the investigation of the consequences that result from the relation religion establishes between man and the universe, for until that relation is settled there is nothing on which philosophy can work.

So also with positive science in the restricted meaning of the word. Such science always has been, and always will be, merely the investigation and study of all such objects and phenomena as, in consequence of a certain relation religion has set up between man and the universe, appear to demand investigation.

Science always has been and will be, not the study of 'everything', as scientists now naïvely suppose (that is impossible, for there are an incalculable quantity of objects that might be studied), but only of such things as religion (in due order and according to their degree of im from among the incalculable quantity of objects and conditions, awaiting examination. And ther not one and indivisible, but there are as n there are religions. Each religion selects a range of objects for investigation, and therefore the science of each different time and people inevitably bears the character of the religion from whose point of view it sees its objects.

Thus pagan science, re-established at the Renaissance and now flourishing in our society under the title of Christian, always was, and continues to be, merely an investigation of all those conditions from which man may obtain the greatest welfare, and of all such phenomena as can be made to promote that end. Brahman and Buddhist philosophic science was always merely the investigation of those conditions under which man escapes from the sufferings that oppress him. Hebrew science (the Talmud) was always merely the study and explanation of the conditions which man had to observe in order to fulfil his contract with God and to keep the chosen people at the height of their vocation. Church-Christian science has been and is an investigation of the conditions under which salvation can be obtained by man. True Christian science, such as is only now being born, is an investigation of the conditions enabling man to know the demands of the Supreme Will from whence he came, and how to apply those demands to life.

Neither philosophy nor science can establish man's relation to the universe, for that relation must be established before any philosophy or science can begin. They cannot do it for this further reason—that science, including philosophy as part of it, investigates phenomena intellectually—independently of the investigator's position or the feelings he experiences. But man's relation to the world is defined not by intellect alone but also by feeling and the whole combination of his spiritual forces. However much you may assure a man and explain to him, that all that truly exists is only idea; or that everything consists of atoms; or that the essence of life is substance, or will; or that heat, light, movement and electricity are different manifestations of one and the same energy; to a being who feels, suffers, rejoices, fears and hopes, it will all fail to explain his place in the universe.

That place, and consequently his relation to the universe,

is shown to him by religion, which says to him: 'The world exists for you, therefore take from life all you can get from it,' or: 'You are a member of a chosen nation loved by God, therefore serve that nation, do all that God has demanded, and you together with your nation will receive the greatest welfare obtainable,' or: 'You are an instrument of the Supreme Will which has sent you into the world to perform an appointed task; learn that Will and fulfil it and you will do for yourself the best it is possible for you to do.'

To understand the statements of philosophy and science, preparation and study are necessary, but for religious comprehension they are not necessary: it is given to everyone, even to the most limited and ignorant of men.

For a man to know his relation to the world around him or to its source, he needs neither philosophic nor scientific knowledge (an abundance of knowledge burdening the consciousness is rather a hindrance), but he needs, if but for a time, to renounce the cares of the world, to have a consciousness of his material insignificance, and to have sincerity—conditions most often met with (as is said in the Gospels) among children and among the plainest, unlearned folk. That is why we often see that the simplest, least-learned, and least-educated people quite clearly, consciously, and easily, assimilate the highest Christian understanding of life, while very learned and cultured men continue to stagnate in crude paganism. So, for instance, there are most refined and highly educated people who see the meaning of life in personal enjoyment or in avoidance of suffering, as did the very wise and highly educated Schopenhauer, or in the salvation of the soul by Sacraments and means of grace, as highly educated Bishops have done, while an almost illiterate Russian peasant sectarian sees the meaning of life, without any mental effort, as it was seen by the greatest sages of the world (Epictetus, Marcus Aurelius, Seneca)—in acknowledging oneself an instrument of God's will, a son of God.

But you will ask me: 'What is the essence of this non-philosophic, non-scientific kind of knowledge? If it is neither philosophic nor scientific, what is it? How is it definable?' To these questions I can only reply that, as religious knowledge is that on which all other knowledge rests, and as it precedes all other knowledge, we cannot define it, for we have no means enabling us to do so. In theological language this knowledge is called revelation and, if one does not attach a mystic meaning to the word 'revelation', that term is quite correct; for this knowledge is not obtained by study, nor by the efforts of one man or of many men, but only by one man or many men accepting that manifestation of infinite wisdom, which is gradually revealing itself to mankind.

Why were people unable, ten thousand years ago, to understand that the meaning of life is not limited to the welfare of one's personality, and why did a time come when a higher understanding of life—the family, social, national, State understanding of life—was revealed to them? Why, within historic memory, was the Christian view of life disclosed to men? And why was it disclosed to this man or that people in particular, and why precisely at such a time in one and not in another form? To try to answer these questions by seeking for reasons in the historic conditions of the time, life, and character and special qualities of those who first made this view of life their own and first expressed it, is like trying to answer the question, 'Why does the rising sun light up some objects before reaching others?' The sun of truth rising higher and higher over the world lights up more and more of it, and is reflected first by those objects which are first reached by its illuminating rays and are best fitted to reflect them. But the qualities which make some men more suited to receive the rising truth are not any special active qualities of mind, but on the contrary are passive qualities of heart, rarely coinciding with great and inquisitive intellect: renunciation of the cares of the world, consciousness of one's own material insignificance, and great sincerity, as we see exemplified by all the founders of religion, who were never remarkable either for philosophic or scientific erudition.

In my opinion the chief mistake, and the one which more than any other hinders the true progress of our Christian branch of humanity, lies in the fact that the scientists (who now occupy the seat of Moses)—guiding themselves by the pagan view of life re-established at the time of the Renaissance, and accepting as the essence of Christianity something that is really a rude perversion of it—have decided that Christianity is a condition humanity has outlived, and that the ancient, pagan, State-social view of life held by them (one that is really worn out) is the very highest understanding of life and the one humanity should persistently cling to. Holding this view, they not only do not understand Christianity—that highest view of life humanity is approaching— but they do not even try to understand it.

The chief source of this misunderstanding lies in the fact that the scientists, parting company with Christianity and recognizing that their science does not accord with it, have decided that the fault lies with Christianity and not with their science. That is to say, they are pleased to believe not what is really the case, that their science is eighteen hundred years behind Christianity, which already influences a large part of contemporary society, but that Christianity has lagged eighteen hundred years behind science.

From this reversal of roles comes the astonishing fact that no people have a more confused conception of the essence and true importance of religion, of morality, or of life, than scientists; and the yet more astonishing fact that the science of to-day—while accomplishing really great success in investigating the phenomena of the material world—turns out to be of no use for the direction of human life, or even does actual harm.

And therefore I think that certainly it is neither philosophy nor science that determines man's relation to the universe, but it is *always religion*.

So to your first question, 'What do I understand by the word *religion*,' I reply: *Religion is a relation man sets up between himself and the endless and infinite universe, or its source and first cause.*

From this answer to the first question the answer to the second follows naturally.

If religion is a relation man establishes towards the universe—a relation which determines the meaning of life—then *morality* is the indication and explanation of such human activity as naturally results from men holding this or that relation towards the universe. And as only two such fundamental relations are known to us, if we consider the pagan, social relation as an enlargement of the personal, or three if we count the social, pagan relation separately—it follows that only three moral teachings exist: the primitive, savage, personal; the pagan, family, State, or social; and the Christian or divine teaching of service to man or to God.

From the first of these relations of man to the universe flows the teaching of morality common to all pagan religions that have at their base the striving after welfare for the separate individual, and that therefore define all the conditions yielding most welfare to the individual and indicate means to obtain such welfare. From this relation to the world flow the pagan teachings: the Epicurean in its lowest form; the Mohammedan teaching of morality which promises coarse personal welfare in this and the next world; the Church-Christian teaching of morality aiming at salvation —that is, at the welfare of one's personality, especially in the other world; and also the worldly utilitarian morality aiming at the welfare of the individual only in this world.

From the same teaching, which places the aim of life in personal welfare and therefore in freedom from personal suffering, flow the moral teaching of Buddhism in its crude form and the worldly doctrine of the pessimist.

From the second, pagan relation of man to the universe, which sees the aim of life in securing welfare for a group of individuals, flow the moral teachings which demand that man should serve the group whose welfare is regarded as the aim of life. According to that teaching personal welfare is only allowable to the extent to which it can be obtained for the whole group of people who form the religious basis of life. From that relation to the universe flow the well-known Roman and Greek moral teachings in which personality always sacrifices itself for society, and also the Chinese morality. From this relation flows also the Jewish morality—the

subordination of one's own welfare to that of the chosen people—and also the Church and State morality of our own
times, which demands the sacrifice of the individual for the
good of the State. From this relation to the universe flows
also the morality of most women, who sacrifice their whole
personality for the benefit of their family and especially for
their children.

All ancient history, and to some extent medieval and modern history, teems with descriptions of deeds of just this family, social, or State morality. And the majority of people to-
day—though they think their morality is Christian because
they profess Christianity—really hold this family, State, pagan
morality, and hold it up as an ideal when educating the
young generation.

From the third, the Christian, relation to the universe—
which consists in man's considering himself to be an instrument of the Supreme Will for the accomplishment of its ends
—flow the moral teachings which correspond to that understanding of life, elucidating man's dependence on the Supreme Will and defining its demands. From that relation of
man to the universe flow all the highest moral teachings
known to man: the Pythagorean, the Stoic, the Buddhist, the
Brahminical, and the Taoist, in their highest manifestations.
and the Christian teaching in its real meaning, demanding
renunciation of one's personal will—and not only of one's
own welfare, but even of that of one's family, society, and
country—for the sake of fulfilling the will of him who sent us
into a life; a will revealed by our conscience. From the first,
the second, or the third of these relations to the infinite
universe or to its source, flows each man's real, unfeigned
morality, no matter what he may profess or preach as morality or in what light he may wish to appear.

So that a man who considers the reality of his relation to
the universe to lie in obtaining the greatest welfare for himself—however much he may say he considers it moral to live
for his family, for society, for the State, for humanity, or for
the performance of God's will—and however artfully he may
pretend and may deceive men, will still always have as his

real motive of action simply his individual welfare; so that when a choice has to be made he will not sacrifice his own personality for his family or State, nor to do the will of God, but will sacrifice them all for his own sake. Since he sees the meaning of life only in personal welfare he cannot do otherwise until such time as he alters his relation to the universe.

And similarly one whose relation to life consists in the service of his own family (as is the case with most women), or of his clan or nation (as among members of the oppressed nationalities and among men politically active in times of strife)—no matter how much he may declare himself to be a Christian, his morality will always be family or national and not Christian, and when any conflict arises between family or social welfare on one side, and that of his personality or the fulfilment of the will of God on the other, he will inevitably choose the service of the group for whom, in his view of life, he exists: for only in such service does he see the meaning of his life. And in the same way a man who regards his relation to the world as consisting in fulfilling the will of Him who sent him hither—however much you may impress upon him that he should (in accord with the demands of his personality, or of his family, his nation, empire, or all humanity) commit acts contrary to the Supreme Will of which the operation of the reason and love wherewith he is endowed makes him aware—will always sacrifice all human ties rather than fail to comply with the Will that has sent him here: for only in such compliance does he discern a meaning for his life.

Morality cannot be independent of religion, for not only is it a consequence of religion—that is, a consequence of the relation in which a man feels that he stands towards the universe—but it is implicit (*impliquée*, as the French say) in religion. Every religion is an answer to the question: 'What is the meaning of my life?' And the religious answer involves a certain moral demand, which may follow or may precede the explanation of the meaning of life. To the question, 'What is the meaning of life?' the reply may be: 'The meaning of life lies in the welfare of the individual, therefore make use of all the advantages within your reach'; or, 'The meaning of life lies in the welfare of a certain group of people, therefore serve that group with all your strength'; or, 'The meaning of life lies in fulfilling the will of Him that sent you, therefore try with all your strength to know that will and to fulfil it.' Or the same question may be answered in this way: 'The meaning of your life lies in your personal enjoyment, for that is the object of man's existence'; 'The meaning of your life lies in serving the group of which you consider yourself a member, for that is your destiny'; or, 'The meaning of your life lies in the service of God, for that is your destiny.'

Morality is included in the explanation of the meaning of life that religion gives, and can therefore in no way be separated from religion. This truth is particularly evident in the attempts of non-Christian philosophers to deduce a doctrine of the highest morality from their philosophy. Such philosophers see that Christian morality is indispensable, that we cannot live without it; they even see that it is an already existing fact, and they want to find some way to attach it to their non-Christian philosophy and even to put things in such a way that Christian morality may seem to result from their pagan social philosophy. That is what they attempt, but their very efforts show more clearly than anything else that Christian morality is not merely independent of pagan philosophy, but that it stands in complete contradiction to that philosophy of individual welfare, or of liberation from individual suffering, or of social welfare.

The Christian ethics, which in accord with our religious conception of life we acknowledge, demand not only the sacrifice of one's personality for the group, but the renunciation alike of one's personality and of one's group for the service of God; but pagan philosophy only investigates means of obtaining the greatest welfare for the individual or for the group of individuals, and therefore a contrast is inevitable. And there is only one way of hiding this contrast—namely, by piling up abstract conditional conceptions one on another, and keeping to the misty domain of metaphysics.

That is what most of the post-Renaissance philosophers have done, and to this circumstance—the impossibility of making the demands of Christian morality (which have been admitted in advance) accord with a philosophy built on pagan foundations—must be attributed the terrible unreality, obscurity, unintelligibility, and estrangement from life, that characterizes modern philosophy. With the exception of Spinoza (whose philosophy develops from truly Christian roots in spite of the fact that he did not consider himself a Christian) and Kant (a man of genius, who admittedly treated his system of ethics as not dependent on his metaphysics), all the philosophers, even the brilliant Schopenhauer, evidently devised artificial connexions between their ethics and their metaphysics.

It is felt that Christian ethics are something that must be accepted in advance, standing quite firmly, not dependent on philosophy and in no need of the fictitious props put to support them; and it is felt that Philosophy merely devises certain propositions in order that ethics may not contradict her but may rather be bound to her and appear to flow from her. All such propositions, however, only appear to justify Christian ethics while they are considered in the abstract. As soon as they are applied to questions of practical life, the non-correspondence, and more, the evident contradiction between the philosophic basis and what we consider to be morality, appears in full strength.

The unfortunate Nietzsche, who has latterly become so celebrated, rendered a valuable service by his exposure of this contradiction. He is incontrovertible when he says that all rules of morality, from the point of view of the current non-Christian philosophy, are mere lies and hypocrisy and that it is much more profitable, pleasant and reasonable, for a man to devise his own Supermen (Uebermenschen) and be one of them, than to be one of the mass which has to serve as the scaffold for these Supermen. No philosophical constructions founded on the pagan-religious view of life can prove to anyone that it is more profitable or wiser for him to live, not for a welfare he desires, comprehends, and sees to be possible for himself or for his family or his society, but for another's welfare—undesired, not understood, and unattainable by his puny human power. Philosophy founded on an understanding of life limited to the welfare of man will never be able to prove to a rational man, who knows that he may die at any moment, that he ought, and that it is good for him to forgo his own desired, understood, and undoubted welfare—not even for any certain welfare to others (for he can never know what will result from his sacrifices), but merely because it is right or good to do so: that it is a categorical imperative.

To prove this from the point of view of pagan philosophy is impossible. To prove that people are all equal—that it is better for a man to sacrifice his life in the service of others than to trample on the lives of others, making them serve him—one must redefine one's relation to the universe: one must prove that man's position is such that he has no option, since the meaning of his life lies only in the execution of the will of Him that sent him, and the will of Him that sent him is that he should give his life to the service of men. And such a change in man's relation to the universe comes only from religion.

Thus it is with the attempts to deduce Christian morality from, and to reconcile it with, the fundamental positions of pagan science. No sophistries or subtleties of thought can destroy this simple and clear position, that the law of evolution, which lies at the base of all the science of to-day, is founded on a general, eternal, and unalterable law—the law of the struggle for existence and the survival of the fittest; and that therefore each man, to attain his own and his group's welfare, should try to be that 'fittest' and to make his group such, in order that he and his group should not perish, but some other man or group that is less fit.

However much some naturalists, frightened by the logical consequences of this law and by their application to human life, may try to perplex the matter with words and to exorcise this law—their efforts only make still more evident the irresistibility of that law, which rules the life of the whole organic world, and therefore that of man regarded as an animal.

Since I began writing this article, a Russian translation has appeared of an article by Mr. Huxley, composed of a speech on Evolution and Ethics[4] delivered by him to some English Society. In this article the learned Professor—like our well-known Professor Bekétov and many others who have written on the same subject, and with as little success as his predecessors—tries to prove that the struggle for existence does not infringe morality, and that side by side with the acknowledgement of the struggle for existence as a fundamental law of life, morality may not merely exist but even progress. Mr. Huxley's article is full of all kinds of jokes, verses, and general views on ancient religion and philosophy, and is consequently so florid and complicated that it is only with great effort that one is able to reach its fundamental thought. That thought however is as follows: The law of evolution runs counter to the moral law; this was known to the ancient Greeks and Hindus. The philosophy and religion of both those peoples brought them to the doctrine of self-renunciation. That doctrine, the author thinks, is not correct; the correct one is this: A law exists, which the author calls the cosmic law, in accord with which all beings struggle against one another and only the fittest survive. Man also is subject to this law; and thanks only to it has man become what he now is. But this law runs counter to morality. How then can it be reconciled with morality? That can be accomplished in this way: A law of social progress exists which seeks to check the cosmic process and to replace it by another, an ethical, process, the object of which is the survival, not of the fittest but of the best in an ethical sense. Where this ethical process sprang from, Mr. Huxley does not explain, but in his twentieth foot-note he says that the basis of this process is, on the one hand that people, like animals, prefer to be in company and therefore suppress in themselves qualities

---

[4] Thomas Huxley's Romanes Lecture, delivered in 1894, and contained in *Evolution and Ethics*, issued by Macmillan & Co.—A. M.

harmful to society; and on the other hand that the members
of a society forcibly suppress actions contrary to social welfare. It seems to Mr. Huxley that this process obliging men to
curb their passions for the sake of preserving the group of
which they are members, and for fear of being punished if
they disturb the order of their group, supplies that ethical
law the existence of which he wishes to demonstrate. It seems
to Mr. Huxley in the naïveté of his soul, that in English society
as it exists to-day—with its Irish problem, the poverty of its
lowest classes, the insensate luxury of the rich, its trade in
opium and spirits, its executions, its slaughter or extermination of tribes for the sake of trade and politics, its secret vice
and its hypocrisy—the man who does not infringe the police
regulations is a moral man guided by the ethical law. He
forgets that the qualities needful to maintain the society in
which a man lives may be useful for that society—as the
members of a band of robbers may be useful to that band,
and as in our own society we find a use for the qualities of
executioners, jailers, judges, soldiers, and hypocrite-priests,
&c.—but that these qualities have nothing in common with
morality.

Morality is something continually developing and growing,
and therefore conformity to the existing rules of a certain
society and their preservation by means of the axe or the
scaffold (to which Mr. Huxley alludes as to instruments of
morality), will not only not tend to the maintenance, but will
be an infringement, of morality. And on the contrary every
infringement of the existing order—such as were not only
the infringements committed by Jesus and his disciples of the
regulations of a Roman province, but the infringements of
present-day regulations by one who refuses to take part in
legal proceedings, military service, or the payment of taxes
levied for warlike preparations—will not only not be an
infringement of morality, but will be an inevitable condition
of its manifestation.

Every cannibal who perceives that he should not eat his
fellow men and who acts accordingly, infringes the order
of his society. And therefore though action infringing the or-

der of any society *may* be immoral, every truly moral action which pushes forward the limits of morality is always *sure* to be an infringement of the order of society. If therefore a law has appeared in society in accord with which people sacrifice their personal advantages for the preservation of the integrity of their group, that law is not the ethical law, but on the contrary will generally be a law contrary to all ethics —that same law of the struggle for existence, but in a hidden latent form. It is the same struggle for existence, but carried over from the individual to a group of individuals. It is not the cessation of the fight, but only a backward swinging of the arm to strike a harder blow.

If the law of the struggle for existence and the survival of the fittest is the eternal law of all life (and it cannot but be admitted to be so when we regard man as an animal)—then no tangled discussions about social progress and an ethical law supposed to flow from it, or to spring up from no one knows where just when we happen to need it (like a *deus ex machina*), can disturb that law.

If social progress, as Mr. Huxley assures us, collects people into groups, then the struggle and the survival will continue among those families, clans, and nations, and the struggle will not only not be more moral, but it will be even more cruel and more immoral than that between individuals, as we see in actual life. Even if we admit the impossible, and suppose that in another thousand years all humanity will, by social progress alone, be united into one whole and form a single nation and a single State—even then (not to mention that the struggle abolished between nations and States will continue between man and the animal world, and will always remain a struggle—that is, will remain an activity quite excluding the possibility of the Christian morality we confess)— even then the struggle between individuals forming this union and between the groups of families, clans, and nationalities, will not be diminished but will continue in a new form, as we see in all aggregations of individuals, families, races, and States. The members of a family quarrel and fight with one another as well as with outsiders, and often to a greater de-

gree and with more venom. It is just the same thing in the
State; among people living in one State a struggle continues just as with people outside the State, only it is carried
on under other forms. In the one case the slaughter is done
with arrows and knives, in the other it is done by hunger. And
if both in the family and in the State the weak are saved, that
is not done by social union, but occurs because love and self-
sacrifice exist among the people united in families and in
States. If, outside the family, only the fittest of two children
survives, while in a good mother's family both remain alive,
this does not result from union into families, but from the
fact that the mother possesses love and self-sacrifice. And
neither self-sacrifice nor love can result from a social process.

To assert that a social process produces morality is like asserting that the construction of stoves produces heat.

Heat comes from the sun, and stoves produce heat only
when fuel (the result of the sun's work) is put into them.
Just so morality comes from religion. Special forms of social
life produce morality only when the results of religious influence—which is morality—are put into them.

Stoves may be heated and give warmth, or may not be
heated and may remain cold; just as social forms may contain morality and thus have a moral influence on society, or
may not contain morality and so remain without influence on
society.

Christian morality cannot be based on a pagan or social
conception of life and cannot be deduced either from philosophy or from non-Christian science; and not only can it
not be deduced from them, but it cannot even be reconciled
with them.

That is how the matter has always been understood by
every serious and strictly consistent philosophy and science,
which said, quite reasonably: 'If our propositions do not tally
with morality, so much the worse for morality', and continued their investigations.

Ethical treatises not founded on religion, and even secular
catechisms, are written and taught, and people may suppose

that humanity is guided by them; but that only seems to be the case, because people are really guided not by those treatises and catechisms but by the religions which they have always possessed and still possess, whereas these treatises and catechisms only counterfeit what flows naturally from religion.

The dictates of secular morality not based on a religious teaching are just like the action of a man who, though ignorant of music, should take the conductor's seat and begin to wave his arms before the experienced musicians who were performing. The music would continue for awhile by its own momentum and because of what the musicians had learned from former conductors; but the waving of a stick by a man ignorant of music would obviously not merely be useless, but would in course of time certainly confuse the musicians and disorganize the orchestra. A similar confusion begins to take place in people's minds at the present time in consequence of attempts made by leading men to teach people a morality not founded on that highest religion which begins to be assimilated, and has already been partly assimilated, by Christian humanity.

It is indeed desirable to have moral teaching unmixed with superstition, but the fact is that moral teaching is a result of a certain relation man holds towards the universe or towards God. If that relation is expressed in forms which seem to us superstitious, we should, to put the matter right, try to express that relation more reasonably, clearly, and exactly, or even to destroy the former relation (now become inadequate) of man to the universe and substitute for it one that is higher, clearer, and more reasonable; but we should in no case devise a so-called secular, non-religious morality founded on sophistry or simply founded on nothing at all.

The attempts to found a morality apart from religion, are like the attempts of children who, wishing to transplant a flower that pleases them, pluck it from the roots that seem to them unpleasing and superfluous, and stick it rootless into the ground. Without religion there can be no real, sincere morality, just as without roots there can be no real flower.

So in answer to your two questions, I say: *'Religion is a certain relation established by man between his separate personality and the infinite universe or its Source. And morality is the ever-present guide to life, which results from that relation.'*

[December 28, o.s., 1894.]

REASON AND RELIGION

A Letter to an Inquirer

◇◇◇◇◇◇◇

You ask me:

1. Should men of no special intellectual gifts seek to express in words truths they have reached relating to the inner life?

2. Is it worth while to try to attain full and clear understanding of one's inner life?

3. How in moments of struggle or doubt are we to know whether it is conscience that speaks to us, or whether it is intellect bribed by our infirmities? (For brevity's sake, I have restated this third question in my own words, without, I hope, altering your meaning.)

These three questions, it seems to me, are all summed up in the second; for if we should not try to attain full and clear understanding of our inner life, then also we should not and cannot express in words the truths we have reached, and in moments of doubt we shall have nothing to guide us in distinguishing between conscience and false reasoning. But if it is right to seek the greatest clearness one's mental powers can attain (whether those powers be great or small), then we should also express in words the truths we have reached and by those truths, elucidated to the utmost and expressed in words, we must be guided in moments of struggle or doubt. And therefore I answer your root question in the affirmative; namely, that every man in order to accomplish the purpose for which he was sent here and to attain true well-being (the two always accord) should exert the whole strength of his mind to elucidate for himself the religious foundations on which he rests, that is to say, he should clear up the purpose of his life.

Among uneducated navvies, whose work is paid for by the cubic fathom, I have often met with a prevalent conviction that mathematical calculations are deceptive and should not be trusted. Whether this is because they do not know mathematics, or because those who calculate the earth they have dug up often intentionally or unintentionally cheat them, the fact remains that a disbelief in the sufficiency or applicability of mathematics for the estimation of quantities has firmly established itself among these uneducated labourers, and for most of them has become an unquestioned verity which they do not even consider it necessary to prove. A similar opinion has established itself among people whom I may safely call *irreligious*—an opinion to the effect that reason cannot solve religious questions, that the application of reason to these questions is the chief source of errors, and that to solve religious questions by reason is an act of wicked pride.

I mention this because the doubt expressed in your questions as to whether one should try to attain full and clear understanding, can only arise from the supposition that reason cannot be applied to the solution of religious questions. Yet that supposition is as strange and as obviously false as the supposition that calculation cannot solve mathematical questions.

Man has received direct from God only one instrument wherewith to know himself and to know his relation to the universe—he has no other—and that instrument is reason: and suddenly he is told that his reason may be used to elucidate his home, family, business, political, scientific or artistic problems, but may not be used to clear up the very thing for which it was chiefly given him. It would seem that to clear up the most important truths, those on which his whole life depends, man must on no account use his reason, but must recognize such truths apart from his reason, though apart from his reason man can know nothing. People say: 'Recognize by inspiration, by faith'; but the fact is that man cannot even believe apart from his reason. If a man believes one thing and not another, he does this only because his reason tells him he should not believe this but should believe that. To say that a man should not be guided by reason, is the same as to say to a man carrying a lamp in a dark catacomb that to find the way out he must extinguish his lamp and be guided, not by light but by something else.

But perhaps it will be said (as you say in your letter) that not all men are gifted with great intellect, and especially not with capacity to express their thoughts; and by an unskilful expression of their thoughts about religion they may therefore occasion error. To that I will reply in the words of the Gospel, that what is hidden from the wise is revealed to babes. And this saying is not an exaggeration or a paradox (as we are accustomed to consider sayings in the Gospels that do not please us), but is a statement of the simplest and most indubitable truth, namely, that to every being in the world a law is given which that being should follow, and that to enable him to perceive this law every being has received suitable organs. And therefore every man is gifted with reason, and by that reason the law he should follow is revealed to each man. That law is hidden only from those who do not wish to follow it, and who, in order not to obey the law, reject reason, and instead of using the reason given to them wherewith to discern truth, accept on faith the guidance of others who have also rejected reason.

The law man should follow is so simple that it is accessible to every child; especially as man need not rediscover this law of his life. Those who lived before us discovered and expressed it, and a man need only verify by his own reason the propositions he finds expressed in tradition—accepting or rejecting them. But he must not do as people advise who prefer not to obey the law: he must not check his reason by tradition, but contrariwise must check tradition by reason. Traditions may come from man and be false, but reason certainly comes from God and cannot be false. And therefore no specially great capacities are needed to know and express the truth; we need only believe that reason is not only the highest, the divine quality in man, but that it is the only instrument he possesses for the attainment of truth.

Special talents and intellectual gifts are needed, not for the knowledge and statement of truth but for the invention and statement of falsehood. Once they abandon the indications of reason and instead of believing them credulously accept what is offered to them as truth, people pile up and credulously accept such complex, unnatural, and contradictory propositions (usually in the guise of laws, revelations, and dogmas), that to express them and connect them with any truth really needs great subtlety of mind and exceptional gifts. One need only imagine to oneself a man of our world, educated in the religious beliefs of any one of the Christian Churches—Catholic, Russo-Greek Orthodox, or Protestant— who should wish to elucidate the religious principles with which he has been inoculated in childhood and to connect them with real life—what a complex intellectual labour he would have to perform in order to adjust all the contradictions contained in the faith with which his education had inoculated him: a God who is the Creator and is good, creates evil, condemns people, demands a ransom and so on; and we ourselves profess a law of love and forgiveness yet we execute people, make war, take their produce from the poor, and the like.

For the disentanglement of these insoluble contradictions, or rather in order to hide them from oneself, great ability and special mental endowments are necessary; but to know the law of one's life, or, as you express it, to attain full and clear understanding of one's belief, no special mental gifts are required—we only need be careful not to accept anything contrary to reason, not to deny our reason, to guard our reason religiously, and believe in it alone. If the meaning of his life seems obscure to a man, this does not prove that his reason is incompetent to explain that meaning; it only indicates that he has credulously accepted too much that is irrational, and that what has not been verified by reason must be set aside.

And therefore my answer to your root question as to whether we must strive to attain a clear understanding of our inner life, is that that is the most necessary and important thing we can do in life. It is necessary and important because the only reasonable meaning of our life consists in fulfilment of the will of God who has sent us here. But the will of God is known, not by some extraordinary miracle, the writing of the law by the finger of the Deity on stone tablets, the compilation by the aid of the Holy Ghost of an infallible book, or by the infallibility of some holy man or collection of men, but only by the use of reason by all men, transmitting both by deed and by word, one to another, the consciousness of truth that is ever more and more elucidating itself to them. That knowledge never has been, nor ever will be, complete, but it ever increases as humanity advances: the longer we live the more clearly we know God's will, and, consequently, the more we know what we should do to fulfil it. And so I think the clearing up by each man (however small he may seem to himself or to others—the least are the greatest) of all religious truth accessible to him, and its expression in words (for expression in words is one sure sign of complete clearness in thought), is one of the chief and most holy duties of man.

I shall be very glad if my reply in any degree satisfies you.

[November 26, 1894.]

A REPLY TO THE SYNOD'S EDICT OF EXCOMMUNICATION, AND TO LETTERS RECEIVED BY ME CONCERNING IT

'He who begins by loving Christianity better than truth, will proceed by loving his own sect or church better than Christianity, and end in loving himself better than all.'—
COLERIDGE.

At first I did not wish to reply to the Synod's Edict about me, but it has called forth very many letters in which correspondents unknown to me write—some of them scolding me for rejecting things I never rejected, others exhorting me to believe in things I have always believed in, others again expressing an agreement with me which probably does not really exist and a sympathy to which I am hardly entitled. So I have decided to reply both to the Edict itself—indicating what is unjust in it—and to the communications of my unknown correspondents.

The Edict of the Synod has in general many defects. It is either illegal or else intentionally equivocal; it is arbitrary, unfounded, untruthful, and is also libellous, and incites to evil feelings and deeds.

It is illegal or intentionally equivocal; for if it is intended as an Excommunication from the Church, it fails to conform to the Church regulations subject to which Excommunications can be pronounced; while if it is merely an announcement of the fact that one who does not believe in the Church and its dogmas does not belong to the Church—that is self-evident, and the announcement can have no purpose other than to pass for an Excommunication without really being one, as in fact happened, for that is how the Edict has been understood.

It is arbitrary, for it accuses me alone of disbelief in all the points enumerated in the Edict; whereas many, in fact almost all educated people, share that disbelief and have constantly expressed and still express it both in conversations, in lectures, in pamphlets, and in books.

It is unfounded because it gives as a chief cause of its publication the great circulation of the false teaching wherewith I pervert the people—whereas I am well assured that hardly a hundred people can be found who share my views, and the circulation of my writings on religion, thanks to the Censor, is so insignificant that the majority of those who have read the Synod's Edict have not the least notion of what I may have written about religion—as is shown by the letters I have received.

It contains an obvious falsehood, for it says that efforts have been made by the Church to show me my errors but that these efforts have been unsuccessful. Nothing of the kind ever took place.

It constitutes what in legal terminology is called a libel, for it contains assertions known to be false and tending to my hurt.

It is, finally, an incentive to evil feelings and deeds, for as was to be expected it evoked in unenlightened and unreasoning people anger and hatred against me, culminating in threats of murder expressed in letters I received. One writes: 'Now thou hast been anathematized, and after death wilt go to everlasting torments and wilt perish like a dog . . . anathema upon thee, old devil . . . be damned.' Another blames the Government for not having as yet shut me up in a monas-

tery, and fills his letter with abuse. A third writes: 'If the
Government does not get rid of you, we will ourselves make
you shut your mouth,' and the letter ends with curses.
'May you be destroyed—you blackguard!' writes a fourth, 'I
shall find means to do it . . .' and then follows indecent
abuse. After the publication of the Synod's Edict I also
noticed indications of anger of this kind in some of the
people I met. On the very day (February 25) when the Edict
was made public, while crossing a public square I heard the
words: 'See! there goes the devil in human form,' and had
the crowd been composed of other elements I should very
likely have been beaten to death, as happened some years
ago to a man at the Pantaléymon Chapel.

So that altogether the Synod's Edict is very bad, and the
statement at the end that those who sign it pray that I may
become such as they are does not make it any better.

That relates to the Edict as a whole; as to details, it is
wrong in the following particulars. It is said in the Edict: 'A
writer well known to the world, Russian by birth, Orthodox
by baptism and education—Count Tolstóy—under the seduc-
tion of his intellectual pride has insolently risen against the
Lord and against his Christ and against his holy heritage,
and has publicly, in the sight of all men, renounced the Orthodox Mother Church which has reared him and educated
him.'

That I have renounced the Church which calls itself Orthodox is perfectly correct.

But I renounced it not because I had risen against the
Lord, but on the contrary only because with all the strength
of my soul I wished to serve him. Before renouncing the
Church, and fellowship with the people which was inexpressibly dear to me, I—having seen some reasons to doubt the
Church's integrity—devoted several years to the investigation of its theoretic and practical teachings. For the theory,
I read all I could about Church doctrine and studied and
critically analysed dogmatic theology; while as to practice,
for more than a year I followed strictly all the injunctions of
the Church observing all the fasts and all the services. And I

became convinced that Church doctrine is theoretically a crafty and harmful lie, and practically a collection of the grossest superstitions and sorcery, which completely conceals the whole meaning of Christ's teaching.[1]

And I really repudiated the Church, ceased to observe its ceremonies, and wrote a will instructing those near me that when I die they should not allow any servants of the Church to have access to me, but should put away my dead body as quickly as possible without having any incantations or prayers over it, just as one puts away any objectionable and useless object that it may not be an inconvenience to the living.

As to the statements made about me, that I devote the 'literary activity and the talent given to him by God, to disseminating among the people teachings contrary to Christ and to the Church', and that, 'in his works and in letters issued by him and by his disciples in great quantities over the whole world, but particularly within the limits of our dear fatherland, he preaches with the zeal of a fanatic the overthrow of all the dogmas of the Orthodox Church and the very essence of the Christian faith'—this is not true. I never troubled myself about the propagation of my teaching. It is true that for myself I have expressed in writings my understanding of Christ's teaching and have not hidden these works from those who wished to become acquainted with them, but I never published them myself. Only when they have asked me about

---

[1] One need only read the Prayer-Book and follow the ritual which is continually performed by the Orthodox priests and is considered a Christian worship of God, to see that all these ceremonies are nothing but different kinds of sorcery adapted to all the incidents of life. That a child in case of death should go to Paradise, one has to know how to oil him and how to immerse him while pronouncing certain words; in order that a mother may cease to be unclean after child-birth, certain incantations have to be pronounced; to be successful in one's affairs, to live comfortably in a new house, that corn may grow well, that a drought may cease, to recover from sickness, to ease the condition in the next world of one who is dying,— for all these and a thousand other incidents there are certain incantations which are pronounced by a priest at a certain place, for a certain consideration.—L. T.

it have I told people how I understand Christ's teaching. To those that asked, I said what I thought and (when I had them) gave them my books.

Then it is said that 'he denies God worshipped in the Holy Trinity, the Creator and Protector of the universe; denies our Lord Jesus Christ, God-man, Redeemer and Saviour of the world, who suffered for us men and for our salvation and was raised from the dead; denies the immaculate conception of the Lord Christ as man, and the virginity before his birth and after his birth of the Most Pure Mother of God.' That I deny the incomprehensible Trinity; the fable, which is altogether meaningless in our time, of the fall of the first man; the blasphemous story of a God born of a virgin to redeem the human race—is perfectly true. But God, a Spirit; God, love; the only God—the Source of all—I not only do not deny, but I attribute real existence to God alone and I see the whole meaning of life only in fulfilling His will, which is expressed in the Christian teaching.

It is also said: 'He does not acknowledge a life and retribution beyond the grave.' If one is to understand, by life beyond the grave, the Second Advent, a hell with eternal torments, devils, and a Paradise of perpetual happiness—it is perfectly true that I do not acknowledge such a life beyond the grave; but eternal life and retribution here and everywhere, now and for ever, I acknowledge to such an extent that, standing now at my age on the verge of my grave, I often have to make an effort to restrain myself from desiring the death of this body—that is, birth to a new life; and I believe every good action increases the true welfare of my eternal life and every evil action decreases it.

It is also stated that I reject all the Sacraments. That is quite true. I consider all the Sacraments to be coarse, degrading sorcery, incompatible with the idea of God or with the Christian teaching, and also as infringements of very plain injunctions in the Gospels. In the Baptism of Infants I see a palpable perversion of the whole meaning which might be attached to the baptism of adults who consciously accepted Christianity; in the performance of the Sacrament of Marriage over those who are known to have had other sexual unions, in the permission of divorce, and in the consecration of the marriages of divorced people, I see a direct infringement both of the meaning and of the words of the Gospel teaching.

In the periodical absolution of sins at Confession I see a harmful deception which only encourages immorality and causes men not to fear to sin.

Both in Extreme Unction and in Anointing I see methods of gross sorcery—as in the worship of icons and relics, and as in all the rites, prayers, and exorcisms which fill the Prayer-Book. In the Sacrament I see a deification of the flesh and a perversion of Christian teaching. In Ordination I see (beside an obvious preparation for deception) a direct infringement of the words of Jesus, which plainly forbid anyone to be called teacher, father, or master.[2]

It is stated finally, as the last and greatest of my sins; that 'reviling the most sacred objects of the faith of the Orthodox people, he has not shrunk from subjecting to derision the greatest of Sacraments, the Holy Eucharist.'[3] That I did not shrink from describing simply and objectively what the priest does when preparing this so-called Sacrament is perfectly true; but that this so-called Sacrament is anything holy, and that it is blasphemy to describe it simply, just as it is performed, is quite untrue. Blasphemy does not consist in calling a partition a partition, and not an iconostasis,[4] and a cup a cup, and not a chalice, &c.; but it is a most terrible, continual, and revolting blasphemy that men (using all possible means of deception and hypnotization) should assure children and simple-minded folk that if bits of bread are cut

---

[2] 'But be not ye called Rabbi: for one is your Master, and all ye are brethren. And call no man your father upon the earth: for one is your Father, which is in heaven. Neither be ye called masters: for one is your Master, even Christ.'—Matt. xxiii. 8-10.

[3] See chapter xxxix, book i, of *Resurrection;* but see also, as a probable provocative of Tolstoy's Excommunication, the description of the Head of the Holy Synod in chapter xxvii, book ii, of that work. —A. M.

[4] The iconostasis in Russo-Greek churches corresponds somewhat both to the Western altar-rails and to a rood-screen.—A. M.

up in a particular manner while certain words are pronounced over them, and if they are put into wine,[5] God will enter into those bits of bread, and any living person named by the priest when he takes out one of these sops will be healthy, and any dead person named by the priest when he takes out one of these sops will be better off in the other world on that account, and that into the man who eats such a sop God himself will enter.

Surely that is terrible!

They undertake to teach us to understand the personality of Christ, but his teaching—which destroys evil in the world and blesses men so simply, easily, and undoubtedly, if only they do not pervert it—is all hidden, is all transformed into a gross sorcery of washings, smearing with oil, gestures, exorcisms, eating of bits of bread, &c., so that of the true teaching nothing remains. And if at any time some one tries to remind men that Christ's teaching consists not in this sorcery, not in public prayer, liturgies, candles, and icons, but in loving one another, in not returning evil for evil, in not judging or killing one another—the anger of those to whom deception is profitable is aroused, and with incomprehensible audacity they publicly declare in churches, and print in books, newspapers and catechisms, that Jesus never forbade oaths (swearing allegiance or swearing in courts of law), never forbade murder (executions and wars), and that the teaching of non-resistance to evil has with Satanic ingenuity been invented by the enemies of Christ.[6]

What is most terrible is that people to whom it is profitable not only deceive adults, but (having power to do so) deceive children also—those very children concerning whom Jesus pronounced woe on him who deceives them. It is terrible that these people for their own petty advantage do such fearful

---

[5] In the Greek Church the priest mixes the sacramental bread with the wine before administering it to the communicant. The reader will note in this article allusions to several practices (baptism by immersion, unction, &c.) which do not exist in the Church of England, or are differently carried out.—A. M.

[6] Speech by Ambrosius, Bishop of Khárkov.—L. T.

evil, hiding from men the truth Jesus revealed, and that gives blessing a thousandfold greater than the gains these men obtain for themselves. They behave like a robber who kills a whole family of five or six people to carry off an old coat and tenpence in money. They would willingly have given him all their clothes and all their money not to be killed, but he could not act otherwise.

So it is with the religious deceivers. It would be worth while keeping them ten times better and letting them live in the greatest luxury, if only they would refrain from ruining men by their deceptions. But they cannot act differently. That is what is awful. And therefore we not only may, but should, unmask their deceptions. If there be a sacred thing, it is surely not what they call Sacraments, but just this very duty of unmasking their religious deceptions when one detects them.

When a Tchouvásh smears his idol with sour cream or beats it, I can refrain from insulting his faith and can pass it by with equanimity, for he does these things in the name of a superstition of his own, foreign to me, and he does not interfere with what to me is holy. But I cannot endure it passively when with their barbarous superstitions, men (however numerous, however ancient their superstitions, and however powerful they may be) preach gross sorcery in the name of the God by whom I live, and of that teaching of Christ's which has given life to me and is capable of giving life to all men.

And if I call what they are doing by its name, I only do my duty and what I cannot refrain from doing because I believe in God and in the Christian teaching. If they call the exposure of their imposture 'blasphemy', that only shows the strength of their deception, and should increase the efforts to destroy this deception, made by those who believe in God and in Christ's teaching, and who see that this deception hides the true God from men's sight.

They should say of Christ—who drove bulls and sheep and dealers from the temple—that he blasphemed. Were he to come now and see what is done in his name in church, he would surely with yet greater and most just anger throw out

all these horrible altar-cloths,[7] lances, crosses, cups and candles and icons and all the things wherewith the priests—
carrying on their sorcery—hide God and his truth from mankind.

So that is what is true and what is untrue in the Synod's
Edict about me. I certainly do not believe in what they say
they believe in. But I believe in what they wish to persuade
people that I disbelieve in.

I believe in this: I believe in God, whom I understand as
Spirit, as Love, as the Source of all. I believe that he is in
me and I in him. I believe that the will of God is most clearly
and intelligibly expressed in the teaching of the man Jesus,
whom to consider as God and pray to, I esteem the greatest
blasphemy. I believe that man's true welfare lies in fulfilling
God's will, and his will is that men should love one another
and should consequently do to others as they wish others to
do to them—of which it is said in the Gospels that in this is
the law and the prophets. I believe therefore that the meaning of the life of every man is to be found only in increasing
the love that is in him; that this increase of love leads man,
even in this life, to ever greater and greater blessedness, and
after death gives him the more blessedness the more love he
has, and helps more than anything else towards the establishment of the Kingdom of God on earth: that is, to the establishment of an order of life in which the discord, deception, and
violence that now rule will be replaced by free accord, by
truth, and by the brotherly love of one for another. I believe
that to obtain progress in love there is only one means:
prayer—not public prayer in churches, plainly forbidden by
Jesus,[8] but private prayer, like the sample given us by Jesus,

---

[7] The altar-cloths referred to are those containing fragments of holy
relics, on which alone mass can be celebrated. The 'lances' are
diminutive ones with which the priest cuts bits out of the holy
bread, in remembrance of the lance that pierced Christ's side.—
A. M.

[8] 'And when thou prayest, thou shall not be as the hypocrites are:
for they love to pray standing in the synagogues and in the corners
of the streets, that they may be seen of men. Verily I say unto you,
They have their reward. But thou, when thou prayest, enter into

consisting of the renewing and strengthening in our own consciousness of the meaning of our life and of our complete dependence on the will of God.

Whether or not these beliefs of mine offend, grieve, or
prove a stumbling-block to anyone, or hinder anything, or
give displeasure to anybody, I can as little change them as I
can change my body. I must myself live my own life and I
must myself alone meet death (and that very soon), and
therefore I cannot believe otherwise than as I—preparing to
go to that God from whom I came—do believe. I do not believe my faith to be the one indubitable truth for all time,
but I see no other that is plainer, clearer, or answers better to
all the demands of my reason and my heart; should I find
such a one I shall at once accept it, for God requires nothing
but the truth. But I can no more return to that from which
with such suffering I have escaped, than a flying bird can re-
enter the eggshell from which it has emerged.

'He who begins by loving Christianity better than truth,
will proceed by loving his own sect or church better than
Christianity, and end in loving himself (his own peace)
better than all,' said Coleridge.

I travelled the contrary way. I began by loving my Orthodox faith more than my peace, then I loved Christianity more
than my Church, and now I love truth more than anything in
the world. And up to now truth for me corresponds with
Christianity as I understand it. And I hold to this Christianity,
and to the degree in which I hold to it I live peacefully and
happily, and peacefully and happily approach death.

---

thy closet, and when thou hast shut thy door, pray to thy Father
which is in secret; and thy Father which seeth in secret shall reward thee openly. But when ye pray, use not vain repetitions, as
the heathen do: for they think that they shall be heard for their
much speaking. Be not therefore like unto them: for your Father
knoweth what things ye have need of, before ye ask him. After this
manner therefore pray ye: Our Father,' &c.—Matt. vi. 5-13.
[April 4, o.s., 1901.]

WHAT IS RELIGION, AND WHEREIN LIES ITS ESSENCE?

I

In all human societies at certain periods of their existence, a time has come when religion has first swerved from its original purpose, then, diverging more and more, has lost sight of that purpose, and finally has petrified into fixed forms so that its influence on men's lives has become ever less and less.

At such times the educated minority cease to believe in the established religious teaching, and only pretend to hold it because they think it necessary to do so in order to keep the mass of the people to the established order of life; but the mass of the people, though by inertia they keep to the established forms of religion, no longer guide their lives by its demands but guide them only by custom and by the State laws.

That is what has repeatedly occurred in various human societies. But what is now happening in our Christian society has never happened before. It has never before happened that the rich, ruling, and more educated minority, which has most influence on the masses, has not only disbelieved the existing religion, but been convinced that no religion at all is any longer needed, and instead of influencing those who are doubtful of the truth of the generally professed religion to accept some religious teaching more rational and clear than the prevalent one, has influenced them to regard religion in general as a thing that has outlived its day and is now not merely a useless, but even a harmful, social organ, like the vermiform appendix in the human body.

Religion is regarded by such men not as something known to us by inward experience, but as an external phenomenon —a disease, as it were, which overtakes certain people and which we can only investigate by its external symptoms.

Religion, in the opinion of some of these men, arose from attributing a spirit to various aspects of Nature (animism); in the opinion of others, it arose from the supposed possibility of communicating with deceased ancestors; in the opinion of others again it arose from fear of the forces of Nature. But, say the learned men of our day, since science has now proved that trees and stones cannot be endowed with a spirit, that dead ancestors do not know what is done by the living, and that the aspects of Nature are explainable by natural causes —it follows that the need for religion has passed, as well as the need for all those restrictions with which (in consequence of religious beliefs) people have hitherto hampered themselves. In the opinion of these learned men there was a period of ignorance: the religious period. That has long been outlived by humanity, though some occasional atavistic indications of it still remain. Then came the metaphysical period, which is now also outlived. But we enlightened people are living in a scientific period: a period of positive science which replaces religion and will bring humanity to a height of development it could never have reached while subject to the superstitious teachings of religion.

Early in 1901 the distinguished French savant Berthelot delivered a speech[1] in which he told his hearers that the day of religion has passed and religion must now be replaced by science. I refer to this speech because it is the first to my hand and because it was delivered in the metropolis of the educated world by a universally recognized savant. But the same thought is continually and ubiquitously expressed in every form, from philosophic treatises down to newspaper *feuilletons.*

M. Berthelot says in that speech that there were formerly two motors moving humanity: Force and Religion; but that

---

[1] See the *Revue de Paris,* January, 1901.—L. T.

these motors have now become superfluous, for in their place we have *science*. By *science* M. Berthelot (like all devotees of science) evidently means a science embracing the whole range of things man knows, harmoniously united, co-ordinated, and in command of such methods that the data it obtains are unquestionably true. But as no such science really exists—and what is now called science consists of a collection of haphazard, disconnected scraps of knowledge, many of them quite useless, and such as instead of supplying undoubted truth very frequently supply the grossest delusions, exhibited as truth to-day but refuted to-morrow—it is evident that the thing M. Berthelot thinks must replace religion is something nonexistent. Consequently the assertion made by M. Berthelot and by those who agree with him, to the effect that science will replace religion, is quite arbitrary and rests on a quite unjustifiable faith in the infallibility of science—a faith similar to the belief in an infallible Church.

Yet men who are said to be educated, and who consider themselves so, are quite convinced that a science already exists which should and can replace religion and which has even already replaced it.

'Religion is obsolete: belief in anything but science is ignorance. Science will arrange all that is needful and one must be guided in life by science alone.' This is what is thought and said both by scientists themselves and also by those men of the crowd who, though far from scientific, believe in the scientists and join them in asserting that religion is an obsolete superstition and that we must be guided in life by science only: that is, in reality, by nothing at all, for science by reason of its very aim (which is to study all that exists) can afford no guidance for the life of man.

II

The learned men of our times have decided that religion is not wanted, and that science will replace it or has already done so; but the fact remains that, now as formerly, no human society and no rational man has existed or can exist with-

out a religion. I use the term *rational* man because an irrational man may live, as the beasts do, without a religion. But
a rational man cannot live without one, for only religion gives
a rational man the guidance he needs, telling him what he
should do and what first and what next. A rational man cannot live without religion precisely because reason is characteristic of his nature. Every animal is guided in its actions
(apart from those to which it is impelled by the need to satisfy its immediate desires) by a consideration of the direct
results of its actions. Having considered those results by such
means of comprehension as it possesses, an animal makes its
actions conform to those consequences and it always un-
hesitatingly acts in one and the same way in accord with
those considerations. A bee, for instance, flies for honey and
stores it in the hive because in winter it will need food for
itself and for the young, and beyond these considerations it
knows and can know nothing. So also a bird is influenced
when it builds its nest or migrates from the north to the south
and back again. Every animal acts in a like way when it does
anything not resulting from direct, immediate necessity, but
prompted by considerations of anticipated results. With
man however it is not so. The difference between a man and
an animal lies in the fact that the perceptive capacities possessed by an animal are limited to what we call instinct,
whereas man's fundamental perceptive capacity is reason. A
bee collecting honey can have no doubts as to whether it is
good or bad to collect honey, but a man gathering in his corn
or fruit cannot but consider whether he is diminishing the
prospects of obtaining future harvests and whether he is not
depriving his neighbour of food. Nor can he help wonder-
ing what the children whom he now feeds will grow up like—
and much else. The most important questions of conduct in
life cannot be solved conclusively by a reasonable man, just
because there is such a superabundance of possible consequences which he cannot but be aware of. Every rational
man knows, or at least feels, that in the most important questions of life he can guide himself neither by personal impulses
nor by considerations of the immediate consequences of his

activity—for the consequences he foresees are too numerous and too various and are often contradictory one to another, being as likely to prove harmful as beneficial to himself and to other people. There is a legend which tells of an angel who descended to earth and, entering the house of a devout family, slew a child in its cradle; when asked why he did so, he explained that the child would have become the greatest of malefactors and would have destroyed the happiness of the family. But it is thus not only with the question, Which human lives are useful, useless, or harmful? A reasonable man cannot decide any of the most important questions of life by considerations of their immediate results and consequences. A reasonable man cannot be satisfied with the considerations that guide the actions of an animal. A man may regard himself as an animal among animals—living for the passing day; or he may consider himself as a member of a family, a society, or a nation, living for centuries; or he may and even must (for reason irresistibly prompts him to this) consider himself as part of the whole infinite universe existing eternally. And therefore reasonable men should do, and always have done, in reference to the infinitely small affairs of life affecting their actions, what in mathematics is called *integrate:* that is to say, they must set up, besides their relation to the immediate facts of life, a relation to the whole immense Infinite in time and space conceived as one whole. And such establishment of man's relation to that whole of which he feels himself to be a part, from which he draws guidance for his actions, is what has been called and is called Religion. And therefore religion always has been, and cannot cease to be, a necessary and indispensable condition of the life of a reasonable man and of all reasonable humanity.

III

That is how religion has always been understood by men who were not devoid of the highest (that is, religious) consciousness, which distinguishes man from the beasts. The word religion itself comes either from *relegere, religens,* revering the Gods; or, as has been commonly supposed, from *religare,* to bind (in obligation to the higher powers). The oldest and most common definition of religion is that *religion is the link between man and God.* 'Les obligations de l'homme envers Dieu: voilà la religion' (Man's obligations to God: that is religion) says Vauvenargues.[2] A similar meaning is given to religion by Schleiermacher[3] and by Feuerbach,[4] who acknowledge *the basis of religion to be man's consciousness of his dependence on God.* 'La religion est une affaire entre chaque homme et Dieu' (Religion is a matter between each man and God).—Bayle.[5] 'La religion est le résultat des besoins de l'âme et des effets de l'intelligence' (Religion is the outcome of the needs of the soul and of the effects of intelligence).— B. Constant.[6] *'Religion is a particular means by which man realizes his relation with the superhuman and mysterious forces on which he considers himself dependent.'*—Goblet d'Alviella.[7] *'Religion is a definition of human life, based on the connexion between the human soul and that mysterious spirit whose dominion over the world and over himself man recognizes, and with which he feels himself united.'*—A. Réville.[8]

So that the essence of religion has always been understood —and is now understood by men not deprived of the highest human characteristic—to be the establishment by man of

---

[2] Luc de Clapiers, Marquis de Vauvenargues (1715-1774), author of *Introduction à la Connaissance de l'Esprit humain,* and of *Réflexions* and *Maximes.* —A. M.

[3] Friedrich E. D. Schleiermacher (1768-1834), author of *Der Christliche Glaube* and many other theological works.—A. M.

[4] L. A. Feuerbach (1804-1872), author of *Das Wesen des Christenthums* (which was translated into English by George Eliot).— A. M.

[5] Pierre Bayle (1647-1706), author of the *Dictionnaire historique et critique,* which exercised a great influence during the eighteenth century, especially on the Continent.—A. M.

[6] Henri Benjamin Constant de Rebeque (1767-1830), politician, and author of *De la Religion.*—A. M.

[7] Eugène Goblet, Comte d'Alviella (1846-   ), author of *Evolution religieuse contemporaine* and other works.—A. M.

[8] A. Réville (1826-1906), Protestant theologian of the advanced school, author of many works on religion.—A. M.

a relation between himself and the infinite Being or Beings whose power he feels over him. And this relation—however different it may be for different nations and at different times —has always defined for men their destiny in the world; from which guidance for their conduct has naturally flowed. A Jew understood his relation to the Infinite to be that he was a member of a nation chosen by God from among all nations, and that he had therefore to observe in the sight of God the agreement made by God with his people. A Greek understood his relation to be that, being dependent on the representatives of eternity—i.e. on the Gods—he ought to do what pleased them. A Brahman understands himself to be a manifestation of the infinite Brahma, and considers that he ought, by renunciation of life, to strive towards union with that highest being. A Buddhist considered, and considers, his relation to the Infinite to be that, passing from one form of life to another, he inevitably suffers, and these sufferings proceed from passions and desires, and therefore his business is to strive to annihilate all passions and all desires and so pass into Nirvana. Every religion is the setting up between man and the infinite life to which he feels himself allied, of some relation from which he obtains guidance for his conduct. And therefore if a religion does not establish any relation between man and the Infinite (as, for instance, is the case with idolatry or sorcery), then it is not a real religion but only a degeneration. If even religion establishes some relation between man and God but does this by means of assertions not accordant with reason and present-day knowledge, so that one cannot really believe the assertions—that also is not a religion but only a counterfeit. If a religion does not unite the life of a man with the infinite life, again it is not a religion. Nor does a belief in propositions from which no definite direction for human activity results constitute a religion.

True religion is a relation, accordant with reason and knowledge, which man establishes with the infinite life surrounding him, and it is such as binds his life to that infinity and guides his conduct.

IV

Though there never was an age when, or a place where, men lived without a religion, yet the learned men of to-day say, like Molière's 'Involuntary Doctor' who asserted that the liver is on the left side: *Nous avons changé tout cela* (We have changed all that); and they think that we can and should live without any religion. But religion, nevertheless, remains what it has been in the past: the chief motor and heart of human societies; and without it, as without a heart, human life is impossible. There have been and are many different religions—for the expression of man's relation to the Infinite and to God or the Gods differs at different times and in different places according to the stages of development of different nations—but never in any society of men, since men first became rational creatures, could they live, or have they lived, without a religion.

It is true that there have been, and sometimes are, periods in the life of nations when the existing religion has been so perverted and has lagged so far behind life as to cease to guide it. But this cessation of its action on men's lives (occurring at times in all religions) has been but temporary. It is characteristic of religion—as of all that is really alive—that it is born, develops, grows old, dies and again comes to life, and comes to life ever in forms more perfect than before. After a period of higher development in religion a period of decrepitude and lifelessness always follows, usually to be succeeded in its turn by a period of regeneration and the establishment of a religious doctrine wiser and clearer than before. Such periods of development, decrepitude, and regeneration have occurred in all religions. In the profound religion of Brahmanism, as soon as it began to grow old and to petrify into fixed and coarse forms not suited to its fundamental meaning, came on one side a renascence of Brahmanism itself, and on the other the lofty teachings of Buddhism, which advanced humanity's comprehension of its relation to the Infinite. A similar decline occurred in the Greek and Roman religions and then, following the lowest depths of that decline, appeared Christianity. The same thing occurred again with Church-Christianity, which in Byzantium degenerated into idolatry and polytheism. To counter-balance this perverted Christianity there arose on one hand the Paulicians,[9] and on the other (in opposition to the doctrine of the Trinity and to Mariolatry) came strict Mohammedanism with its fundamental dogma of One God. The same thing happened again with Papal Medieval Christianity, which evoked the Reformation; so that periods when religion weakens in its influence on the majority of men are a necessary condition of the life and development of all religious teachings. This occurs because every religious teaching in its true meaning, however crude it may be, always establishes a relation between man and the Infinite, which is alike for all men. Every religion regards men as equally insignificant compared to Infinity; and therefore every religion contains the conception of the equality of all men before that which it regards as God: whether that be lightning, wind, a tree, an animal, a hero, or a deceased king (or even a living one, as occurred in Rome). So that the admission of the equality of man is an inevitable and fundamental characteristic of every religion. But as equality among men never has existed anywhere in actual life and does not now exist, it has happened that as soon as a new religious teaching appeared (always including a confession of equality among all men)[10] then at once those people for whom inequality was profitable tried to hide this essential feature by perverting the teaching itself. This has always happened wherever a new religious teaching has appeared. And it has been done for the most part not consciously, but merely because those to whom inequality was profitable—the rulers and the rich—in order to

[9] The Paulicians were a sect who played a great part in the history of the Eastern Church (seventh to twelfth centuries). They rejected the Church view of Christ's teaching and were cruelly persecuted. —A. M.

[10] That is to say, that all are equal in the sight of God; that human laws and customs should give them an equal right to life, liberty, and the pursuit of happiness; and that men should treat one another as brothers.—A. M.

feel themselves justified by the teaching without having to alter their position, have tried by all means to attach to the religious teaching an interpretation sanctioning inequality. And naturally a religion so perverted that those who lorded it over others could consider themselves justified in so doing —when passed on to the common people instilled in them also the idea that submission to those who exercise authority is demanded by the religion they profess.

V

All human activity is evoked by three motive causes: Feeling, Reason, and Suggestion, the last-named being the same thing that doctors call hypnotism. Sometimes man acts only under the influence of feeling—simply striving to get what he desires. Sometimes he acts solely under the influence of reason, which shows him what he ought to do. Sometimes, and most frequently, man acts because he himself or other people have suggested an activity to him, and he unconsciously submits to the suggestion. Under normal conditions of life all three influences play their part in prompting a man's activity. Feeling draws him towards a certain activity; reason judges of this activity in the light of present circumstances, as well as by past experience and future expectation; and suggestion, apart from feeling and reason, causes a man to carry out the actions evoked by feeling and approved by reason. Were there no feeling man would undertake nothing; if reason did not exist, man would yield at once to many contradictory feelings, harmful to himself and to others; were there no capacity of yielding to one's own or other people's suggestion, man would have unceasingly to experience the feeling that prompted him to a particular activity and keep his reason continually intent on the verification of the expediency of that feeling. And therefore all these three influences are indispensable for even the simplest human activity. If a man walks from one place to another, this occurs because feeling has impelled him to move from one place to another, reason has approved of this intention and dictated means for its accomplishment (in this case—stepping along a certain road), and the muscles of the body obey and the man moves along the road indicated. While he is going along, both his feeling and his reason are freed for other activity, which could not be the case but for his capacity to submit to suggestion. This is what happens with all human activities and, among the rest, with the most important of them—religious activity. Feeling evokes the need to establish a man's relation to God; reason defines that relation; and suggestion impels man to the activity flowing from that relation. But this is so only as long as religion remains unperverted. As soon as perversion commences, the part played by suggestion grows ever stronger and stronger and the activity of feeling and of reason weakens. The methods of suggestion are always and everywhere the same. They consist in taking advantage of man at times when he is most susceptible to suggestion (during childhood, and at important occurrences of life: deaths, births, or marriages), and then acting on him by means of art: architecture, sculpture, painting, music, and dramatic performances, and while he is in a condition of receptivity (comparable to that produced on individuals by semi-hypnotization), instilling into him whatever the suggestors wish.

This process may be observed in all ancient religions: in the lofty religion of Brahmanism degenerating into gross idolatry of multitudinous images in various temples accompanied by singing and the smoke of incense; in the ancient Hebrew religion preached by the prophets, changing into a worship of God in a gorgeous temple with ostentatious songs and processions; in the lofty religion of Buddhism, transforming itself—with its monasteries and images of Buddha and innumerable ostentatious rites—into impenetrable Lamaism; and in Taoism with its sorcery and incantations.

Always in all religious teachings when they began to be perverted, their guardians, having brought men into a state in which their reason acted but feebly, employed every effort to suggest and instil into men whatever they wished them to believe. And in all religions it was found necessary to suggest the same three things, which serve as a basis for all the per-

versions to which a degenerating religion is exposed. First it
is suggested that there are men of a particular kind who alone
can act as intermediaries between man and God (or the
Gods); secondly that miracles have been and are performed,
proving and confirming the truth of what is told by these intermediaries between man and God; and thirdly that there
are certain words—repeated verbally or written in books—
which express the unalterable will of God (or of the Gods),
and which are therefore sacred and infallible. And as soon as
these propositions are accepted under the influence of hypnotism, then also all that the intermediaries between man and
God say is also accepted as sacred truth, and the chief aim of
the perversion of religion is attained, namely: the concealment
of the law of human equality, and even the establishment
and assertion of the greatest inequality; the separation into
castes, the separation into chosen people and Gentiles, into
orthodox and heretics, saints and sinners. This very thing has
occurred and is occurring in Christianity: complete inequality
among men has been admitted, and they are divided not only
(with reference to their comprehension of the teaching) into
clerics and laity, but (with reference to social position) into
those who have power and those who ought to submit to
power—which in accord with the teaching of Paul is acknowledged as having been ordained of God.

VI

Inequality among men, not only as clergy and laity, but
also as rich and poor, masters and slaves, is established by the
Church-Christian religion as definitely and glaringly as by
other religions. Yet judging by what we know of Christian
teaching in its earliest form in the Gospels, it would seem that
the chief methods of perversion made use of in other religions
had been foreseen, and a clear warning against them had
been uttered. Against a priestly caste it was plainly said that
no man may be the teacher of another ('Call no man your
father—neither be ye called masters'). Against attributing
sanctity to books it was said that the spirit is important but

not the letter, that man should not believe in human traditions, and that all the law and the prophets (that is, all the
books regarded as sacred writing) amount only to this, that
we should do to others as we wish them to do to us. If nothing is said against miracles, and if in the Gospels themselves
miracles are described which Jesus is supposed to have performed, it is nevertheless evident from the whole spirit of the
teaching that Jesus based the proof of the validity of his
doctrine not on miracles but on the merits of the teaching itself. ('If any man willeth to do his will, he shall know of the
teaching, whether it be of God, or whether I speak from myself.') And, above all, Christianity proclaims the equality of
men, no longer merely as a deduction from man's relation to
the infinite, but as a basic doctrine of the brotherhood of all
men, resulting from their being acknowledged as sons of God.

It seems therefore as though it should have been impossible
to pervert Christianity so as to destroy the consciousness of
equality among men. But the human mind is subtle, and
(perhaps unconsciously or semi-consciously) a quite new
dodge was devised to make inoperative the warnings contained in the Gospels and this plain pronouncement of equality among men. This dodge consisted in attributing infallibility not only to certain writings but also to a certain set of
men called The Church, who have a right to hand on this
infallibility to people they themselves select.

A slight addition to the Gospels was invented, telling how
Christ, when about to go up into the sky, handed over to certain men the exclusive right—not merely to teach others divine truth (according to the literal text of the Gospel he be-
queathed at the same time the right, not generally utilized,
of being invulnerable by snakes, or poisons)[11]—but also to
decide which people should be saved or the reverse, and,
above all, to confer this power on others. And the result was
that as soon as this idea of a Church was firmly established,

---

[11] 'Go ye into all the world, and preach the Gospel. . . . And
these signs shall follow them that believe; in my name . . . they
shall take up serpents; and if they drink any deadly thing, it shall
not hurt them.'—Mark xvi. 15-18.

all the Gospel warnings hindering the perversion of Christ's teaching became inoperative, for the Church was superior both to reason and to the writings esteemed sacred. Reason was acknowledged to be the source of errors, and the Gospels were explained not as common sense demanded but as suited those who constituted the Church.

And so all the three former methods of perverting religion —a priesthood, miracles, and the infallibility of scriptures— were admitted in full force into Christianity. Intermediaries between God and man were admitted because the need and fitness of having such intermediaries was recognized by the Church; the validity of miracles was acknowledged because the infallible Church testified to them; and the sanctity of the Bible was acknowledged because it was acknowledged by the Church.

And Christianity was perverted as all other religions had been, but with this difference, that just because Christianity most clearly proclaimed its fundamental principle—the equality of all men as sons of God—it was necessary most forcibly to pervert its whole teaching in order to hide this fundamental principle. And by the help of this conception of a Church this has been done to a greater extent than in any other religion. So that really no religion has ever preached things so immoral or so evidently incompatible with reason and with contemporary knowledge, as the doctrines preached by Church-Christianity. Not to speak of all the absurdities of the Old Testament, such as the creation of light before the sun, the creation of the world six thousand years ago, the housing of all the animals in the Ark; or of the many immoral horrors, such as injunctions to massacre children and whole populations at God's command; not to speak even of the absurd Sacrament of which Voltaire used to say that, though there have been and are many absurd religious doctrines, there never before was one in which the chief act of religion consisted in eating one's own God,—not to dwell on all that, what can be more absurd than that the Mother of God was both a mother and a Virgin; that the sky opened and a voice spoke from up there; that Christ flew into the sky and sits somewhere up there at the right hand of his father; or that God is both One and Three, not three Gods like Brahma, Vishnu, and Shiva, but One and yet Three? And what can be more immoral than the terrible doctrine that an angry and revengeful God punishes all men for Adam's sin, and sent his son on earth to save them, knowing beforehand that men would kill him and would therefore be damned; and that salvation from sin consists in being baptized, or in believing that all these things really happened, and that the son of God was killed by men that men might be saved, and that God will punish with eternal torments those who do not believe this?

So that, leaving aside things some people consider as additions to the chief dogmas of this religion—things such as various relics, icons of various Mothers of God,[12] prayers asking for favours and addressed to saints each of whom has his own speciality—and not to speak also of the Protestant doctrine of predestination—the very foundations of this religion, admitted by all and formulated in the Nicene Creed, are so absurd and immoral and run so counter to right feeling and to common sense, that men cannot believe in them. Men may repeat any form of words with their lips, but they cannot believe things that have no meaning. It is possible to say with one's lips: 'I believe the world was created six thousand years ago'; or, 'I believe Christ flew up into the sky and sat down next to his Father'; or, 'God is One and at the same time Three'—but no one can believe these things, for the words have no sense. And therefore men of our modern world who profess this perverted form of Christianity really believe in nothing at all.

And that is the peculiar characteristic of our time.

---

[12] The wonder-working icons of the Kazán, Iberian, and many other 'Mothers of God', are all paintings of Mary the mother of Jesus, to which various miraculous powers were attributed in Russia.—A. M.

VII

People in our time do not believe in anything, yet, using a false definition of faith which they take from the *Epistle to the Hebrews* (wrongly ascribed to Paul), they imagine they have faith. Faith according to that definition is 'the substance of things hoped for, the evidence of things not seen' (Heb. xi. 1). But—not to mention the fact that faith cannot be a 'substance', since it is a mental condition and not an objective reality—faith is also not 'the evidence of things not seen', for the 'evidence' referred to in the Epistle, as the context shows, is simply credulity, and credulity and faith are two different things.[13]

Faith is neither hope nor credulity, but a special state of the soul. Faith is man's consciousness that his position in the world is such as obliges him to do certain things. Man acts in accord with his faith not because, as is said in our Russian Catechism, he believes in the unseen as in the seen, nor because he hopes to attain his expectation, but only because having defined his position in the universe he naturally acts according to that position. An agriculturist cultivates the land, and a navigator sets out to sea, not because, as the Catechism says, they believe in the unseen or hope to receive a reward for their activity (such hope exists, but it is not what guides them), but because they consider that activity to be their calling. So also a religiously believing man acts in a certain way, not because he believes in the unseen or expects a reward for his activity, but because, having understood his posi-

---

[13] What is fundamental in the above argument is, that the author of the *Epistle to the Hebrews* defines faith without indicating that it relates man to God *rationally* and *supplies guidance for conduct;* while in Tolstóy's apprehension these are just the essential characteristics of faith, as of religion. The paragraph has been altered in this edition because, as Tolstóy first wrote it, it was aimed chiefly against the Russian and Slavonic versions of Hebrews xi. 1, and was therefore perplexing to English readers. It has now been worded to fit the English authorized version, and can with equal ease be worded to fit the Greek text.—A. M.

tion in the universe, he naturally acts in accord with that position. If a man has decided that his position in society is that of a labourer, an artisan, an official, or a merchant, then he considers it necessary to work; and as a labourer, an artisan, an official, or a merchant, he does his work. Just so do men in general, who one way or other have defined their position in the world, necessarily and naturally act in accord with that definition (which sometimes is rather a dim consciousness than a definition). Thus, for instance, a man having defined his position in the world as that of a member of a nation chosen by God, which in order to enjoy God's protection must fulfil His demands, will live in such a way as to fulfil those demands; another man, having defined his position on the supposition that he has passed and is passing through various forms of existence and that on his actions more or less depends his better or worse future, will be guided in life by that definition; and the conduct of a third man, who has defined his position as that of a chance combination of atoms in which a consciousness has been temporarily kindled which must be extinguished for ever, will differ from that of the two first.

The conduct of these men will be quite different because they have defined their positions differently—that is to say, they have different faiths. Faith is the same thing as religion, only with this difference: that by the word *religion* we imply something observed outside us, while what we call *faith* is the same thing, only experienced by man within himself. Faith is a relation man is conscious of towards the infinite universe, and from this relation the direction of his activity results. And therefore true faith is never irrational or incompatible with present-day knowledge, and it cannot be its characteristic to be supernatural or absurd, as people suppose, and as was expressed by a Father of the Church who said: '*Credo quia absurdum*' (I believe because it is absurd). On the contrary, the assertions of true faith, though they cannot be proved, never contain anything contrary to reason or incompatible with human knowledge, but always explain that in life which without the conception supplied by faith would appear irrational and contradictory.

Thus, for instance, an ancient Hebrew believing in a Supreme, Eternal, All-powerful Being who created the universe, the world, the animals, man, &c., and who has promised to patronize His people if they will keep His Law—did not believe in anything irrational or incompatible with his knowledge, but on the contrary this faith explained to him many things in life, which without such a faith would have been inexplicable to him.

In the same way a Hindu who believes that our souls have lived in animals and that according to the good or evil life led they pass into higher or lower animals—by the help of this faith explains to himself many things that without it would be inexplicable to him.

It is the same with a man who considers life an evil, and the aim of life to be peace attainable by the annihilation of desire. He believes in nothing unreasonable, but on the contrary in something that makes his outlook on life more reasonable than it was without that faith.

It is the same with a true Christian who believes that God is the spiritual Father of all men and that the highest human blessedness is attainable by man when he acknowledges his sonship to God and the brotherhood of all mankind.

All these faiths, if they cannot be demonstrated, are in themselves not irrational, but on the contrary give a more rational meaning to occurrences in life which without them seem irrational and contradictory. Moreover all these beliefs, by defining man's position in the universe, inevitably demand conduct in accord with that position. And therefore if a religious teaching asserts irrational propositions which explain nothing but only help to confuse man's understanding of life —then it is not a faith, but only a perversion of faith which has already lost the chief characteristic of true faith and instead of demanding anything from men has become their pliant tool. One of the chief distinctions between true faith and its perversion is that in a perverted faith man demands that God, in return for sacrifices and prayers, should fulfil his wishes and serve man. But in a true faith man feels that God demands from him the fulfilment of His will: demands that man should serve God.

And just this faith is lacking among the men of our time— they do not even understand what it is like, and by faith they mean, either repeating with their lips what is given to them as the essence of faith, or the performance of ceremonies which, as Church-Christianity teaches, help them to attain their desires.

VIII

People in our world live without any faith. One part, the educated, wealthy minority, having freed themselves from the Church hypnotism, believe in nothing at all, and look upon every faith as an absurdity or merely as a useful means of keeping the masses in subjection. The immense, poor, un-educated majority—consisting of people who with few exceptions are really sincere—being still under the hypnotism of the Church, think they believe in what is suggested to them as a faith, although it is not really a faith, for instead of elucidating to man his position in the world it only darkens it.

This situation, and the relations of the non-believing, insincere minority to the hypnotized majority, are the conditions which shape the life of our so-called Christian world. And this life—both of the minority which holds in its hands the means of hypnotization, and of the hypnotized majority— is terrible, both on account of the cruelty and immorality of the ruling classes and of the crushed and stupefied condition of the great working masses. Never at any period of religious decline has the neglect and forgetfulness of the chief characteristic of all religion, and of Christianity in particular— the principle of human equality—fallen to so low a level as it has reached in our time.

A chief cause in our time of the terrible cruelty of man to man—besides the complete absence of religion—is the refined complexity of life which hides from men the consequences of their actions. However cruel the Attilas and Genghis-Khans and their followers may have been, the process of personally killing people face to face must have been unpleasant to them and the consequences of the slaughter must have been still more unpleasant: the lamentations of the kindred of the slain and the presence of the corpses. So that the consequences of their cruelty tended to diminish it. But to-day we kill people by so complex a transmission and the consequences of our cruelty are so carefully removed and hidden from us, that there are no effects tending to restrain cruelty, and the cruelty of one set of men towards another is ever increasing and increasing till it has reached dimensions it never attained before.

I think that nowadays if—I do not say some prominent villain such as Nero, but—some most ordinary man of business wished to make a pond of human blood for diseased rich people to bathe in when ordered to do so by their learned medical advisers, he would not be prevented from arranging it if only he observed the accepted and respectable forms: that is, did not use violence to make people shed their blood but got them into such a position that they could not live without shedding it; and if also he engaged priests and scientists: the former to consecrate the new pond as they consecrate cannons, ironclads, prisons, and gallows; and the latter to find proofs of the necessity and justifiability of such an institution, as they have found proofs of the necessity for wars and brothels.[14]

The fundamental principle of all religion—the equality of men—is so forgotten, neglected, and buried under all sorts of absurd dogmas in the religion now professed, and in science this same inequality (in the theory of the struggle for existence and survival of the fittest) is so acknowledged to be a necessary condition of life—that the destruction of millions

---

[14] Laws similar to our 'Contagious Diseases Preventions Act' of 1864 (supported by the Royal College of Physicians and Surgeons in 1866) existed in Russia, as well as a regular system of licensing houses of ill-fame.—A. M.

of human lives for the convenience of a ruling minority is considered a most usual and necessary event, and is continually going on.

Men of to-day do not know how to express sufficient delight over the splendid, unprecedented, colossal progress achieved by technical science during the nineteenth century.

There is no doubt that never in history was such material progress made in mastering the powers of Nature as during the nineteenth century. But also there is no doubt that never in history was there such an example of immoral life freed from any force restraining man's animal inclinations, as that given by our ever-increasingly bestialized Christian humanity. The material progress achieved in the nineteenth century has really been great; but that progress has been bought, and is being bought, by such neglect of the most elementary demands of morality as humanity never before was guilty of, even in the days of Genghis-Khan, Attila, or Nero.

There is no doubt that the ironclads, railroads, printing-presses, tunnels, phonographs, Röntgen-rays, and so forth, are very good. They are all very good, but what are also good —good, as Ruskin says, beyond comparison with anything else—are human lives, such as those of which millions are now mercilessly ruined for the acquisition of ironclads, railways, and tunnels, which instead of beautifying life disfigure it. To this the usual reply is that appliances are already being invented, and will with time be invented, to check such destruction of human life as is now going on—but this is untrue. As long as men do not consider all men their brothers and do not consider human lives the most sacred of all things—on no account to be sacrificed, since to support them is the very first and most immediate of duties—that is, as long as men do not treat each other religiously, they will always ruin one another's lives for the sake of personal advantage. No one will be so silly as to agree to spend thousands of pounds if he can attain the same end by spending a hundred pounds— with a few human lives that are at his disposal thrown in. On the railroad in Chicago about the same number of people are crushed each year. And the owners of the railroads, quite naturally, do not adopt appliances which would prevent these people from being crushed, for they have calculated that the annual payments to the injured and to their families come to less than the interest on the cost of such appliances.

Very possibly these men who ruin human lives for their own profit may be shamed by public opinion or otherwise compelled to provide the appliances. But as long as men are not religious, and do their deeds to be seen of men and not as in the sight of God, they will, after providing appliances in one place to secure people's lives, in other matters again treat human lives as the best material out of which to make a profit.

It is easy to conquer Nature, and to build railways, steamers, museums, and so forth, if one does not spare human lives. The Egyptian Pharaohs were proud of their pyramids, and we are delighted with them, forgetting the millions of slaves' lives that were sacrificed for their erection. And in the same way we are delighted with our exhibition-places, ironclads, and trans-oceanic cables—forgetting with what we pay for these things. We should not feel proud of all this till it is all done by free men and not by slaves.

Christian nations have conquered and subdued the American Indians, Hindus, and Africans, and are now conquering and subduing the Chinese, and are proud of doing so. But really these conquests and subjugations do not result from the Christian nations being spiritually superior to those conquered, but contrariwise from their being spiritually far inferior to them. Leaving the Hindus and Chinese out of account, even among the Zulus there were, and still are, some sort of obligatory religious rules prescribing certain actions and forbidding others; but among our Christian nations there are none at all. Rome conquered the world just when Rome had freed itself from every religion. The same, only to a greater degree, is the case now with the Christian nations. They are all in one and the same condition of having rejected religion; and, therefore, notwithstanding dissensions among themselves they are all united and form one confederate band of robbers, among whom theft, plunder, depravity, and murder goes on, individually or collectively, without causing

the least compunction of conscience, and even with the greatest self-complacency, as occurred the other day in China.
Some believe in nothing and are proud of it; others pretend
to believe in what they for their own advantage hypnotize
the common folk into accepting as a faith; while others again
—the great majority, the common people as a whole—accept
as a faith the hypnotic suggestions to which they are subject,
and slavishly submit to all that is demanded of them by the
dominant and unbelieving hypnotizers.

And what these hypnotizers demand is what Nero and all
like him, who have tried in some way to fill the emptiness of
their lives, have always demanded: the satisfaction of their
insane and superabounding luxury. Luxury is obtained in no
other way than by enslaving men, and as soon as there is
enslavement, luxury increases, and the increase of luxury inevitably drags after it an increase of slavery, for only people
who are cold and hungry and bound down by want, will continue all their lives long doing not what *they* want but what
is wanted only for the pleasure of their masters.

IX

In the sixth chapter of the Book of Genesis there is a profound passage in which the author says that God, before the
Flood, having seen that the spirit He had given to men that
they might serve Him was used by them only to serve their
own desires, became so angry with men that He repented of
having created them, and, before entirely destroying them,
decided to shorten the life of man to a hundred and twenty
years. And the very thing that then, according to the Bible,
so provoked God's anger that it caused Him to shorten man's
life, is again going on among the people of our Christian
world.

Reason is the power which enables men to define their relation to the universe, and as all men stand in one and the
same relation to the universe it follows that religion—which
is the elucidation of that relation—unites men. And union

among men affords them the highest attainable welfare both
physical and spiritual.

Complete union with the highest and most perfect reason,
and therefore complete welfare, is the ideal towards which
humanity strives; and all religions unite people by supplying
identical answers to all men of any given society when they
ask what the universe is and what its inhabitants are; and by
uniting them it brings them nearer to the attainment of welfare. But when reason diverging from its natural function
(that of determining man's relation to God, and what his
activity should be conformably to that relation), is used in
the service of the flesh and for angry strife with other men
and other fellow creatures, and when it is even used to justify
this evil life, so contrary to man's nature and to the purpose
for which he is intended—then those terrible calamities result under which the majority of men are now suffering, and
a state is reached that makes any return to a reasonable and
good life seem almost impossible.

Pagans united by the crudest religious teaching are far
nearer the recognition of truth than the pseudo-Christian
nations of our day who live without any religion, and among
whom the most advanced people are themselves convinced—
and suggest to others—that religion is unnecessary and that
it is much better to live without any.

Among the pagans men may be found who, recognizing
the inconsistency of their faith with their increasing knowledge and with the demands of their reason, produce or adopt
a new religion more in accord with the spiritual condition of
their nation and acceptable to their compatriots and co-
believers. But men of our world—some of whom regard religion as an instrument wherewith to keep common folk in
subjection, while others consider all religion absurd, and yet
others (the great majority of the nation), while living under
the hypnotism of a gross deception think they possess true
religion—become impervious to any forward movement and
incapable of any approach towards truth.

Proud of their improvements in things that relate to the

bodily life, as well as of their refined, idle reasonings (in which they aim not only at justifying themselves, but also at proving their superiority to any other people of any age of history), they petrify in ignorance and immorality while feeling fully assured that they stand on an elevation never before reached by humanity, and that every step forward along the path of ignorance and immorality raises them to yet greater heights of enlightenment and progress.

X

Man naturally wishes to bring his bodily (physical) and his rational (spiritual) activity into conformity. He cannot be at peace until he has reached that conformity in one way or other. But it is attainable in two different ways. One way is for a man to decide by the use of his reason on the necessity or desirability of a certain action or actions and then to behave accordingly; the other way is for a man to commit actions under the influence of his feelings, and then to invent intellectual explanations or justifications for what he has done.

The first method of making one's actions conform to one's reason is characteristic of men who have some religion and on the basis of its precepts decide what they ought and what they ought not to do. The second method is generally characteristic of men who are not religious and have no general standard by which to judge the quality of actions, and who therefore always set up a conformity between their reason and their actions, not by subjecting the latter to their reason, but (after acting under the sway of feeling) by using reason to justify what they have done.

A religious man—knowing what is good and what is bad in his own activity and in that of others and knowing also why one thing is good and another is bad—when he sees a contradiction between the demands of reason and his own or other men's actions, will employ the whole force of his reason to find means to destroy these contradictions by learning how best to bring his actions into agreement with the demands of his reason. But a man without religion—who has no standard whereby to judge the quality of actions apart from the pleasure they afford him—yielding to the sway of his feelings (which are most various and often contradictory), involuntarily falls into contradictions, and having fallen into contradictions tries to solve or hide them by arguments more or less elaborate and clever but always untruthful. And therefore while the reasoning of truly religious men is always simple, direct, and truthful, the mental activity of men who lack religion becomes particularly subtle, complex, and insincere.

I will take the most common example: that of a man who is addicted to vice—that is, is not chaste, not faithful to his wife, or being unmarried indulges in vice. If he is a religious man he knows that this is wrong, and all the efforts of his reason are directed to finding means to free himself from his vice: avoiding intercourse with adulterers and adulteresses, increasing the amount of his work, arranging a strict life for himself, not allowing himself to look on a woman as on an object of desire, and so forth. And all this is very simple and everyone can understand it. But if the incontinent man is not religious, he at once begins to devise all sorts of explanations to prove that falling in love with women is very good. And then we get all sorts of most complex, cunning, and subtle considerations about the affinity of souls, about beauty, about the freedom of love, and so on; and the more these spread the more they darken the question and hide the essential truth.

Among those who lack religion the same thing happens in all spheres of activity and of thought. To hide underlying contradictions, complex, subtle disquisitions are piled up which, by filling the mind with all sorts of unnecessary rubbish, divert men's attention from what is important and essential, and make it possible for them to petrify in the deceit in which, without noticing it, the people of our world are living.

'Men loved the darkness rather than the light; for their works were evil,' says the Gospel. 'For every one that doeth ill hateth the light, and cometh not to the light, lest his works should be reproved.'

And therefore the men of our world, having, in conse-

quence of their lack of religion, arranged a most cruel, animal, and immoral life, have also brought their complex,
subtle, unprofitable activity of mind—hiding the evil of this
kind of life—to such a degree of unnecessary intricacy and
confusion that the majority of them have quite lost the capacity to distinguish good from evil or false from true.

There is not a single question the men of our world can approach directly and simply: all questions—economic, national, political (whether home or foreign), diplomatic or
scientific, not to mention questions of philosophy and religion
—are presented so artificially and incorrectly and are
swathed in such thick shrouds of complex, unnecessary dis-
putations—such subtle perversions of meanings and words,
such sophistries and disputes—that all arguments about such
questions revolve on one spot, connected with nothing, and
like driving-wheels without a connecting strap, effect nothing
except the one object for which they were produced: to hide
from oneself and from others the evil in which men live and
the evil they commit.

XI

In every domain of what is now called science one and the
same feature is encountered baffling the mental efforts men
direct to the investigation of various domains of knowledge.
This feature is that all these scientific investigations evade the
essential question calling for an answer, and examine side-
issues the investigation of which brings one to no definite result but becomes more intricate the farther one advances.
Nor can this be otherwise in a science which selects the objects of its investigation haphazard and not according to the
demands of a religious conception of life defining what should
be studied and why, what first and what afterwards. For
instance, in the now fashionable subjects of Sociology and
Political Economy it would seem that there is really only one
question: 'How is it, and why is it, that some people do nothing while others are working for them?' (If there is another
question: 'Why do people work separately, hindering one an-

other, and not together in common as would be more profitable?' that question is included in the first. For were there no inequality there would be no strife.) It would seem that there ought to be only that one question, but science does not even think of propounding and replying to it but commences its discussions from afar off and conducts them so that its conclusions can never either solve or assist the solution of the fundamental problem. Discussions are started concerning what used to be and what now is, and the past and the present are regarded as something as unalterable as the course of the stars in the heavens, and abstract conceptions are devised—value, capital, profit, and interest—and a complex play of wits (which has now already continued for a hundred years) results among the disputants. In reality the question can be settled very easily and simply.

Its solution lies in the fact that as all men are brothers and equals, each should act towards others as he wishes them to act towards him; and therefore the whole matter depends on the destruction of a false religious law and the restoration of the true religious law. The advanced people of Christendom, however, not only refuse to accept that solution, but on the contrary try to hide from men the possibility of such a solution, and therefore devote themselves to the idle play of intelligence which they call science.

The same thing takes place in the domain of Jurisprudence. There would seem to be only one essential question: 'How is it that there are men who allow themselves to perpetrate violence on others, to fleece them, confine them, execute them, send them to the wars, and so on?' The solution of that question is very simple if it be examined from the only point of view suitable to the subject—the religious. From a religious point of view man must not and should not subject his neighbour to violence, and therefore only one thing is needful for the solution of the question—namely, to destroy all superstitions and sophistries which allow of violence, and to instil into men religious principles clearly excluding the possibility of violence.

But the advanced men, instead of doing this, devote all

their wits to the task of hiding from others the possibility and necessity of such a solution. They write mountains of books about all sorts of laws: civil, criminal, police, Church, commercial, &c., and expound and dispute about these—fully assured that they are doing something not only useful but very important. To the question, 'Why, among men who are naturally equal, may some judge, coerce, fleece, and execute others?'—they give no reply, and do not even acknowledge the existence of such a question. According to their doctrine this violence is not committed by men but by some abstraction called The State. And similarly, in all realms of knowledge, the learned men of to-day evade and are silent about the essential questions and hide the underlying contradictions.

In the realm of history, the only essential question is: 'How did the workers (who form nine hundred and ninety-nine thousandths of the whole of humanity) live?' To this question we get nothing like an answer; the question is ignored, while whole mountains of books are written by historians of one school to tell of the stomach-aches of Louis XI, the horrors committed by Elizabeth of England or Iván the Terrible of Russia, of who were their Ministers, and of what verses and comedies were written by literary men to amuse these Kings and their Mistresses and Ministers. Meanwhile the historians of another school tell us in what sort of country a people lived, what they ate, what they sold, what clothes they wore —and in general about things that could have no influence on the people's true life, but were results of their religion, which the historians of this class imagine to be itself a result of the food the people ate and the clothes they wore.

Yet an answer to the question: 'How did the workers live?' cannot be given till we acknowledge religion to be the essential condition of a people's life. And the reply is therefore to be found in the study of the religions believed in by the nations: for these brought them to the position in which they lived.

In the study of Natural History one would think there was little need to darken men's common sense, but even here, following the bent of mind which contemporary science has adopted, instead of giving the most natural replies to the questions: 'What is the world of living things (plants and animals) and how is it subdivided?' an idle, confused, and perfectly useless chatter is started (directed chiefly against the Biblical account of the creation of the world) as to how organisms came into existence—which really one neither needs to know nor can know, for this origin, however we may explain it, always remains hidden from us in endless time and space. But on this theme, theories and refutations and supplementary theories are invented, filling millions of books, the unexpected result arrived at being: That the law of life which man should obey is the struggle for existence.

More than that, in consequence of the absence of any guidance from religious principle, the applied sciences—such as Technology and Medicine—inevitably diverge from their reasonable purpose and take a false direction. Thus Technology is directed not to lightening the toil of the people, but to achieving improvements needed only by the rich and which will therefore yet more widely separate the rich from the poor, the masters from their slaves. If some advantages from these inventions and improvements—some crumbs—do reach the working classes, this is not at all because they were intended for the people, but only because by their nature they could not be kept from them.

It is the same with medical science, which has advanced in its false direction till it has reached a stage at which only the rich can command it, while from their manner of life and their poverty (and as a result of the fact that the questions relating to the amelioration of the life of the poor have been neglected) the mass of the people can only avail themselves of it under conditions that most clearly show how medical science has diverged from its true purpose.

But this avoidance and perversion of essential questions is most strikingly seen in what is now called Philosophy. There would seem to be one essential question for philosophy to answer: 'What must I do?' And in the philosophy of the Christian nations answers to this question—though combined with very much that is unnecessary and confused, as in the case of

Spinoza, Kant (in his *Critique of Practical Reason*), Schopenhauer, and particularly Rousseau—have at any rate been given. But latterly, since Hegel (who taught that whatever exists is reasonable) the question: 'What must we do?' has been pushed into the background and philosophy directs its whole attention to the investigation of things as they are and to making them fit into a prearranged theory. That was the first downward step. The next step, leading human thought to a yet lower level, was the acknowledgement of the law of the struggle for existence as fundamental, merely because that struggle can be observed among plants and animals. Under the influence of that theory it is assumed that the destruction of the weakest is a law which should not be checked. Finally came the third step, when the semi-sane Nietzsche's puerile efforts at originality, which do not even present anything complete or coherent but are as it were immoral, offhand jottings of utterly baseless thoughts, were accepted by advanced people as the last word of philosophic science. In reply to the question: 'What must we do?' the advice is now plainly offered: 'Live as you please, paying no attention to the lives of others.'

If anyone doubted the terrible state of stupefaction and bestiality to which our Christian humanity has descended— without speaking of the crimes recently committed in South Africa and China, which were defended by priests and accepted as achievements by all the great ones of the earth— the extraordinary success of the writings of Nietzsche would alone suffice to supply an unanswerable proof. Some disjointed writings—aiming most obtrusively at effect—appear, written by a man suffering from megalomania, a bold but limited and abnormal German. Neither by their talent nor validity have these writings any claim on public attention. In the days of Kant, Leibnitz, or Hume, or even fifty years ago, such writings, far from attracting attention, could not even have appeared. But in our days all the so-called educated classes of humanity are delighted with the ravings of Herr Nietzsche; they dispute about him and explain him, and innumerable copies of his works are printed in all languages.

Turgénev humorously says that there are such things as 'reversed platitudes', and that they are often used by people lacking in talent but desirous of attracting attention. Everyone knows for instance that water is wet: but suddenly someone seriously asserts that water is dry—not ice, but water is dry; and such an opinion, if confidently expressed, attracts attention.

In the same way, the whole world knows that virtue consists in subduing one's passions and in self-renunciation. This is known not by Christians only (with whom Nietzsche imagines he is fighting), but it is an eternal and supreme law which all humanity has recognized—in Brahmanism, Buddhism, Confucianism, and in the ancient Persian religion. And suddenly a man appears who announces his discovery that self-renunciation, mildness, meekness, love—are all vices which are ruining humanity (he refers to Christianity, forgetting all the other religions). It is comprehensible that such an assertion should at first perplex people. But after thinking a little and failing to find in his writings any proofs supporting this vague assertion, every rational man ought to reject such books and only be surprised that nowadays there is no nonsense too arrant to find a publisher. With the works of Nietzsche that course has not been adopted. The majority of pseudo-enlightened people seriously discuss the theory of 'Supermen', and acclaim its author as a great philosopher—a successor to Descartes, Leibnitz, and Kant.

And all this has happened because the majority of pseudo-enlightened men of to-day dislike anything reminding them of virtue or of its chief basis: self-renunciation and love—things that restrain and condemn the animal life they lead; and they gladly welcome a doctrine of egotism and cruelty—however poorly, unintelligibly, and disjointedly expressed—which justifies the system of founding one's own happiness and greatness upon the lives of others: the system in which they live.

XII

Christ reproached the Scribes and Pharisees because they took the keys of the Kingdom of Heaven but neither themselves entered in nor let others enter.

The learned scribes of to-day do the same: they have now taken the keys not of the Kingdom of Heaven but of enlightenment, and neither enter in nor let others enter.

The hierophants, the priests, by all sorts of deception and hypnotism, have instilled into people an idea that Christianity is not a teaching proclaiming the equality of all men and therefore destructive of the whole present system of life; but that on the contrary it supports the existing order of things and bids us differentiate people, like the stars, and regard them as belonging to different orders—acknowledging any existing authority as ordained of God and obeying it absolutely; in fact, suggesting to the oppressed that their position is what God wishes it to be, and that they ought to put up with it meekly and humbly, submitting to their oppressors who need not be meek or humble, but should—as Emperors, Kings, Popes, Bishops, and secular or spiritual magnates of various kinds—correct others by teaching and punishing them, while themselves living in splendour and luxury which it is the duty of those in subjection to supply. And the ruling classes, thanks to this false teaching, which they strongly support, rule over the people, obliging them to furnish means of support for their rulers' idleness, luxury, and vices. And the only men who have freed themselves from this hypnotism—the scientific people—those therefore who alone are able to free the people from their oppression, do not do it though they say they wish to; but instead of doing what might attain that end they do just the opposite, imagining that they thereby serve the people.

One would think these men—even from casually observing what it is that those who hold the masses in subjection are most afraid of—might see what really moves men and what really keeps them down in the places they now occupy, and would direct their whole force to that source of power. They not only do not do this, however, but consider such action quite useless.

It is as if these men did not wish to see the facts. They assiduously and sincerely do all sorts of different things for the people, but do not do the one thing primarily needful; and their activity is like the activity of a man trying to move a train by exerting his muscles, when he need only get on the engine and do what he constantly sees the engine-driver do: move a lever to let steam into the cylinders. That steam is men's religious conception of life. And the advanced men need only notice the eagerness with which those in authority retain control of that motive power—by means of which the rulers lord it over the masses—to understand to what they must direct their efforts in order to free the people from slavery.

What does the Sultan of Turkey guard and to what does he cling for support? And why does the Russian Emperor on arriving at a town go first of all to kiss an icon or the relics of some saint? And why, in spite of all the varnish of culture he so prides himself on, does the German Kaiser in all his speeches—seasonably or unseasonably—speak of God, of Christ, of the sanctity of religion, of oaths, &c.? Simply because they all know that their power rests on the army, and that the army—the very possibility of such a thing as an army existing—rests on religion. And if wealthy people are generally particularly devout: making a show of believing, going to Church, and observing the Sabbath—it is all done chiefly because an instinct of self-preservation warns them that their exceptionally advantageous position in the community is bound up with the religion they profess.

These people often do not know in what way their privileges rest on religious deception, but their instinct of self-preservation warns them of the weak spot in that on which their power rests, and they first of all defend that place. Within certain limits these people always allow, and have allowed, socialistic and even revolutionary propaganda, but the foundations of religion they never allow to be touched.

And therefore if history and psychology do not suffice to enable the advanced men of to-day—the learned, the Liberals, the Socialists, the Revolutionists and Anarchists—to discover what it is that moves the people, this visible indication should suffice to convince them that the motive power lies not in material conditions but only in religion.

Yet strange to say the learned, advanced people of to-day, who understand and discuss the conditions of life of various nations very acutely, do not see what is so obvious that it strikes one's eye. If these men intentionally leave the people in their religious ignorance for the sake of retaining their own profitable position among the minority, this is a terrible, revolting fraud. Men who act so are the very hypocrites Christ especially denounced—the only people He did in fact denounce—and He denounced them because no monsters or malefactors ever brought so much evil into human life as is brought by these men.

But if they are sincere, the only explanation of so strange an eclipse of reason is, that just as the masses are hypnotized by a false religion, so also are the pseudo-enlightened men of to-day hypnotized by a false science which has decided that the chief motor-nerve that now as heretofore actuates humanity, has become altogether useless and can be replaced by something else.

XIII

This delusion or deceit of the scribes—the educated men of our world—is the peculiarity of our times, and in this lies the cause of the miserable condition in which Christian humanity now lives, as well as of the brutalization into which it is sinking deeper and deeper.

It is usual for the advanced, educated classes of our world to assert that the false religious beliefs held by the masses are of no special importance, and that it is not worth while and is unnecessary to struggle against them directly, as was done by Hume, Voltaire, Rousseau and others. Science, they think—that is to say, the disconnected, casual information they disseminate among the people—will of itself attain that end, and man, having learned how many million miles it is from the earth to the sun, and what metals exist in the sun and the stars, will cease to believe in Church doctrines.

This sincere or insincere assertion or assumption covers either a great delusion or a terrible deception. From the very earliest years of childhood—the years most susceptible to suggestion, when those who train children cannot be sufficiently careful what they transmit to them—a child is hypnotized with the absurd, immoral dogmas of so-called Christian religion, irreconcilable with our reason and knowledge. He is taught the dogma of the Trinity, which healthy reason cannot hold; the coming of one of the three Gods to earth for the salvation of the human race, and his resurrection and his ascent into heaven; is taught to expect a second coming, and punishment in eternal torments for disbelief in these dogmas; also he is taught to pray for what he wants; and many other things. And when all this (incompatible as it is with reason, contemporary knowledge, and man's conscience) is indelibly stamped on the child's impressionable mind, he is left to himself to find his way as he can amid the contradictions which flow from these dogmas he has accepted and assimilated as unquestionable truths. No one tells him how he may or should reconcile these contradictions, or if the theologians do try to reconcile them their attempts only confuse the matter more than before. So little by little the man becomes accustomed to suppose that reason cannot be trusted (and the theologians strongly support this notion) and therefore anything is possible, and that there is no capacity in man by means of which he can himself distinguish good from evil or falsehood from truth, and that in what is most important for him—his actions —he should be guided not by his reason but by what others tell him. It is evident what a terrible perversion of man's spiritual world such an education must produce, reinforced as it is in adult life by all the means of hypnotization which, by the aid of the priests, is continually exercised upon the people.

If a man of strong spirit with great labour and suffering does succeed in freeing himself from the hypnotism in which he has been educated in childhood and held in mature life, the perversion of his mind, produced by the persuasion that he must distrust his own reason, can still not pass without leaving traces—just as in the physical world the poisoning of an organism with some powerful virus cannot pass without leaving its trace. It is natural for such a man, having freed himself from the hypnotism of this deceit and hating the falsehood from which he has just escaped, to adopt the view advocated by advanced men and to regard every religion as an obstacle in the path along which humanity is progressing. And having adopted that opinion such a man becomes, like his teachers, devoid of principle—that is devoid of conscience, and guided in life merely by his desires. Nor does he condemn himself for this, but considers that it places him on the highest plane of mental development attainable by man.

That is what may happen with men of strong minds. The less strong, though they may be roused to doubts, will never completely free themselves from the deception in which they were brought up, but adopting or inventing various cunningly devised, cloudy theories to justify the absurd dogmas they have accepted, and living in a sphere of doubts, mist, sophistries and self-deception, they will co-operate in the mystification of the masses and oppose their enlightenment.

But the majority of men, having neither the strength nor the opportunity to struggle against the hypnotism exercised over them, will live and die generation after generation, as they now do—deprived of man's highest welfare, which is a truly religious understanding of life—and will remain docile tools of the classes that rule over them and deceive them.

And it is this terrible deception that advanced and learned men consider unimportant and not worth directly attacking. The only explanation of such an assertion, if those who make it are sincere, is that they are themselves under the hypnotism of a false science; but if they are not sincere then their conduct is explained by the fact that an attack on established beliefs is unprofitable and often dangerous. In any case, one way or another, the assertion that the profession of a false religion does no harm—or though harmful is unimportant—

and that one can therefore disseminate enlightenment without destroying religious deception, is quite untrue.

Mankind can be saved from its ills only by being freed both from the hypnotism in which the priests are holding it and from that into which the learned are leading it. To pour anything into a full bottle one must first empty out what it contains. And similarly it is necessary to free men from the deception of their false faith in order that they may be able to adopt a true religion, that is, a correct relation (in accord with the development humanity has attained) towards the Source of all—towards God,—and that from this relation they may obtain guidance for their actions.

XIV

'But is there any true religion? Religions are endlessly various, and we have no right to call one of them true just because it most nearly suits our own taste'—that is what people say who look at the external forms of religion as at some disease from which they feel themselves free but from which other people still suffer. But this is a mistake; religions differ in their external forms but they are all alike in their fundamental principles. And it is just these fundamental principles of all religions which constitute that true religion which alone to-day is natural to all men, and the acceptance of which can alone save men from their calamities.

Mankind has lived long, and just as it has produced and improved its practical inventions through successive generations, so also it could not fail to produce and improve those spiritual principles which have formed the bases of its life, as well as the rules of conduct that resulted from those principles. If blind men do not see these, that does not prove that they do not exist.

This religion of our times, common to all men, exists not as some sect with all its peculiarities and perversions, but as a religion consisting of those principles which are alike in all the widespread religions known to us and professed by more than nine-tenths of the human race; and that men are not yet completely brutalized is due to the fact that the best men of all nations hold to this religion and profess it, even if unconsciously, and only the hypnotic deception practised on men by the aid of the priests and scientists now hinders men from consciously adopting it.

The principles of this true religion are so natural to men that as soon as they are put before them they are accepted as something quite familiar and self-evident. For us the true religion is Christianity in those of its principles in which it agrees, not with the external forms, but with the basic principles of Brahmanism, Confucianism, Taoism, Hebraism, Buddhism, and even Mohammedanism. And just in the same way, for those who profess Brahmanism, Confucianism, and so on —true religion is that of which the basic principles agree with those of all other religions. And these principles are very simple, intelligible, and clear.

These principles are: that there is a God, the origin of all things; that in man dwells a spark from that Divine Origin, which man can increase or decrease in himself by his way of living; that to increase this divine spark man must suppress his passions and increase love in himself; and that the practical means to attain this result is to do to others as you would they should do to you. All these principles are common to Brahmanism, Hebraism, Confucianism, and Mohammedanism. (If Buddhism supplies no definition of God, it nevertheless acknowledges That with which man commingles, and into Which he is absorbed when he attains to Nirvana. And That with which man commingles or into Which he is absorbed in Nirvana, is the same Origin that is called God in Hebraism, Christianity, and Mohammedanism.)

'But that is not religion,' is what men of to-day will say who are accustomed to consider that the supernatural, i.e. the unmeaning, is the chief sign of religion. 'That is anything you like: philosophy, ethics, ratiocination—but not religion.' Religion, according to them, must be absurd and unintelligible (*Credo quia absurdum*). Yet it was only from these very principles, or rather in consequence of their being preached as religious doctrines, that—by a long process of perversion—all those absurd miracles and supernatural occurrences were elaborated which are now considered to be the fundamental signs of every religion. To assert that the supernatural and irrational form the essential characteristic of religion is like observing only rotten apples, and then asserting that a flabby bitterness and a harmful effect on the stomach are the prime characteristics of the fruit called Apple.

Religion is the definition of man's relation to the Source of all things and of man's purpose in life which follows from that relation, and it supplies rules of conduct resulting from that purpose. And the universal religion, whose first principles are alike in all the faiths, fully meets the demands of this understanding of religion. It defines the relation of man to God as being that of a part to the whole; from this relation it deduces man's purpose, which is to increase the divine element in himself; and this purpose involves practical demands on man in accord with the rule, Do to others as you wish them to do to you.

People often doubt, and I myself at one time doubted, whether such an abstract rule as, Do to others as you wish them to do to you, can be as obligatory a rule and guide for action as the simpler rules: to fast, pray, and take communion, &c. But an irrefutable reply to that doubt is supplied, for instance, by the spiritual condition of a Russian peasant who would rather die than spit out the Sacrament onto a manure heap, but who is yet ready to kill his brothers at the command of men.

Why should demands flowing from the rule of doing to others as you wish them to do to you—such, for instance, as not killing one's brother man, not reviling, not committing adultery, not revenging oneself, not taking advantage of the need of one's brethren to satisfy one's own caprice, and many others,—why should not they be instilled as forcibly and become as binding and inviolable as the belief in the sanctity of the Sacraments, or of images, &c., now is to men whose faith is founded more on credulity than on any clear inward consciousness?

XV

The truths of the religion common to all men of our time are so simple, so intelligible, and so near the heart of each man, that it would seem only necessary for parents, rulers, and teachers to instil into children and adults—instead of the obsolete and absurd doctrines (in which they themselves often do not believe) about Trinities, virgin-mothers, redemptions, Indras, Trimurti, and Buddhas and Mohammeds who fly away into the sky—those clear and simple truths the metaphysical essence of which is that the spirit of God dwells in man; and the practical rule of which is that man should do to others as he wishes them to do to him—for the whole life of humanity to change. If only—in the same way that it is now instilled into children and confirmed in adults that God sent His son to redeem Adam's sin, and that He established His Church which must be obeyed, as well as rules deduced from these beliefs, telling when and where to pray and make offerings, when to refrain from such and such food, and on what days to abstain from work—if only it were instilled and confirmed that God is a spirit whose manifestation is present in us, the strength of which we can increase by our lives: if only this and all that naturally flows from this were instilled in the same way that quite useless stories of impossible occurrences, and rules of meaningless ceremonies deduced from those stories, are now instilled—then, instead of purposeless strife and discord, we should very soon (without the aid of diplomatists, international law, peace-congresses, political economists, and Socialists in all their various subdivisions) see humanity living a peaceful, united, and happy life guided by the one religion.

But nothing of the kind is done: not only is the deception of false religion not destroyed and the true one not preached, but on the contrary men go farther and farther away from the possibility of accepting the truth.

The chief cause of people not doing what is so possible,

natural, and necessary, is that men to-day, in consequence of having lived so long without religion, are so accustomed to establish and defend their existence by violence, by bayonets, bullets, prisons, and gallows, that it seems to them as if such an arrangement of life were not only normal, but were the only one possible. Not only do those who profit by the existing order think so, but even those who suffer from it are so stupefied by the hypnotism exercised upon them that they also consider violence to be the only means of securing good order in human society. Yet it is just this arrangement and maintenance of the commonweal by violence that does most to hinder people from comprehending the causes of their sufferings and consequently from being able to establish a true order.

The results of it are such as might be produced by a bad or malicious doctor who should drive a malignant eruption inwards, thereby cheating the sick man and making the disease worse and its cure impossible.

To people of the ruling classes who enslave the masses and think and say: *'Après nous le déluge,'* [15] it seems very convenient by means of the army, the priesthood, the soldiers, and the police, as well as by threats of bayonets, bullets, prisons, workhouses, and gallows, to compel the enslaved people to remain in stupefaction and enslavement, and not to hinder the rulers from exploiting them. And the ruling men do this, calling it the maintenance of good order, but there is nothing that so hinders the establishment of a good social order as this does. In reality, far from being the establishment of good order, it is the establishment of evil.

If men of our Christian nations still possessing some remnants of those religious principles which in spite of everything yet live in the people, had not before them the continual example of crime committed by those who have assumed the duty of guarding order and morality among men—the wars, executions, prisons, taxation, sale of intoxicants and of opium —they would never have thought of committing one-hun-

---

[15] Madame de Pompadour's remark, 'After us the deluge.'—A. M.

dredth of the evil deeds—the frauds, violence and murders
—which they now commit in full confidence that such deeds
are good and natural for men to commit.

The law of human life is such that the only way to improve
it, whether for the individual or for a society of men, is by
means of inward, moral growth towards perfection. All attempts of men to better their lives by external action—by violence—serve as the most efficacious propaganda and example of evil, and therefore not only do not improve life, but on
the contrary increase the evil which, like a snowball, grows
larger and larger and removes men more and more from the
only possible way of truly bettering their lives.

In proportion as the practice of violence and crime, committed in the name of the law by the guardians of order and
morality, becomes more and more frequent and cruel, and is
more and more justified by the hypnotism of falsehood presented as religion, men will be more and more confirmed in
the belief that the law of their life is not one of love and service to their fellows, but is one demanding that they should
strive with and devour one another.

And the more they are confirmed in that thought, which
degrades them to the level of the beasts, the harder will it be
to shake off the hypnotic trance in which they are living, and
to accept as the basis of their life the true religion of our time,
common to all humanity.

A vicious circle has been established: the absence of religion
makes possible an animal life based on violence; an animal
life based on violence makes emancipation from hypnotism
and an adoption of true religion more and more impossible.
And therefore men do not do what is natural, possible,
and necessary in our times: do not destroy the deception and
simulacrum of religion, and do not assimilate and preach the
true religion.

XVI

Is any issue from this enchanted circle possible, and if so,
what is it?

At first it seems as if the Governments, which have taken on themselves the duty of guiding the life of the people for their benefit, ought to lead us out of this circle. That is what men who have tried to alter the arrangements of life founded on violence and to replace them by a reasonable arrangement based on mutual service and love, have always supposed. So thought the Christian reformers, and the founders of various theories of European Communism, and so also thought the celebrated Chinese reformer Mo Ti,[16] who for the welfare of the people proposed to the Government not to teach schoolchildren military sciences and exercises, or give rewards to adults for military achievements, but to teach both children and adults the rules of esteem and love, and give rewards and encouragement for feats of love. So also thought, and think, many religious peasant-reformers, of whom I have known and now know several, beginning with Sutáev and ending with an old man who has now five times presented a petition to the Emperor, asking him to decree the abrogation of false religion and to order that true Christianity be preached.

It seems to men natural that the Government—which justifies its existence on the score of its care for the welfare of the people—must, to secure that welfare, wish to use the only means which can never do people any harm and can only produce the most fruitful results. Government however has not only never taken upon itself this duty, but on the contrary has always and everywhere maintained with the greatest jealousy any false, effete religion prevalent at the period, and has in every way persecuted those who have tried to inform the people of the principles of true religion. In reality this cannot be otherwise; for if Governments were to expose the falsity of the present religions and to preach the true one, it would be as if a man were to cut down the branch on which he is sitting.

But if Government will not do this work it would seem cer-

---

[16] Mo Ti (or Mih Teih) lived a little before Mencius (about 372-289 B.C.) who wrote against the former's doctrine of universal love. —A. M.

tain that those learned men who having freed themselves from
the deception of false religion say they wish to serve the common people whose labour has provided for their education
and support, are bound to do it. But these men, like the Government, do not do it: first, because they consider it inex-
pedient to risk unpleasantness and to suffer the danger of
persecution at the hands of the ruling classes for exposing
a fraud which Government protects and which in their opinion
will disappear of itself; secondly, because, considering all religion to be an effete error, they have nothing to offer the people in place of the deception they are expected to destroy.

There remain those great masses of unlearned men who are
under the hypnotic influence of Church and Government deception, and who therefore believe that the simulacrum of religion which has been instilled into them is the one true religion and that there is and can be no other. These masses
are under a constant and intense hypnotic influence. Generation after generation they are born and live and die in the
stupefied condition in which they are kept by the clergy and
the Government; and if they free themselves from that influence they are sure to fall into the school of the scientists who
deny religion—when their influence becomes as useless and
harmful as the influence of their teachers.

So that for some men the work is unprofitable, while for
others it is impossible.

XVII

It looks as if no issue were possible.

And indeed for irreligious men there is not, and cannot be,
any issue from this position; those who belong to the higher,
governing classes, even if they pretend to be concerned for
the welfare of the masses, will never (guided by worldly aims,
they can never) seriously attempt to destroy the stupefaction
and servitude in which these masses live, and which make it
possible for the upper classes to rule over them. In the same
way, men belonging to the enslaved masses cannot, while
guided by worldly motives, wish to make their own hard posi-

tion harder by entering on a struggle against the upper classes to expose a false teaching and to preach a true one. Neither of these sets of men has any motive to do this, and if they are intelligent they will never attempt it.

But it is otherwise for religious people: men such as those who—however perverted a society may be—are always to be found guarding with their lives the sacred fire of religion without which human life could not exist. There are times (and our time is such) when these men are unnoticed, when —as among us in Russia—despised and derided by all, their lives pass unrecorded; in exile, in prisons, and in penal battalions. Yet they live, and on them depends the rational life of humanity. And it is just these religious men—however few they may be—who alone can and will rend asunder that enchanted circle which keeps men bound. They can do it, because all the disadvantages and dangers which hinder a worldly man from opposing the existing order of society not only do not impede a religious man, but rather increase his zeal in the struggle against falsehood, and impel him to confess by word and deed what he holds to be divine truth. If he belongs to the ruling classes he will not only not wish to hide the truth out of regard for his own advantageous position, but on the contrary, having come to hate such advantages he will exert his whole strength to free himself from them and to preach the truth, for he will no longer have any other aim in life than to serve God. If he belongs to the enslaved, then in the same way, unbiased by the wish, common among those of his position, to improve the conditions of his physical life, such a man will have no aim but to fulfil the will of God by exposing falsehood and confessing truth; and no suffering or threats will make him cease to live in accord with that purpose which he has recognized in his life. They will both act thus, as naturally as a worldly man exerts himself and puts up with privations to obtain riches or to please a ruler from whom he expects to receive advantages. Every religious man acts thus, because a human soul enlightened by religion no longer lives merely by the life of this world, as irreligious people do, but lives an eternal, infinite life, for which suffering and death in this life are as insignificant as are blisters on his hands or weariness of limbs to a ploughman when he is ploughing a field.

These are the men who will rend asunder the enchanted circle in which people are now confined. However few such men there may be, however humble their social position, however poor in education or ability, as surely as fire lights the dry steppe, so surely will these people set the whole world aflame and kindle all the hearts of men, withered by long lack of religion and now thirsting for a renewal of life.

Religion is not a belief, settled once for all, in certain supernatural occurrences supposed to have taken place once upon a time, nor in the necessity for certain prayers and ceremonies; nor is it, as the scientists suppose, a survival of the superstitions of ancient ignorance which in our time has no meaning or application to life; but religion is a certain relation of man to eternal life and to God, a relation accordant with reason and contemporary knowledge, and it is the one thing that alone moves humanity forward towards its destined aim.

A wise Hebrew proverb says, 'The soul of man is the lamp of God.' Man is a weak and miserable animal until the light of God burns in his soul. But when that light burns (and it burns only in souls enlightened by religion) man becomes the most powerful being in the world. Nor can this be otherwise, for what then acts in him is no longer *his* strength but the strength of God.

So this is what religion is and in what its essence consists.

[February, 1902.]

ON

PEACE

❖❖❖❖❖❖❖❖❖❖❖❖❖❖❖❖❖❖❖❖❖❖❖❖❖❖❖❖

CHRISTIANITY AND PATRIOTISM

Preface

The Franco-Russian celebrations that took place in France in October of last year (1893) aroused in me, as well probably as in many other people, at first a feeling of amusement, then of perplexity, and at last of indignation, which I wished to express in a short magazine article. But as I considered the chief causes of that strange phenomenon more and more seriously I arrived at the opinions I now present to the reader.

Russians and Frenchmen have lived for many centuries knowing one another and sometimes coming into friendly but more often unfortunately into very hostile relations with one another, aroused by their governments. And now suddenly, because a French squadron visited Kronstadt two years ago and its officers came ashore and ate a great deal in various places and drank a quantity of various kinds of wine while listening to and uttering many false and foolish words, and because a similar Russian squadron visited Toulon last year and its officers went to Paris and ate and drank a great deal while hearing and uttering still more false and foolish words, it has come to pass that not only the men who ate, drank, and talked, but all those who were present and even those who were not present but merely heard and read of it in the papers—all these millions of Russian and French people suddenly imagined themselves to be particularly fond of one another, that is, that all the French love all the Russians and all the Russians love all the French.

These feelings were expressed in France during October in most extraordinary ways.

This is how the reception of the Russian sailors is described in *Sélsky Véstnik* (*Rural News*), a paper that collects its information from all the other newspapers:

When the Russian and French vessels met, besides firing salvos they greeted one another with ardent and enthusiastic cries of 'Hurrah!' *'Vive la Russie!'* *'Vive la France!'*

There were also bands of music on many private steamers playing the Russian national anthem, 'God Save the Tsar', and the French *Marseillaise,* and the public in private boats waved hats, flags, handkerchiefs, and bouquets of flowers. There were many barges loaded entirely with peasant men and women and their children who all held bouquets of flowers, and even the children waved their bouquets and shouted with all their might, *Vive la Russie.* At the sight of such popular enthusiasm our sailors were unable to restrain their tears. . . .

The French men-of-war at Toulon were all drawn up in the harbour in two lines and our squadron passed between them, led by the admiral's ironclad which was followed by the other vessels. An extraordinarily solemn moment had arrived.

The Russian flagship fired a salute of fifteen guns in honour of the French squadron, and the French flagship replied with a double salute of thirty guns. The strains of the Russian national anthem thundered from the French ship. The French sailors climbed up their masts and rigging and loud cries of welcome poured forth unceasingly from both squadrons and from the surrounding vessels. The sailors' caps and the hats and handkerchiefs of the spectators were all waved rapturously in honour of the precious guests. From all sides, from the water and from the land, thundered the universal acclaim: 'Hail to Russia! Hail to France!'

In accord with naval usage Admiral Avelan with the officers of his staff went ashore to greet the local authorities. At the landing-stage they were met by the French general naval staff and the senior officers of the port of Toulon. A general friendly shaking of hands ensued amid the thunder of guns and the pealing of bells. The naval band played the national anthem, 'God Save the Tsar', which was drowned by loud cries from the public of 'Long live the Tsar! *Vive la Russie!*' And these cries mingled into one mighty roar eclipsing both the music and the firing of the guns.

Witnesses report that at that moment the enthusiasm of the countless mass of people attained its highest pitch, and that no words can convey the feelings that overflowed in the hearts of all those who were present. Admiral Avelan, bare-headed and accompanied by the Russian and French officers, set out for the head-quarters of the naval administration where he was awaited by the French Minister of Marine.

When receiving the Admiral, the Minister said:

'Kronstadt and Toulon are two places that bear testimony to the sympathy existing between the Russian and the French peoples. You will be welcomed everywhere as cordial friends. The Government and the whole of France greet you, and those who accompany you, as the representatives of "a great and noble people".'

The Admiral replied that he was unable to express all the gratitude he felt. 'The Russian squadron and the whole of Russia,' he said, 'will be grateful for the reception you have given us.'

On taking leave of the Minister after a short conversation the Admiral again thanked him for his welcome, and added:

'I do not wish to part from you without pronouncing the words that are impressed on the hearts of all Russians: "Long live France" ' [1]

Such was the reception at Toulon. In Paris the reception and the festivities were even more extraordinary.

This is how the newspapers described the reception in Paris:

---

[1] *Sélsky Véstnik*, 1893, No. 41.

All looks are directed to the Boulevard des Italiens, whence the Russian sailors are to appear. At last from a long way off the roar of a whole hurricane of exclamations and applause is heard. The roar grows stronger and clearer. The hurricane is evidently drawing nearer. There is a great crush and pressure in the square. The police rush to clear the route to the *Cercle Militaire,* but this proves to be a far from easy task. There is an indescribable crush and pressure among the crowd. . . . At last the head of the procession appears in the square. At the same moment a deafening cry of *Vive la Russie! Vive la Russie!* rises above it. All heads are bared, the public packed tightly at the windows, on the balconies, and even on the roofs, wave hats, flags, and handkerchiefs, and applaud frantically, throwing down from the windows clouds of small, multi-coloured cockades. A whole sea of handkerchiefs, hats, and flags wave above the heads of the crowd standing in the square. *Vive la Russie! Vive la Russie!* shouts that crowd with its hundred-thousand throats. And they strive hard to get the best possible view of their dear guests, stretching out their hands to them and expressing sympathy in every possible way.[2]

Another correspondent writes that the enthusiasm of the crowd approached delirium. One Russian journalist then in Paris describes that procession of sailors as follows:

They say truly that it is an event of world-wide importance, amazing, moving us to tears, uplifting the soul and making it quiver with the love which sees men as brothers and hates blood and violent annexation and the tearing of children from a beloved mother. I have been in a kind of delirium for some hours. I felt it strange and overwhelming to stand at the Gare de Lyons among the representatives of the French Government in their gold-embroidered uniforms, among the members of the municipality in dress-coats, and to hear the cries of *Vive la Russie! Vive le Tsar!* and our national anthem played over and over again. Where was I? What had happened?

---

[2] From the *Nóvoe Vrémya* newspaper.

What magic current had blended all this into one feeling, one comprehension? Does one not indeed feel the presence of the God of love and brotherhood, the presence of some higher ideal that descends on men only at exalted moments? One's heart is so full of something beautiful and pure and elevated that the pen is unable to express it. Words are pale beside what I saw and what I felt. This was not rapture—that word is too banal —it was better than rapture, more picturesque, deeper, more joyful and more varied. It is impossible to describe what it was like at the *Cercle Militaire* when Admiral Avelan appeared on the balcony of the second story. Here words are of no avail. During the service, when the choir were singing in church: 'O Lord, save thy people!'—the triumphal strains of the *Marseillaise* played by a band of wind instruments in the street burst through the open doors. It produced an astonishing impression no words can convey.[3]

II

The Russian sailors who had arrived in France went from one fête to another for a whole fortnight, and during and after each fête they ate, drank, and talked. And the reports of what and where they drank on Wednesday, and what and where they drank on Friday, and of what was then said, was communicated by telegraph to all Russia. As soon as one of the Russian captains drank to the health of France, that fact was immediately announced to the world, and directly the Russian Admiral said: 'I drink to *la belle France!*' those words were at once transmitted all over the world. But more than that, the zeal of the newspapers was such that not only the toasts but even the menus of the dinners were reported, with all the pâtés and hors-d'œuvres consumed at them.

Thus in one newspaper it was stated that the dinner was a work of art:

> Consommé de volailles, petits pâtés.
> Mousse de homard parisienne.

---

[3] *Nóvoe Vrémya,* October 1893.

Noisette de bœuf à la béarnaise.
Faisans à la Périgord.
Casseroles de truffes au champagne.
Chaud-froid de volailles à la Toulouse.
Salade russe.
Croûte de fruits toulonaise.
Parfaits à l'ananas.
Desserts.

In the next number of that paper it was said that: 'In its culinary aspect the dinner left nothing to be desired. The menu was as follows:

Potage livonien et St.-Germain.
Zéphyrs Nantua.
Esturgeon braisé moldave.
Selle de daguet grand veneur. . . .'

In the following day's paper a fresh menu was given. With each menu a description was also given of the drinks swallowed by the festive party, some sort of 'vudka',[4] some sort of Bourgogne vieux, Grand Moët, and so on. In an English newspaper all the intoxicating drinks consumed during these fêtes were enumerated, the quantity of it being so enormous that all the drunkards in Russia and in France could hardly have swallowed it in so short a time.

The speeches made were also reported, but the menus were more varied than the speeches, which invariably consisted of the same words in different combinations and permutations. The meaning of these words was always one and the same: we love each other tenderly and are enraptured that we have suddenly learnt to love each other so tenderly. Our aim is not war, nor *revanche*, nor the recovery of lost provinces: our sole aim is *peace*, the blessings of *peace*, the security of *peace*, the tranquillity and *peace* of Europe. Long live the Russian Emperor and Empress! We love them and we love *peace*. Long live the President of the Republic and his wife! We love them too and we love *peace*. Long live France and Russia, their fleets and their armies! We love the

---

[4] A French misspelling of *vodka*.

army, we love peace, and we love the commander of the squadron!

The speeches generally ended as if with a refrain, with the words: 'Toulon-Kronstadt' or 'Kronstadt-Toulon'. And the names of those places where so many different dishes had been eaten and so many different wines had been drunk, were pronounced as words recalling the most noble and heroic actions of the representatives of both nations—words that left nothing more to be said since all was understood. We love one another and we love peace. Kronstadt-Toulon! What more could be added to that? . . . especially when said to the triumphal music of bands playing two hymns at the same time: the one hymn glorifying the Tsar and imploring God to send him all prosperity, the other cursing all tsars and kings and invoking destruction upon them.

Those who expressed their feeling of love particularly well received orders and rewards, and some people, for similar services or simply from an overflow of love, were presented with very strange and unexpected gifts. Thus the French squadron made the Russian Tsar a present of some sort of golden book in which it seems nothing was written—or at least nothing that anybody needed to know; while the commander of the Russian squadron received an even more surprising object—a peasant plough (a *sokhá*) made of aluminium and covered with flowers—in addition to many other unexpected gifts.

And all these strange actions were accompanied by even stranger religious rites and public prayers to which one supposed the French had long become unaccustomed. So many public prayers as during that brief period had hardly been performed since the time of the Concordat.[5] The French all at once became extraordinarily devout, and carefully hung up in the rooms of the Russian sailors those very images they had so carefully removed from their own schools as pernicious instruments of superstition, and they prayed continu-

---

[5] The Concordat of 1801, concluded between Napoleon and Pope Pius VII.—A. M.

ally. The Cardinals and Bishops prescribed prayers everywhere and themselves offered up the strangest prayers.
Thus a bishop at Toulon at the launching of the ironclad
Jorigiberi prayed to the God of peace, letting it be felt
however that in case of need he could also apply to the God
of war. 'What will be its destiny God alone knows,' said he,
speaking of the newly launched vessel. 'Whether it will
vomit death from its terrible womb is unknown. But if,
having appealed to-day to the God of peace, we have here-
after to appeal to the God of war, we are firmly convinced
that the *Jorigiberi* will go to meet the foe hand in hand with
the mighty vessels whose crews have to-day entered into such
close and brotherly union with our own. But may that pass us
by and the present celebrations leave only peaceful memories,
like the remembrance of the Grand Duke Constantine,[6] who
was present here at the launching of the *Quirinal*, and may
the friendship of France and Russia make two nations the
guardians of peace. . . .'

Meanwhile tens of thousands of telegrams were flying from
Russia to France and from France to Russia. French women
greeted the Russian women. Russian women expressed their
gratitude to the French women. A troupe of Russian actors
greeted the French actors, and the French actors informed
them that they had laid the greeting of the Russian actors
deep in their hearts. Russian graduates of law at the District Court of some town or other announced their rapture to
the French nation. General So-and-so thanked Madame This-
and-that, and Madame This-and-that assured General So-
and-so of the ardour of her sentiments for the Russian nation.
Russian children wrote greetings in verse to French children,
French children replied in verse and in prose. The Russian
Minister of Education testified to the French Minister of Education of the sudden feelings of love for the French enter-
tained by all the teachers and writers under his supervision.
The Society for the Protection of Animals testified its ardent

---

[6] Constantine Nikoláevich, second son of Nicholas I. He was a
General and Admiral, and visited Toulon in 1857.—A. M.

attachment to the French, and a similar announcement was made by the Municipality of Kazán.

The Canon of Arras assured the Most Reverend Chief Priest of the Russian Court clergy that a love of Russia and of his Imperial Majesty Alexander III and his Imperial Family was deeply implanted in the hearts of all the Cardinals and Archbishops of France, and that French and Russian priests alike reverence the Most Holy Virgin and profess an almost identical faith, to which the Most Reverend Chief Priest replied that the prayer of the French clergy for the Imperial Family had echoed joyfully in the hearts of all the Russian people, lovingly attached to their Tsar, and that as the Russian people worshipped the Most Holy Virgin in the same way they confidently relied on France in life and death. Very similar announcements were made by all sorts of generals, telegraph clerks, and grocery-store dealers. They all congratulated somebody on something and thanked somebody for something.

The excitement was so great that most extraordinary things were done, and no one noticed their strangeness. On the contrary, everyone was approving and delighted and made haste to do something of the same sort as quickly as possible in order not to be left behind. If protests were uttered, and even written and printed, against the senselessness of these frenzied proceedings, such protests were either hushed up or shouted down.[7]

---

[7] I know, for example, of the following protest made by Russian students and sent to Paris, but not accepted by a single newspaper:

'An open letter to French students.

'A group of Moscow law students with the University Inspector at their head has recently had the audacity to speak in the name of all Moscow students regarding the Toulon festivities.

'We, the representatives of the Moscow Union of students of various provinces, protest most emphatically against that group's assumption of authority, and against the exchange of greetings that has taken place between it and the French students. We too regard France with warm affection and profound respect, but we so regard her because we see in her a great nation which has in the past constantly been the mouthpiece and herald to the whole world of the great ideals of liberty, equality, and fraternity, and which was foremost in courageously attempting to incorporate those great ideals

To say nothing of the millions of working days wasted on these festivities or the wholesale drunkenness (connived at by all the authorities) of those who took part in them, to say nothing of the senselessness of the speeches that were delivered, most insane and cruel things were done and no one paid any attention to them.

Thus some dozens of people were crushed to death and no one found it necessary to refer to it. A correspondent wrote that a Frenchman told him at a ball that there was now hardly a woman in Paris who would not betray her duty to satisfy the desire of any of the Russian sailors. And all this passed unnoticed as though it ought to be so. There were even cases of unmistakable insanity. One woman for instance

---

in life. The best part of the youth of Russia has always been ready to acclaim France as leader in the struggle for the future welfare of humanity. But we do not regard festivities like those of Kronstadt and Toulon as appropriate occasions for such greetings.

'On the contrary, these festivities represent a sad, though we hope temporary, condition—the desertion by France of her former great historic role. The country which once called upon the whole world to break the chains of despotism and offered its fraternal aid to any people fighting to be free, is now burning incense before the Russian Government, which systematically impedes the normal, organic growth of a people's life, and relentlessly and unscrupulously crushes every aspiration towards enlightenment, freedom, and independence. The Toulon demonstrations are one act of the drama of antagonism created between the two great nations of France and Germany by Napoleon III and Bismarck. That antagonism keeps all Europe under arms and makes Russian absolutism (that absolutism which has always been the support of arbitrary power and despotism against freedom, and of exploiters against the exploited) the arbiter of the political destinies of the world. These festivities evoke in us a feeling of pain for our own country and of regret at the blindness of so considerable a part of French society.

'We are convinced that the younger generation of France will not be carried away by national chauvinism, but that, ready to struggle for the better social conditions towards which humanity advances, it will know how to interpret the present events and what attitude to adopt towards them. We hope our ardent protest may find a sympathetic response in the hearts of the youth of France.

'Union of the Council of the Twenty-four Federated Societies of Moscow Students.'—L. T.

put on a dress of the colours of the French and Russian flags, and having waited for the arrival of the sailors cried: '*Vive la Russie!*' and jumped from the bridge into the river and was drowned.

In general the women played a conspicuous part in all these celebrations and even directed the men. Besides throwing flowers and various ribbons and presenting gifts and addresses, French women flung themselves on the Russian sailors in the streets and kissed them; others for some reason brought their children to them to be kissed, and when the Russian sailors gratified their wish, all those present were moved to ecstasy and wept.

This strange excitement was so infectious that, as one of the correspondents relates, an apparently quite healthy Russian sailor, after witnessing for a fortnight all that was going on around him, leapt from his ship into the sea in broad daylight and swam about shouting: '*Vif lya Frantz!*' When he was pulled out and asked why he had done it, he replied that he had taken a vow to swim round the ship in honour of France.

In this way the excitement grew and grew quite unchecked, like a rolling snowball, and at last not only those on the spot, and not only those who were predisposed and of weak nerves, but even strong and normal people succumbed to the general mood and reached an abnormal condition.

I remember that when carelessly reading one of the descriptions of the triumphal reception of the sailors, I suddenly became aware that a feeling of emotion was being communicated to me and that I was even on the verge of tears. And I had to make an effort to resist that feeling.

III

In the Kiev University Records a Professor of Psychiatry, Sikórsky by name, recently gave an account of a psychical epidemic of Malevanism—as he calls it—which he had investigated in certain villages of the Vasilkóvsky district of the province of Kiev. In Sikórsky's words, that epidemic consisted

essentially in the fact that some people in those villages under
the influence of a leader named Malevánov, imagining that the
world would soon come to an end, altered their whole manner
of life and began giving away their possessions, dressing themselves up, eating and drinking nice things, and ceased working.
The Professor found the condition of these people abnormal.
He says: 'Their extraordinary complacency often passed into
exaltation—a joyful condition lacking external cause. They
were sentimentally disposed, courteous to an extreme, very
talkative, active in their movements, and apt to shed facile
tears of joy that disappeared as easily as they came. They
sold necessities to buy parasols, silk kerchiefs, and the like;
and the kerchiefs served them only as toilet adornments. They
ate many sweetmeats. Their state of mind was always joyous,
and they led an idle life, visiting one another and walking
about. When the evident foolishness of refusing to work was
pointed out to them they always replied with the stereotyped
phrase: "If I want to work I'll work: if I don't want to, why
should I force myself?" '

The learned professor considers that the condition of these
people constitutes a clear case of a psychopathic epidemic,
and advises the government to take measures to prevent its
spreading. He concludes his article with the words: 'Malevanism is the cry of an ailing population. It is its prayer for
deliverance from intoxicants, and for an improvement in educational and sanitary conditions.'

But if Malevanism is the cry of an ailing population and a
prayer for deliverance from intoxicants and harmful social
conditions, what a much more terrible cry from an ailing population, and what an entreaty to be rescued from intoxicants
and false social conditions, is this new malady that has
broken out in Paris, and that with frightful rapidity has mas-
tered the greater part of the urban population of France and
almost the whole of the governmental and privileged classes
of Russia!

And if it is admitted that the mental derangement of the
Malevanists is dangerous, and that the government would do
well to follow the professor's advice and arrange for the con-

finement of some of their leaders in lunatic asylums and monasteries and the banishment of others to remote regions; how much more dangerous should we consider this new epidemic which has appeared in Toulon and Paris and spread all over France and Russia, and how much more necessary must it be, if not for the government then for society, to take resolute measures to prevent the diffusion of such epidemics.

The resemblance between the one and the other epidemic is complete. There is the same extraordinary complacency passing into spontaneous and joyful exaltation, there is the same sentimentality, exaggerated courtesy and loquacity, the same frequent tears of emotion that come and go without reason, the same holiday mood, the same festivities, the same promenading and paying calls, the same dressing up in showy clothes, the same fancy for choice food, the same senseless speeches, the same idleness, the same singing and music, the same direction by the women, and the same clownish poses in *attitudes passionelles* which Sikórsky observed among the Malevanists, and which I understand as meaning those unnatural poses assumed during ceremonious meetings, receptions, and the delivery of speeches at banquets.

The resemblance is complete! The only difference—and it is a very important one for the society in which these things occur—is that in the one case the madness is confined to some dozens of poor peaceful villagers living on their own small means and therefore unable to do violence to their neighbours, and infecting others only by the personal and vocal transmission of their mood; while in the other case it is the madness of millions of people who control vast sums of money and have the means of doing violence to other people (rifles, bayonets, fortresses, ironclads, melinite and dynamite), having moreover at their disposal most powerful means of spreading their madness—postal services, telegraphy, enormous numbers of newspapers, and all sorts of publications which vie with one another in spreading the infection to all ends of the earth. And there is another difference: the first set of people, far from drinking to excess, make no use of intoxicating drinks, while the second set keep themselves in a constant state of semi-intoxication. And therefore, for the society in which such phenomena occur, the difference between the Kiev epidemic (during which, according to Sikórsky's information, no acts of violence or murders were committed) and the one that prevailed in Paris (where twenty women were crushed to death during one procession) is as great as that between a cinder that falls from the grate and lies smouldering on the floor which it will obviously not set alight, and a fire which has already reached the doors and walls of a house. The results of the Kiev epidemic, in the worst case, will be that the peasants of a millionth part of Russia will spend what they have earned by their toil and will not be able to pay the State taxes. But the consequences of the Toulon-Paris epidemic which has seized upon people who wield terrible power, enormous sums of money, weapons of violence, and means of spreading their madness, may and must be terrible.

IV

When a feeble and unarmed old idiot in cap and dressing-gown is mouthing nonsense one may listen to him with compassion without contradicting him, and even humouring him in jest; but when a whole crowd of sturdy madmen armed from head to foot with sharp daggers, swords, and loaded revolvers, have broken out of confinement and are excitedly brandishing their deadly weapons, one cannot humour them, or even feel at ease for an instant. And so it is with the excitement aroused by the French receptions in which French and Russian society is now involved, for those who have succumbed to this epidemic of insanity are in possession of terrible weapons of murder and destruction.

It is true that in all the speeches and toasts uttered during those festivities, and in all the articles about them, it was constantly proclaimed that the object of what was happening was to secure peace. Even the partisans of war spoke not of hatred for those who had seized the lost provinces, but of some sort of love which somehow hates.

The cunning of the mentally afflicted is however well known, and this constant repetition of the sentence: 'We don't want war, we want peace!' and the silence about what is in everyone's mind, is a most menacing symptom.

In his answering toast at the banquet in the Elysée, the Russian ambassador said: 'Before proposing a toast to which not only all within these walls will respond from the very depth of their hearts, but to which all those far and near whose hearts are beating at this moment in unison with ours in all parts of great and beautiful France as well as in all Russia, will respond with equal ardour, allow me to convey to you the expression of our profound gratitude for the words of greeting addressed by you to the Admiral authorized by the Tsar to return the Kronstadt visit. The lofty station you occupy has given emphasis to your words concerning the true significance of the splendid, *peaceful* triumph that is being celebrated with such remarkable unity, loyalty, and sincerity.'

The same quite irrelevant reference to peace is found in the speech of the French President:

'The bonds of love which unite Russia and France,' said he, 'strengthened two years ago by the touching manifestations of which our fleet was the object at Kronstadt, are becoming closer every day, and the honest interchange of our friendly sentiments must inspire all who have at heart the blessing of *peace,* confidence and security'—and so on.

In both speeches the blessings of peace and peaceful celebrations are alluded to quite unexpectedly and irrelevantly.

It is the same with the telegrams exchanged between the Russian Emperor and the French President. The Russian Emperor telegraphed:

> '*Au moment où l'escadre russe quitte la France, il me tient à cœur de vous exprimer combien je suis touché et reconnaissant de l'accueil chaleureux et splendide que mes marins ont trouvé partout sur le sol français. Les témoignages de vive sympathie qui se sont manifestés encore une fois avec tant d'éloquence, joindront un nouveau lien à ceux qui unissent les deux pays et con-*

tribueront, je l'espère, à l'affermissement de la paix générale, objet de leurs efforts et de leurs vœux les plus constants.'

The French President in his reply telegram said:

'La dépêche dont je remercie votre majesté m'est parvenue au moment où je quittais Toulon pour rentrer à Paris. La belle escadre sur laquelle j'ai eu la vive satisfaction de saluer le pavillon russe dans les eaux françaises, l'accueil cordial et spontané que vos braves marins ont recontré partout en France affirment une fois de plus avec éclat les sympathies sincères qui unissent nos deux pays. Ils marquent en même temps une foi profonde dans l'influence bienfaisante que peuvent exercer ensemble deux grandes nations devouées à la cause de la paix.'

Again in both telegrams without rhyme or reason there is a reference to peace which has nothing to do with the reception of the sailors.

There was not a speech or an article in which it was not said that the object of all these orgies was the peace of Europe. At the dinner given by the representatives of the Russian Press everyone spoke of peace. Zola, who recently wrote that war was necessary and indeed beneficial, and M. de Vogüé who has more than once expressed the same opinion in print, did not say a word about war but spoke only of peace. The sittings of the Chamber were opened with speeches about the late celebrations, and the speakers declared that these festivities were the declaration of peace to Europe.

It is just like a man coming into a peaceable company and at every opportunity eagerly assuring those present that he has no intention whatever of knocking anyone's teeth out, blacking their eyes, or breaking their arms, but only wants to pass the evening peaceably. 'Nobody doubts it,' one wishes to say: 'Even if you had such horrible intentions, at any rate don't dare to mention them.'

Many articles about the celebrations actually contained a plain and naïve expression of pleasure that during the festivities no one expressed what, *tacitu consensu*, it had been decided to conceal from everybody, and that only one incautious man (who was promptly removed by the police) shouted aloud what everyone was thinking: '*A bas l'Allemagne!*' In the same way children sometimes are so delighted at having concealed their mischief that their delight betrays them.

Why be so pleased that no one has said anything about war if we really are not thinking of it?

V

No one thinks of war, but milliards of money are spent on warlike preparations, and millions of men are under arms in Russia and in France.

'But this is all done to ensure peace. *Si vis pacem, para bellum. L'empire c'est la paix, la république c'est la paix.*'

But if so, why is it that among us in Russia the military advantage of our alliance with France in case of war with Germany is explained not only in all the newspapers and periodicals published for people supposed to be educated, but even in the *Rural News,* a paper published by the Russian Government for the peasants? There it is impressed on this unfortunate folk, deluded by the government, that 'to be friendly with France is also useful and advantageous for Russia because if, contrary to expectations, the Powers we have mentioned (Germany, Austria, and Italy) decided to violate the peace with Russia, then (though she might, by God's help, hold her own unaided and deal successfully with the very powerful alliance of her enemies) it would not be an easy task, and even a successful struggle would involve great sacrifices and losses'—and so on. (*Rural News,* No. 43, 1893.)

And why is history taught in all French high schools from a primer compiled by Monsieur Lavisse (21st edition, 1899) in which there is the following statement:

> *Depuis que l'insurrection de la Commune a été vaincue, la France n'a plus été troublée. Au lendemain de la guerre, elle s'est remise au travail. Elle a payé aux Allemands sans difficultés l'énorme contribution de guerre de cinq milliards. Mais la France a perdu sa renommée militaire pendant la guerre de 1870. Elle a perdu une*

partie de son territoire. Plus de quinze cent mille hommes qui habitaient nos départements du Haut-Rhin, du Bas-Rhin et de la Moselle, et qui étaient de bons Français, ont été obligés de devenir Allemands. Ils ne sont pas résignés à leur sort. Ils détestent l'Allemagne; ils espèrent toujours redevenir Français. Mais l'Allemagne tient à sa conquête, et c'est un grand pays dont tous les habitants aiment sincèrement leur patrie et dont les soldats sont braves et disciplinés. Pour reprendre à l'Allemagne ce qu'elle nous a pris, il faut que nous soyons de bons citoyens et de bons soldats. C'est pour que vous deveniez de bons soldats que vos maîtres vous apprennent l'histoire de la France. L'histoire de la France montre que dans notre pays les fils ont toujours vengé les désastres de leurs pères. Les Français du temps du Charles VII ont vengé leurs pères vaincus à Crécy, à Poitiers, Azincourt. . . . C'est à vous—enfants élevés aujourd'hui dans nos écoles—qu'il appartient à venger vos pères, vaincus à Sedan et à Metz. C'est votre devoir, le grand devoir de votre vie. Vous devez y penser toujours . . . and so forth.

At the foot of the page there is a series of questions on the above: 'What did France lose as well as a part of her territory? How many Frenchmen were turned into Germans by the loss of that territory? Do those Frenchmen love Germany? What should we do in order some day to regain what Germany has taken from us? . . .'

There are also some *Réflexions sur le livre VII*, in which it is said that 'the children of France should remember our defeats in 1870' and that 'they should feel the burden of that recollection in their hearts', but that 'this recollection should not discourage them: it should, on the contrary, arouse their valour.'

So that if in official speeches peace is talked of with great insistence, the common people, the rising generation, and the Russian and French people in general, are quietly and constantly impressed with the necessity, righteousness, advantageousness, and even the heroism of war.

'We do not think of war. We are only concerned about peace.'

One would be inclined to ask: *Qui diable trompte-t-on ici?* if that question were worth asking, and if it were not all too evident who is the unfortunate victim who is being deceived.

That victim is always and ever the deceived, foolish, working folk—those who with blistered hands have built all those ships, fortresses, arsenals, barracks, cannon, harbours, steamers, and moles, and all these palaces, halls, platforms, and triumphal arches; who have set up and printed all these newspapers and pamphlets, and have procured and brought all these pheasants and ortolans, oysters, and wines that are consumed by the men who are fed, brought up, and kept by them, and who are deceiving them and preparing the most fearful calamities for them. It is always the same kindly, foolish folk, who stand open-mouthed like children, showing their healthy white teeth, naïvely delighted by dressed-up admirals and presidents with flags waving above them, and by fireworks and bands of music; and for whom, before they have time to look round, there will be neither admirals nor presidents nor flags nor bands, but only a desolate battlefield, cold, hunger, and anguish—before them murderous enemies and behind them relentless officers preventing their escape—blood, wounds, suffering, putrefying corpses, and a senseless unnecessary death.

And men like these who are now feasting at the celebrations in Toulon and Paris will sit in a dark cloth tent after a good dinner, with unfinished glasses of good wine before them and with cigars between their teeth, and will indicate, with pins stuck into a map, the spots where such-and-such a quantity of cannon-fodder (made up of these same simple people) must be expended in order to capture such-and-such a position or to obtain this or that ribbon or Order.

VI

'But there is nothing of the kind, there are no warlike intentions,' we are told. 'It is only a case of two nations feeling mutual sympathy and expressing that feeling to one another.

What is there wrong in the representatives of a friendly nation being received with special celebrations and honour by the representatives of another nation? What is there bad in that—even if one admits that the alliance may have significance as a defence against a dangerous neighbour who threatens the peace of Europe?'

It is bad because it is a most obvious and shameless falsehood, lacking any justification. This sudden exceptional love of Russians for French and French for Russians is false. Our implied dislike and distrust of the Germans is also false. And it is still more false to say that the aim of all these unseemly and senseless orgies is to preserve the peace of Europe.

We all know that we have not previously experienced and do not now experience any special love for the French; just as we have not previously experienced and do not now experience any special enmity for the Germans.

We are told that Germany has designs against Russia, that the Triple Alliance threatens our own peace and the peace of Europe, and that our alliance with France equalizes the forces and is therefore a guarantee of peace.

This assertion is so obviously silly that one is ashamed to refute it seriously. For such an alliance to ensure peace all the forces would have to be mathematically equal. If the preponderance is now on the side of the Franco-Russian alliance the danger is still there. It is even greater, for if there was a danger that Wilhelm at the head of a European alliance would disturb the peace, there would be a much greater danger that France—who cannot reconcile herself to the loss of her provinces—would do so. Why, the Triple Alliance called itself the peace-league, though to us it seemed a league of war. And in just the same way the Franco-Russian Alliance cannot appear other than it really is—a league of war.

How then, if peace depends on the balance of power, can one define the units between which an equilibrium must be established? The English are now saying that the alliance of Russia and France threatens them, and that they must form a new alliance. Into how many alliances must Europe be divided to establish an equilibrium? Why, if that is how things are, then the strongest man in any society of people is a danger, and the others should form alliances to counterbalance him.

People ask: 'What is there bad in France and Russia expressing their mutual sympathy in order to ensure peace?'

It is bad because it is a lie, and a lie can never be uttered without doing harm.

The devil is a murderer and the father of lies. Lies always lead to murder, and especially in such a case as this.

Before the Turkish war,[8] just as is the case now, a sudden love was supposed to have sprung up between us Russians and certain Slavonic brethren of ours to whom no one had paid any attention for some hundreds of years; whereas the Germans, French, and English had always been, and still are, incomparably nearer and more akin to us than any of those Montenegrins, Serbians, or Bulgarians. Then, too, similar enthusiasms, receptions, and celebrations were started, fanned by the Aksákovs and Katkóvs who are now mentioned in Paris as models of patriotism. Then, as now, they only spoke of the mutual love that had suddenly sprung up between the Russians and the Slavs. At first, just as now in Paris so then in Moscow, they ate, drank, said silly things to one another and were touched by their exalted feelings, spoke of union and peace, and kept silent about the chief matter—the designs against Turkey. The newspapers worked up the excitement and gradually the government began to take part in the game. Serbia revolted. There were diplomatic notes and semi-official articles. The newspapers lied more and more, invented, and grew heated. And in the end Alexander III, who did not really want war, was unable to avoid consenting to it, and that occurred which we already know: the destruction of hundreds of thousands of innocent people, and the brutalizing and stupefying of millions. And what has been done in Toulon and Paris and is still being done in the newspapers, is obviously leading the same way, or to still worse

---

[8] The Russo-Turkish war of 1877-8.—A. M.

calamities. Various Generals and Ministers will drink to
France, to Russia, to different regiments, armies, and fleets, in
just the same way to the strains of *God Save the Tsar* and
La Marseillaise. The papers will print their lies, the idle crowd
of rich people who do not know what to do with their time
and their energy will babble patriotic speeches and stir up
enmity towards Germany. And however peacefully inclined
Alexander III may be, events will so shape themselves that
he will be unable to refuse his assent to a war which will
be demanded by everyone around him, by all the newspapers, and (or so it always seems in such cases) by the public
opinion of the whole nation. And before we have time to look
round the usual ominous and senseless proclamation will appear in the columns of the press:

'We, by the grace of God autocratic Emperor of all the Rus-
sias, King of Poland, Grand Duke of Finland, &c., &c., announce to all our faithful subjects that for the good of our beloved people entrusted to us by God we have deemed it our
duty before God to send them to the slaughter. May God be
with them.'—and so on.

The bells will peal and long-haired men will dress themselves in gold-embroidered sacks and begin to pray on behalf
of murder. The familiar, age-old, horrible business will re-
commence. The editors of newspapers will set to work to
arouse hatred and murder under the guise of patriotism and
will be delighted to double their sales. Manufacturers, merchants, and contractors for army-stores, will hurry about joyfully in expectation of doubled profits. Officials of all sorts
will busy themselves in the hope of being able to steal more
than usual. Army commanders will bustle here and there,
drawing double pay and rations and hoping to receive various trinkets, ribbons, crosses, stripes, and stars, for murdering
people. Idle ladies and gentlemen will fuss about, entering
their names in advance for the Red Cross and getting ready
to bandage those whom their husbands and brothers are setting out to kill—imagining that they will be doing a most
Christian work thereby.

And hundreds of thousands of simple kindly folk, torn from

peaceful toil and from their wives, mothers, and children, and with murderous weapons in their hands, will trudge wherever they may be driven, stifling the despair in their souls by songs, debauchery, and vodka. They will march, freeze, suffer from hunger, and fall ill. Some will die of disease, and some will at last come to the place where men will kill them by the thousand. And they too, without themselves knowing why, will murder thousands of others whom they had never before seen, and who had neither done nor could do them any wrong.

And when there are so many sick, wounded, and killed that there are not hands enough to pick them up, and when the air is so infected by that rotting cannon-fodder that it becomes unpleasant even to the commanders, then they will stop for a while, the wounded will somehow be picked up, the sick brought in and dumped in heaps where chance may decide, and the dead dug into the ground and sprinkled over with lime. And then once more the whole crowd of deluded men will be led on and on, till those who started the mischief are weary of it, or until those who thought it necessary have got what they wanted.

And so once again men will have been made savage, ferocious, and brutal; and love will wane in the world, and the Christianizing of mankind which had begun will be retarded again for scores or hundreds of years. And once again those for whom it is profitable will declare with assurance that since there was a war, that proves war to be necessary, and they will again begin to prepare future generations for it, perverting them from childhood upwards.

VII

Hence, when such patriotic demonstrations as the Toulon festivities take place, people's wills are bound in advance, though apparently only for the distant future, and they are pledged to the accustomed iniquities that are always the result of patriotism. And everyone who realizes the significance of those festivities cannot but protest against their tacit implication. Thus when those gentlemen, the journalists, assert that every Russian sympathizes with what took place at Kronstadt and Toulon and Paris and that this alliance for life and death is confirmed by the will of the whole people, and when the Russian Minister of Education assures the French ministers that all under his command (the children, scholars, and writers of Russia) share his feelings, and when the commander of the Russian squadron assures the French that all Russia will be grateful for the reception given them, and when the chief priests answer for their flocks with assurances that the prayers of the French for the welfare of the Imperial family are joyfully echoed in the hearts of the Tsar-loving Russian people, and when the Russian ambassador in Paris, who is regarded as the representative of the Russian people, declares, after a dish of *ortolans à la soubise et logopèdes glacées* and with a glass of Grand Moët champagne in his hand, that all Russian hearts beat in unison with his own, which is brimming over with sudden and exceptional love for *la belle France*—then we who are free from that insanity consider it our sacred duty, not only for ourselves but also for tens of millions of Russians, to protest most emphatically against such a statement, and to affirm that our hearts do not beat in unison with those of these gentlemen—the journalists, ministers of education, commanders of squadrons, chief priests, and ambassadors—but on the contrary are filled with indignation and disgust at the pernicious falsehood and wrong which they, consciously or unconsciously, are spreading around by their words and deeds. Let them drink Moët as much as they please, let them write articles and make speeches, but let them do so for themselves alone. We who regard ourselves as Christians cannot allow ourselves to be bound by what these gentlemen are saying and writing.

We cannot allow it because we know what lies hidden under all these drunken ecstasies, speeches, and embraces, which do not look like a confirmation of peace as they assure us, but rather like the orgies and drunkenness criminals indulge in when preparing to co-operate in crime.

VIII

About four years ago the first swallow of the Toulon spring —a French agitator[9] well known as an advocate of war with Germany—came to Russia to pave the way for a Franco-Russian alliance and visited us in the country. He arrived while we were mowing the hay. On returning to the house for lunch we made our visitor's acquaintance, and he immediately told us how he had fought in the war of 1870, had been taken prisoner and had escaped, and how he had sworn a patriotic oath—of which he was evidently proud —not to cease agitating for war with Germany till the integrity and honour of France was restored.

Our circle did not share his conviction that an alliance of Russia with France was necessary for the recovery of France's former frontiers and the restoration of her power and glory and to safeguard ourselves from Germany's evil designs. To his plea that France could not rest satisfied until she recovered her lost provinces, we replied that neither could Prussia rest satisfied until she had avenged herself for Jena, and that if a French *revanche* should now succeed, the Germans would have to re-avenge it and so on without end.

To his plea that the French were in duty bound to rescue their brothers who had been torn from them, we replied that the position of the working-class inhabitants of Alsace-Lorraine under German rule was, for the most part, hardly worse in any respect than it had been under French rule, and that because it would be pleasanter for some Alsatian to be reckoned as French rather than German, and because he, our visitor, wished to vindicate the glory of French arms, it was not worth while to incur the terrible miseries war occasions, and not right even to sacrifice a single human life.

When he said that it was all very well for us to talk like that, since we should speak differently if the Baltic Provinces

---

[9] Paul Déroulède (1846-1914). Author of *Chants du Soldat.*— A. M.

or Poland had been taken from us, we replied that even from a political point of view the loss of Poland or the Baltic Provinces could not be considered a calamity, but might rather be regarded as a benefit, since it would spare us the military force and the political expenditure they require; while from a Christian point of view we could in no case assent to war, since war demands the murder of men, and Christianity not only forbids all murder, but requires the doing of good to all men, accounting them all as brothers without distinction of nationality. A Christian Government when engaging in war should, we said, to be consistent, not only remove the crosses from the churches, convert the church buildings to other purposes, give the clergy other duties, and above all suppress the Gospel—it should also renounce all the precepts of morality that result from the Christian doctrines. *C'est à prendre ou à laisser,* we told him. Until Christianity is abolished people can only be drawn into war by cunning and deception, as is done now.

But we see this cunning and deception and therefore cannot yield to it.

And since we had no band, no champagne, nor anything to befog our senses, our visitor merely shrugged his shoulders and with characteristic French politeness said that he was very grateful for the hospitable reception he had met with in our house, but much regretted that his views had not met with a similar welcome.

IX

After this conversation we went with our guest to the hayfield, and there, hoping to find more sympathy for his ideas among the people, he asked me to translate to my fellow-worker, Prokófy, an old, sickly, ruptured peasant, but still a persistent worker, his plan of action against the Germans, which was to squeeze them between the Russians and the French from both sides. The Frenchman explained this graphically to Prokófy by pressing each side of the man's sweat-soaked hempen shirt with his white fingers, and I remember Prokófy's good-natured surprise and derision when I explained to him the meaning of words and gesture. He evidently took the proposal about squeezing the Germans from both sides as a jest—unable to believe that a grown-up educated man could calmly and soberly speak of war as being desirable.

'Why, if we squeeze them from both sides,' said Prokófy, replying by a jest to what he took to be a jest, 'there would be nowhere for them to move. We must let them out somewhere.'

I translated that reply to my visitor.

'*Dites-lui que nous aimons les Russes,*' said he.

These words evidently surprised Prokófy even more than the proposal to squeeze the Germans, and aroused a certain feeling of suspicion.

'Who does he belong to?' asked Prokófy, distrustfully indicating my visitor with his head.

I said that he was a wealthy Frenchman.

'And what business has he come about?' asked Prokófy.

When I explained that he had come in the hope of getting the Russians to form an alliance with France in case of war with Germany, Prokófy evidently retained his suspicions, and turning to the peasant women who were sitting among the hay-cocks, involuntarily expressed his feeling by shouting to them in a stern voice to go and rake up the loose hay.

'Hey, you crows, you're all asleep! Get to work! Here's a time to deal with the Germans! The hay's not in yet and it looks as if we may have to begin reaping[10] the corn on Wednesday,' said he. And then, as if afraid of having offended the foreign visitor, he added, with a good-natured smile that showed the stumps of his worn teeth: 'You'd better come and work with us and bring the Germans along too, and when we've done work we'll have some merry-making together. The Germans are men too, like ourselves.'

And having said this, Prokófy drew his sinewy arm from between the prongs of the pitchfork on which he was leaning,

---

[10] Or 'go squeezing'.—A. M.

threw the fork on his shoulder and went over to the women. *'Oh, le brave homme!'* exclaimed the polite Frenchman, laughing, and so ended for the present his diplomatic mission to the Russian people.

The sight of those two men, so different from one another— the well-fed elegant Frenchman, in a top-hat and the long overcoat that was then very fashionable, radiant with freshness and self-confidence, with his white hands, unused to work, energetically showing how the Germans must be squeezed; and the shaggy figure of Prokófy, shrivelled up by constant labour, always tired but always at work despite his enormous rupture, with fingers swollen by toil, with wisps of hay in his hair, with slack home-made breeches and down-trodden bark shoes, striding along with an enormous fork of hay on his shoulder, with that step, not lazy but economical in movement, with which a working man always moves—the strong contrast presented by those two men made much clear to me then, and now, after the Toulon-Paris festivities, vividly recurs. One of them personified all those who, fed by the people's toil, afterwards use those same people for cannon-fodder; while the other personified that very cannon-fodder which feeds and protects the others who afterwards so dispose of it.

X

'But two provinces have been taken from France, children torn from a beloved mother. And Russia cannot permit Germany to dictate to her and deprive her of her historic mission in the East, nor risk the chance of being deprived, like the French, of her territory—the Baltic provinces, Poland, and the Caucasus.'

'And Germany cannot tolerate the possibility of losing the advantages she has gained at such cost! And England will not yield her naval supremacy to anyone!'

When such words are uttered it is usually taken for granted that the French, the Russians, the Germans, and the English, ought to be ready to sacrifice everything to regain their lost provinces, to maintain their influence in the East, to preserve their unity and power, or their supremacy on the sea, and so on.

It is taken for granted that the feeling of patriotism is, in the first place, a feeling innate in every man; and secondly that it is such a lofty moral feeling that it should be infused into those in whom it is absent. But neither the one assumption nor the other is correct. I have lived half a century among the Russian people, and during all that time I have never seen or heard a manifestation or expression of patriotism among the great mass of real Russian peasants, with the exception of patriotic formulas learnt in military service or repeated from books by the more superficial and degraded of the people. I have never heard expressions of patriotic feeling expressed by our people. On the contrary, I have constantly heard, from the most serious and respected of the country folk, expressions of complete indifference to, and even contempt for, any kind of patriotic manifestation. I have observed the same thing among the working people of other countries, and educated Frenchmen, Germans, and Englishmen, have repeatedly told me the same thing.

The working people are too much taken up with the task of earning a living for themselves and their families to be able to interest themselves in the political questions that figure as the chief motives of patriotism. The question of Russia's influence in the East, the unification of Germany, the return of France's lost provinces, of the cession of this or that part of one State to another, and so on, does not interest them—not only because they hardly ever know the conditions under which these questions arise, but because the interests of their life are quite apart from national and political interests.

To a man of the people it is always a matter of complete indifference where a frontier is drawn, to whom Constantinople may belong, whether Saxony or Brunswick shall, or shall not, be a member of the German Union, whether Australia or Matabeleland shall belong to England—or even to what government he has to pay his taxes and into which army he must send his sons. The important thing for him is to know how much tax he will have to pay, whether the army service will be a long one, whether he will have to pay for the land over many years, and whether he will get much for his work—all questions quite apart from national and political interests. That is why—despite the intensive efforts made by governments to instil a patriotism into people that is not innate in them, and to suppress the ideas of socialism that are developing among them—socialism is penetrating more and more into the masses of the people, while patriotism, with which they are so carefully inoculated by the government, not only fails to spread, but is disappearing more and more and is only maintained among the upper classes to whom it is profitable.

If it does happen that patriotism takes possession of the crowd, as has now occurred in Paris, it only happens when the masses are subjected to intensive hypnotism by the governments and ruling classes, and such patriotism is only maintained among the people as long as that hypnotic influence is maintained.

So for instance in Russia, where patriotism, in the form of love and devotion to the Faith, the Tsar, and the Fatherland, is grafted onto the Russian people with extraordinary intensity by every instrument in the hands of the government: the Church, the schools, the Press, and all kinds of ceremonies —the Russian working class, the hundred-million Russian people, despite the undeserved reputation bestowed on them as being particularly devoted to their Faith, Tsar, and Fatherland, are in fact the freest of all people from the deception of patriotism and from devotion to Faith, Tsar, and Fatherland. For the most part the Russian peasant knows nothing about the Faith—that Orthodox State faith to which he is supposed to be devoted—and as soon as he recognizes it he rejects it and becomes a rationalist, that is, he adopts a belief which can be neither attacked nor defended. And towards his Tsar (in spite of incessant, intensive attempts to instil a feeling of devotion) his attitude is the same as to all authorities employing violence, that is one if not of condemnation then of complete indifference. While as to his Fatherland (unless one understands it to mean his own village or his own

district) he is either completely ignorant of it or, if he knows
it, he makes no distinction between it and other countries.
Russians now settle quite indifferently in Russia or outside it,
in Turkey or in China, just as they formerly emigrated to
Austria or to Turkey.

XI

My old friend D——[11] who lived alone in the country during
the winter while his wife was in Paris, where he visited her
occasionally, often conversed with his steward—an illiterate
but wise and venerable peasant—who came in the long autumn evenings to bring his report. Among other things, my
friend used to tell him of the advantages of the French system of government as compared with our own. This was on
the eve of the last Polish insurrection (of 1863-4) and the
interference of the French Government with our affairs. At
that time the patriotic Russian Press was burning with indignation at this interference, and so stirred up the ruling
classes that our political relations became very much strained
and there was talk of a war with France.

My friend, having read the papers, told his steward of the
relations between Russia and France, and influenced by the
tone of the Press and being an old military man, said that if
there were a war he would re-enter the army and go to fight
the French. At that time patriotic Russians considered a *revanche* on the French for Sevastopol necessary.

'Why should we fight?' asked the steward.

'Well, how can we allow France to dictate to us?'

'But you yourself say that they are better governed than
we are,' said the steward quite seriously. 'Then why not let
them arrange things for us too?'

And my friend told me he was so taken aback by this com-
ment that he did not know what to reply, and only laughed
as one does on awakening from a deceptive dream.

---

[11] This no doubt was D. A. Dyákov, from whom the character of
Dmítri in *Boyhood* and *Youth* was drawn.—A. M.

Such opinions may be heard from every sober Russian working man who is not under the hypnotic influence of the government.

People speak of the love of the Russian peasantry for their Faith, their Tsar, and their Fatherland, and yet there is not a single Russian peasant community which would hesitate for a moment if they had to choose which of two places to settle in: one in Russia under their 'Little Father the Tsar' (as he is termed in books), with their holy Orthodox Faith, in their adored Fatherland, but with less and poorer land; and one anywhere outside Russia, in Prussia, China, Turkey, or Austria, without their Father, the white Tsar, and without the Orthodox Church, but with more and better land. They would all choose the latter! This we have often seen before and still see to-day.

For every Russian peasant the question under what government he will live (since he knows that whichever it is he will be plundered just the same) has infinitely less importance than—I won't even say whether the water is good, but whether the clay is soft and cabbage grows well.

It might be supposed that this indifference arises from the fact that any government under which they might come would be better than the Russian, since there is none worse in Europe. But that is not so, for as far as I know, the same attitude prevails among English, Dutch, and German peasants who emigrate to America, and among others who come to Russia.

The shifting of the European population from one rule to another, from Turkish to Austrian or from French to German, makes so little difference to working-class conditions that it cannot in any case arouse discontent among the workers unless they are subjected to suggestion from governments and the ruling classes.

XII

In proof of the existence of patriotism, people usually point to manifestations of it on various ceremonial occasions: in

Russia during the coronation,[12] and after the attempt on the Tsar's life on October 17th;[13] in France when war was declared on Prussia; in Germany when victory was celebrated; or during these Franco-Russian festivities.

But one has to know how these manifestations are prepared. In Russia, for instance, during every journey made by the Tsar, men from the peasant communities and the factories are prepared to meet and welcome him.

The enthusiasm of the crowd is for the most part artificially prepared by those to whom it is necessary, and the degree of enthusiasm displayed merely indicates the degree of art of the organizers of that enthusiasm. That art is an old one and its specialists have consequently reached great virtuosity in preparing these ecstasies.

When Alexander II was still heir to the throne and in command of the Preobrazhénsk Regiment, as the heir-apparent usually was, he once drove after dinner to the regiment, which was then in camp. As soon as his carriage was seen, the soldiers, it is recorded, ran out to meet him just as they were in their shirt-sleeves, and greeted their august commander with such enthusiasm that they all raced after the carriage and many of them crossed themselves as they looked up at the Tsetsarévich. All who saw this reception were touched by the naïve devotion and love of the Russian soldiers for the Tsar and his heir, and decided to arrange all sorts of festivities on October 1st in honour of Russia. Many towns and provinces decided to send special deputations to Toulon or Paris to greet the Russian visitors and take them presents as souvenirs of France, or to send them addresses and telegrams of welcome. It was decided that the 1st of October should be regarded everywhere as a national holiday and that the pupils of all educational establishments should be given a holiday on that day, and those in Paris two days. It was decided to remit all fines incurred by officials of the lower ranks, that

---

[12] Of Alexander III in 1883, two years after his accesssion.—A. M.

[13] A terrorist attempt to blow up the train in which Alexander III was travelling was made at Bórki, near Khárkov, in 1888. One of his children was injured.—A. M.

they might remember the 1st of October with gratitude as a day of rejoicing for France.

'To make it easier for the public to visit Toulon and take part in the welcome to the Russian squadron, the railways reduced their fares by half and special trains were provided.'

And then when a whole series of simultaneous measures (such as a government can always take thanks to the power in its hands) has been taken everywhere, and a certain portion of the people, chiefly the scum of the town rabble, has been brought to an abnormally excited condition, people say: 'Look! This is a spontaneous expression of the will of the whole nation.'

Such manifestations as those that have lately taken place in Toulon and Paris, which take place in Germany at receptions of the Emperor or of Bismarck, at the manœuvres in Lorraine, and that are constantly repeated in Russia on every ceremonial occasion, only prove that the means existing for exciting the crowd are so powerful that the government and the ruling classes which control them can always evoke at will whatever manifestation they please. On the other hand nothing so clearly proves the absence of patriotism in the people as these intense efforts now employed by the governments and the ruling classes to arouse it artificially, and the smallness of the results obtained despite all these efforts.

If patriotic feelings were really so innate in the people, they would be left to appear freely of themselves and would not have to be worked up continually by artificial means as well as on special occasions.

Let them cease if but for a while to force the whole Russian people to swear allegiance to each Tsar on his coronation, as is now done, let them cease solemnly pronouncing the customary prayers for the Tsar at every Church service, let them cease making holidays of his birthday and name-day— with the ringing of bells, illuminations, and the prohibition of work; let them cease displaying his portrait everywhere, give up printing his name and the names of his family, and even the pronouns relating to them, in enormous letters in prayerbooks, calendars, and school books; let them cease glorifying him in special books and gazettes devoted entirely to that purpose, and let them cease prosecuting and imprisoning men for the slightest disrespectful word about the Tsar; let them cease doing these things if but for a while, and we should see in how far it is natural for the people—the real working people like Prokófy and the village elder Iván, and all the Russian peasants—to feel (as people assure us and as foreigners believe) adoration for the Tsar, who in one way or other delivers them over into the hands of the landowners and the rich people generally.

So with Russia. And in the same way let them in Germany, France, Italy, England and America, cease doing all that is being strenuously done there too in the same way by the ruling classes to arouse patriotism and devotion and submission to the existing government, and then we should see in how far this supposed patriotism is characteristic of the peoples of our time.

As it is, people are constantly hypnotized from childhood in one and the same direction by all possible means: school books, Church services, sermons, speeches, books, newspapers, poems, and monuments. Some thousands of people are brought together, forcibly or by bribery, and when they have been joined by the loafers who are always glad to see any spectacle, they begin to shout what is shouted before them to the accompaniment of cannon and bands and glitter and brilliance of all kinds, and we are told that this is the expression of the feelings of the whole nation. But in the first place these thousands, or at most tens of thousands, who shout at such celebrations, form but a tiny ten-thousandth part of the whole population. And in the second place, of these tens of thousands of shouting and hat-waving people, the greater part, if not assembled by force as is done among us in Russia, have been artfully lured there by some bait or other. Thirdly, among all those thousands there are scarcely a few dozen who know what it is all about: they would shout and wave their hats in just the same way if the very opposite of what is happening were taking place. And fourthly, the police are present who promptly silence and remove all who shout anything the government does not wish and demand—as was strenuously done during the Franco-Russian celebrations.

In France they acclaimed with similar enthusiasm Napoleon the First's war with Russia, Alexander I, against whom that war was fought, then Napoleon again, then again the Allies, the Bourbons, the Orleans,[14] the Republic, Napoleon III, and Boulanger; while in Russia they acclaim with equal enthusiasm to-day Peter,[15] tomorrow Catherine, afterwards Paul, Alexander, Constantine,[16] Nicholas, The Duke of Leuchtenberg,[17] our brother-Slavs, the King of Prussia, the French sailors, and anyone whom the authorities wish welcomed. And the same thing takes place in England, America, Germany and Italy.

What is called patriotism is merely, in our day, on the one side a certain frame of mind constantly produced and supported among the people by the schools, the Church, and a venal press, for purposes required by the government; and on the other side a temporary excitement aroused in the classes of the lowest mental and moral level by special means adopted by the ruling classes and afterwards given out as an expression of the permanent will of the whole nation. The patriotism of oppressed nationalities is no exception to this. That too is unnatural in the labouring masses, and is artificially fostered in them by the upper classes.

XIII

'But if the working people do not experience patriotic emotions, that is because they have not yet reached the level of that lofty emotion natural to every educated man. If they

---

[14] King Louis-Philippe.—A. M.
[15] Peter III who was assassinated.—A. M.
[16] A brother of Alexander and of Nicholas II. He was proclaimed Emperor by the Decembrist conspirators in 1825.—A. M.
[17] Maximilian Eugène Joseph Napoleon, Duke of Leuchtenberg (son of Eugène de Beauharnais who bought the dukedom of Leuchtenberg). He married Márya Nikoláevna, a sister of Alexander II. ·—A. M.

have not yet reached it, it should be developed in them, and that is just what the government is doing.'

People of the ruling classes say that with such complete conviction that patriotism is a lofty sentiment, that common folk who have not experienced it acknowledge themselves to blame for not feeling it, and try to persuade themselves that they do feel it, or at least pretend to do so.

But what is this lofty feeling the ruling classes think should be developed in the people?

That sentiment, in its most precise definition, is nothing but putting one's own kingdom or people before every other kingdom or people—a feeling fully expressed by the patriotic German song: *Deutschland, Deutschland über alles,* in which it is only necessary to substitute *Russland, Frankreich, Italien,* or any other kingdom, in place of *Deutschland,* to obtain the clearest formula for the lofty feeling of patriotism. No doubt that feeling is very useful and desirable for governments and for the unity of a State, but one cannot help seeing that it is not at all a lofty sentiment, but on the contrary a very stupid and immoral one: stupid because if each kingdom is to consider itself better than any other, it is evident that they will all be wrong; and immoral because it inevitably impels every man who feels it to seek advantages for his own State and people to the detriment of other States and peoples—an impulse directly contrary to the fundamental moral law recognized by all, not to do to others what we do not wish done to us.

Patriotism may have been a virtue in the ancient world when it demanded of a man devotion to the highest ideal then attainable—that of his fatherland. But how can it be a virtue in our time, when it demands what is contrary to the ideal of both our religion and morality, and is a recognition not of the equality and brotherhood of men but of the predominance of one State and one people over all others? But more than that, this sentiment is no longer a virtue in our time but is certainly a vice. Patriotism in its true meaning cannot exist in our time, for there are no material or moral grounds for it.

Patriotism had a meaning in the ancient world when each nation was more or less homogeneous professing one national religion and subject to the absolute power of its divinely appointed ruler, and appeared to itself to be as it were an island in the midst of an ocean of barbarians constantly striving to submerge it.

It is understandable that in such a case patriotism—that is the desire to withstand the attacks of the barbarians, who were not only ready to destroy the social order of the nation but threatened it with plunder, wholesale murder, captivity, enslavement, and the violation of its women—was a natural feeling. It is understandable that to preserve himself and his fellow-countrymen from such disaster a man might put his own people before all others, entertain a hostile feeling for the surrounding barbarians, and kill them to defend his own people.

But what meaning can such a feeling have in our Christian times? On what grounds and for what objects can a Russian of our time go and kill Frenchmen and Germans, or how can a Frenchman kill Germans, when—however ill-educated he may be—he knows very well that the men of other kingdoms and peoples against whom his patriotic enmity is aroused are not barbarians but Christians, just such people as he is, often of the same creed and profession as he, desiring peace and a peaceful exchange of labour, and who are for the most part united with him either by the common interests of work, that is by trade, by spiritual interests, or by both of these? So that very often men of one kingdom are nearer and more necessary to men of another kingdom than to their own countrymen, as is the case with commercial folk, with workmen connected with employers of other nationalities, and especially with learned men and artists.

Besides, the very conditions of life have so changed now that what we call our country—which we are supposed to distinguish in some way from all the rest—has ceased to be as clearly defined as it was in ancient times when the people forming one nation belonged to one race, one State, and one religion: the patriotism of the Egyptians, Jews, or Greeks, for instance, who when defending their fatherland were also defending their religion, their nationality, their native land and their State.

But how can an Irishman in the United States express his patriotism to-day, when by his religion he belongs to Rome, by his birth to Ireland, and as a citizen to the United States? And the Czech in Austria, the Pole in Russia, Prussia, and Austria, the Hindu in the British Empire, and the Tartar and the Armenian in Russia and Turkey, are in a similar position. But leaving aside these several subject nationalities, even men of the most homogeneous States, such as Russia, France, and Prussia, can no longer feel the sentiment of patriotism which was natural to the ancients, for very often the chief interests of their lives (sometimes domestic, when their wives are of another nation, sometimes economic, when their capital is invested abroad, sometimes spiritual, scientific, or artistic) are not in their own country but outside it, in that State against which their patriotic enmity is being aroused.

And above all, patriotism is impossible in our time because however we have tried during nineteen hundred years to conceal the meaning of Christianity, it has nevertheless permeated our life, and controls it to such a degree that even the coarsest and most stupid people cannot now fail to see the complete incompatibility of patriotism with the moral principle by which they live.

XIV

Patriotism was a necessity in the formation and consolidation of strong States composed of heterogeneous populations and needing defence against barbarians. But when Christian enlightenment had transformed those States from within, giving to them all the same basic principles, patriotism became the sole obstacle to that union among nations for which Christian consciousness had prepared them.

Patriotism in our day is a cruel tradition surviving from an outlived past. It is maintained only by inertia and because governments and the ruling classes, feeling that their power and even their existence is bound up with it, persistently excite and maintain it among the people by cunning and by violence. Patriotism in our time resembles scaffolding which was needed for the erection of the walls of a building, and which though it now obstructs the use of the building is still not removed because its existence is profitable to certain people.

For a long time past Christian nations have not had, nor could have had, reasons for quarrelling. One cannot even imagine how or why Russian and German workmen, working peacefully together on their frontiers and in their cities, should begin to quarrel with one another. Still less can one imagine enmity between a Kazán peasant supplying grain to a German, and the German who supplies him with scythes and machines. It is the same with French, German, and Italian workmen. And it is absurd even to speak of a quarrel between learned men, artists, and writers of different nationalities, absorbed in the same general interests independently of nationality and politics.

But the governments cannot let the people be quiet—that is, in peaceful relations with one another—for the chief, if not the sole, justification for the existence of governments lies in pacifying and adjusting their hostile relations. And so the governments provoke those hostile relations under the guise of patriotism, and then make a show of pacifying them. It is like a gypsy who, having sprinkled pepper under his horse's tail and lashed him in his stall, leads him out hanging onto his halter and pretending that he can hardly control the excited animal.

We are assured that the governments are anxious to preserve peace between the peoples. But how do they preserve it?

Men live on the banks of the Rhine in peaceful intercourse with one another, when all at once, in consequence of various disputes and intrigues between kings and emperors, war begins, and it seems necessary to the French government to declare some of those inhabitants to be French. Centuries pass: the people have grown used to the position, when enmity again arises between the governments of the great nations and a war is started on very empty pretexts, and it seems necessary to the Germans to declare these men Germans again, and ill will is aroused between all the French and the Germans.

Or Germans and Russians are living quietly on their frontier, peaceably exchanging services and the products of labour, and all at once those same institutions which exist for the purpose of maintaining peace between nations begin quarrelling, commit one folly after another, and can find nothing better to do than the childish trick of punishing themselves merely to get their own way and mortify their opponents (in this case very conveniently for themselves, for those who institute a tariff war do not suffer from it themselves—others have to do that). A customs war is started, such as was recently waged between Russia and Germany. And by the help of the newspapers ill will is aroused between Germans and Russians, which is further inflamed by the Franco-Russian festivities, and may at any moment lead to a bloody war.

I have cited these last two instances of how governments influence the people and arouse their hostility to other nations, because they are modern instances. But there is not a single war in all history which has not been evoked by governments and by governments alone, quite independently of the advantage of the people, for whom a war, even a successful one, is always harmful.

The governments assure their peoples that they are in danger of being attacked by other nations or by foes in their midst, and that the only way to escape that danger is by slavish obedience to their governments. This is seen very plainly during revolutions and dictatorships, and it occurs always and everywhere where there is arbitrary rule. Every government explains its existence and justifies all its violence on the ground that if it were not there things would be worse. Having convinced the people that they are in danger, the governments dominate them. And when the peoples are dominated by governments the latter compel them to attack each other. And in this way a belief in the governments' assurance of the danger of attacks by other nations is confirmed among the peoples.

Divide et impera.

Patriotism in its simplest, clearest, and most indubitable meaning is nothing but an instrument for the attainment of the government's ambitious and mercenary aims, and a renunciation of human dignity, common sense, and conscience by the governed, and a slavish submission to those who hold power. That is what is really preached wherever patriotism is championed.

Patriotism is slavery.

The advocates of peace by means of arbitration reason thus: two animals cannot divide their prey except by fighting: children act thus also, and so do barbarians and the barbarous nations. But rational men settle their disagreements by discussion, persuasion, and by referring the decision of the question to disinterested and reasonable people, and the nations of our day ought to act so. These arguments seem quite correct. The peoples of our time have reached a period of enlightenment and have no enmity towards one another and could settle their differences in a peaceful manner. But the argument is only correct in so far as it applies to the people alone, and only if the people are not under the sway of their governments. People in subjection to their governments cannot be rational, for subjection to government is already an indication of the utmost irrationality.

What use is it to talk of the reasonableness of men who promise in advance to fulfil everything (including the murder of men) commanded by government—that is, by men who have happened to get into the position of rulers?

Men who can undertake to fulfil with unquestioning submission all that is decreed by men they do not know, living in Petersburg, Vienna, or Paris, cannot be rational; and the governments—that is, the men wielding such power—can still less be reasonable. They cannot but misuse such insensate and terrible power and cannot but be crazed by wielding it.

For this reason peace between nations cannot be attained by the reasonable method of conventions and arbitrations so long as that submission of the peoples to governments, which is always irrational and pernicious, still continues.

But the subjection of men to government will always continue as long as patriotism exists, for every ruling power rests on patriotism—on the readiness of men to submit to power for the sake of the defence of their own people and country, that is, their State, from the dangers supposed to threaten them. The power of the French kings over their people before the Revolution rested on such patriotism, and so did the power of the Committee of Public Safety after the Revolution, and on that same patriotism the power of Napoleon (both as Consul and Emperor) was built up, and the power of the Bourbons after the overthrow of Napoleon, and then of the Republic and of Louis-Philippe, and then again of the Republic and again of Napoleon III, and then once more of the Republic; and on that same patriotism the power of Boulanger was all but established.

It is terrible to say that there is not, and has never been, any act of collective violence by one set of people upon another that has not been perpetrated in the name of patriotism. In the name of patriotism the Russians have fought against the French and the French against the Russians. In the name of patriotism the Russians and the French are now preparing to fight against the Germans, and in the name of patriotism the Germans are preparing to fight on two fronts. And it is not wars alone. In the name of patriotism the Russians are oppressing the Poles and the Germans the Slavs, and in the name of patriotism the Communists slaughtered the men of Versailles and the men of Versailles the Communists.

XV

It would seem that the spread of education, improved means of transport, and increased intercourse between different nations, the growth of the public Press, and above all the decreasing danger from other nations, should make it more and more difficult, and at last impossible, to maintain the deception of patriotism.

But the fact is that those very means of general superficial education, increased facilities for travel and intercourse, and especially the growth of the Press, more and more controlled by the governments, give them nowadays such possibilities of exciting feelings of mutual hostility between the nations that though the uselessness and harmfulness of patriotism has become increasingly obvious, the influence exerted by governments and the ruling classes to arouse patriotism among the people has increased to an equal extent.

The only difference between past and present is, that as many more people now share in the advantages afforded by patriotism to the upper classes, many more people take part in spreading and keeping up that amazing superstition.

The more difficult governments find it to retain their power, the more people they share it with.

Formerly a small group of rulers held the power: emperors, kings, dukes, and their officials and warriors. But now that power and the advantages it affords are shared not only by the officials and clergy, but also by large and even small capitalists, landowners, bankers, members of the legal professions, teachers, rural functionaries, learned men, artists, and especially writers for the Press. And all these people, consciously or unconsciously, spread the deception of patriotism necessary for the maintenance of their advantageous position. And thanks to the fact that the means of deception have become greater and that an ever greater number of people now participate in it, it is so successfully carried out that despite the greater difficulty of the deception the people are as much deceived as ever.

A hundred years ago the illiterate masses, having no conception of whom their government consisted, or of the nations that surrounded them, blindly obeyed the local officials and nobles by whom they were enslaved. And it was enough for the government to keep those officials and nobles under its control by means of bribes and rewards, for the masses obediently to fulfil what was demanded of them. But now, when the masses can for the most part read and know more or less of whom their government consists and what nations surround them; when men of the people continually and easily move from place to place carrying news of what is being done in the world, mere demands that people shall fulfil the government's orders are no longer sufficient. It is necessary also to befog the just ideas which the people have of life, and to instil into them other conceptions of the conditions of their life and of the attitude of other nations towards them.

And thanks to the development of the Press, of education, and of the facilities for travel, the governments, having their agents everywhere, by means of decrees, Church teaching, schools and newspapers, instil into the people the wildest and most perverse conception of their interests, and of the mutual relations of the peoples and their characteristics and intentions. And the people are so oppressed by toil that they have neither time nor opportunity to understand the significance and test the justice of the ideas instilled into them, and submit implicitly to the demands thus imposed upon them in the name of their welfare.

And those of the people who have freed themselves from constant toil and secured some education, and who it would seem might therefore understand the deception to which they had been exposed, are submitted to such threats, bribes, and hypnotization by the government, that almost without exception they promptly pass over to its side, and obtaining advantageous and well-paid posts as teachers, priests, officers, or officials, begin to share in spreading the deception which ruins their fellows. It is as if at the doors of education snares were placed in which all who in one way or other escape from amid the masses crushed by toil, are inevitably caught.

At first when one understands all the cruelty of this deception one feels indignant with those who from personal, covetous aims, or from vanity, promote this cruel deception which ruins not only men's bodies but also their souls, and one wishes to expose these cruel deceivers. But the fact is that the deceivers act as they do, not because they wish to deceive but because they can hardly act otherwise. And their deception is not Machiavellian—not done with a consciousness of the deception they are producing—but for the most part with a naïve conviction that they are doing something good and elevated—in which conviction they are continually supported by the sympathy and approval of all those around them. It is true that dimly feeling that their power and advantageous position depends on that deception they are involuntarily attracted to it, but they act as they do not from a wish to cheat the people, but because they think that what they are doing is of use to them.

So the emperors and kings with their ministers, perform their coronations, manœuvres, reviews, and visits to one another during which, dressed up in various uniforms, they move from place to place and consult together with serious faces how to keep peace between supposedly hostile people (to whom it would never occur to fight), and are fully convinced that all they are doing is extremely valuable and reasonable.

In just the same way all the ministers, diplomats, and officials of all sorts, dressing themselves up in their uniforms with various ribbons and crosses and anxiously writing their obscure, involved, and useless communications, reports, instructions, and projects, on fine paper all carefully docketed, are fully convinced that without their activity the whole life of the people would cease or fall to pieces.

The military too, attired in their ludicrous costumes and seriously discussing what rifles and cannon kill people best, are fully convinced that their manœuvres and parades are very important and necessary for the people.

The clergy who preach patriotism, and the journalists and writers of patriotic poems and school-books who receive a generous remuneration for them, have the same conviction, and the organizers of festivities such as the Franco-Russian ones share it also and are sincerely moved when they pronounce their patriotic speeches and toasts. All these people perform their role unconsciously, because it is necessary or because their whole life is built on that deception and they can do nothing else. Meanwhile those very actions evoke sympathy and approval from all those among whom they are performed. Being all bound up with one another they not only approve and justify one another's actions and activity— emperors and kings justifying the doings of the military, the officials, and the clergy; and the military, officials, and clergy, the doings of the emperors and kings and of one another— but the common crowd (especially in towns), seeing no intelligible meaning in all that is being done by these people, involuntarily attribute to it a peculiar and almost supernatural significance. The crowd see, for instance, that triumphal arches are erected, that men dress up in crowns, uniforms, and sacerdotal vestments, that fireworks are displayed, cannon are fired, bells are rung, regiments march with bands playing, papers and telegrams fly about, and couriers rush from place to place, while anxious men in strange attire ride incessantly from place to place, say and write something, and so on; and not being in a position to ascertain that all this is being done (as is actually the case) without the least necessity, the crowd attribute to it a special, mysterious, and important significance, and greet all these shows with ecstatic cries or silent respect. And these expressions, sometimes of delight and always of respect, strengthen the confidence of those who are doing all these silly things.

Not long ago Wilhelm II ordered himself a new throne with some special ornamentation, and having dressed himself up in a white uniform with a cuirass, tight breeches, and a helmet with a bird on it, and having also put on a red mantle, came out to his subjects and sat down on that new throne, fully convinced that this was a necessary and very important affair. And his subjects not only saw nothing ridiculous in it but considered the sight a very solemn one.

XVI

For a very long time past the power of the governments over the peoples has not rested on force, as it did in the days when one people conquered another and held it in subjection by force of arms, or when the rulers had legions of armed janissaries, *oprichniki,* and armed guards amid an unarmed people. For a long time past the power of the governments has rested on what is called public opinion.

There is a public opinion that patriotism is a great moral sentiment, and that people should consider their own nation and State as the best in the world; and this results in a public opinion that it is right and proper to acknowledge the authority of the government and to submit to it, that it is right and proper to serve in the army and submit to its discipline, that it is right and proper to give one's earnings to the government in the form of taxes, that it is right and proper to accept the decisions of the courts, and that it is right and proper to accept as divine truth whatever the emissaries of the government deliver to us.

And once such a public opinion exists, a mighty power is established, controlling in our days milliards of money, an organized mechanism of administration, the postal services, telegraphy, telephones, disciplined armies, the law courts, the police, a submissive clergy, schools, and even newspapers; and this power maintains among the people the public opinion needed for its own maintenance.

The power of the governments rests on public opinion, and possessing power they can always support the sort of public opinion they require by their whole organization, officials, law courts, schools, the Church, and even the Press. Public opinion produces the power, power produces public opinion; and it seems as if there were no escape from this position.

And that would really be the case if public opinion were something fixed and unchanging and if governments could always produce the public opinion they desired.

But fortunately that is not so. In the first place, public opinion is not something constant, unchanging and stagnant, but on the contrary is something continually changing and moving with the movement of mankind. And secondly, public opinion not only cannot be produced at will by governments, but is what produces governments and gives or deprives them of power.

If public opinion seems to remain stationary, and is now what it was decades ago, or if it oscillates in some particular respects as though returning to a former state (now, for instance, abolishing a republican government and replacing it by a monarchy, and now again destroying a monarchy and replacing it by a republic)—this only seems so when we look at the external manifestations of public opinion which are artificially produced by the governments. We need only regard public opinion in relation to the whole life of the people to see that public opinion, like time, never stands still, but is always moving, always going persistently forward along the path by which humanity is advancing, just as the spring moves steadily forward along the way the sun leads it, despite delays and fluctuations. So that, though in its external aspects the position of the peoples of Europe is almost the same to-day as it was fifty years ago, the peoples' relation to it is quite different. Though there are the same rulers, armies, wars, taxes, luxury and poverty, Catholicism, Orthodoxy, and Lutheranism as before, in the old days they existed because public opinion demanded them, whereas now they exist only because the governments artificially keep up what was once a living public opinion.

If we often fail to notice this movement of public opinion, just as we fail to notice the movement of the river when we are swimming with the current, that is because the unnoticed changes of public opinion which constitute its movement take place within ourselves.

Public opinion is by its nature a constant and irresistible movement. If it seems to us to stand still, that is because there are everywhere people who at a certain phase of public opinion have secured for themselves an advantageous position and afterwards use every effort to give it permanence and prevent the emergence of what is new and real and what, though not as yet fully expressed, is already alive in people's consciousness. And such men, retaining an outlived public opinion and concealing the new one, are those who now constitute the governments and the ruling classes, and who profess patriotism as a necessary condition of human life.

The means these people control are enormous, but as public opinion is something ever fluid and growing, all their efforts cannot but be in vain: what is old decays and what is young grows.

The longer nascent public opinion is checked the more does it grow and the more strongly will it find expression. The governments and the ruling classes try with all their might to keep up the old patriotic public opinion on which their power rests and to restrain manifestation of the new opinion which will destroy it. But to retain the old and stop the new is possible only within certain limits, just as a dam can only hold running water back to a certain extent.

However much the governments may try to excite in people the old public opinion of the heroism of patriotism—now no longer natural to them—men of our time no longer believe in it, but believe ever more and more in the solidarity and brotherhood of all nations. Patriotism does not now offer men anything but a most terrible future; while the brotherhood of all the people is an ideal which becomes ever more and more intelligible and desirable to mankind. And so the transition from the old, outlived public opinion to the new one must inevitably be accomplished. That transition is as inevitable as the fall of the last dry leaves in spring and the opening out of the young ones from the swollen buds.

And the longer that transition is postponed the more insistent it becomes and the more obvious is its inevitability.

Indeed, it is only necessary to consider what we profess both as Christians and simply as men of our time—to think of those moral principles by which we are guided in our social, family, and personal life, and of the position in which we have placed ourselves in the name of patriotism—to realize what a degree of contradiction there is between our consciousness and that which, through the intensive efforts of the government, is still considered to be our public opinion. It is only necessary to reflect on the most ordinary demands of patriotism, which are presented to us as something very simple and natural, to realize to what an extent those demands contradict that real public opinion which we all share. We all consider

ourselves free, educated, humane men, and even Christians;
yet we are in such a position that if Wilhelm takes offence at
Alexander to-morrow, or Mr. N. N. writes a lively article on
the Eastern question, or Prince So-and-so plunders some
Bulgarians or Serbs, or some Queen or Empress takes offence
at something, we—educated, humane Christians—must all
go to kill people whom we do not know and towards whom,
as towards all men, we are well disposed.

If that has not yet happened we are indebted, so people
assure us, to Alexander the Third's pacific disposition or to
the fact that his son Nicholas Alexándrovich[18] is to marry
Victoria's granddaughter. But were someone else in Alexander's place or should Alexander's disposition change, or should
Nicholas Alexándrovich marry Amelia instead of Alex, then
we shall rush to rip out each other's guts as if we were wild
beasts.

Such is the supposed public opinion of our time, and opinions of that kind are calmly repeated in all the most progressive and liberal organs of the Press.

If we, Christians for a thousand years, have not yet cut one
another's throats, it is only because Alexander the Third does
not allow us to do so.

Surely that is terrible!

XVII

No feats of heroism are needed to bring about the greatest
and most important changes in the life of humanity; neither
the arming of millions of men, nor the construction of new
railways and machines, nor the organization of exhibitions or
Trades Unions, nor revolutions, nor barricades, nor dynamite
outrages, nor the perfection of aerial navigation, and so forth.
All that is necessary is a change of public opinion.

And for that change no effort of thought is demanded, no

---

[18] In November 1894 he ascended the throne of Russia as Nicholas
II. A month later he married Princess Alexandra of Hesse, the
daughter of Queen Victoria's second daughter, the Princess Alice.
—A. M.

refutation of any existing thing, and no planning of anything new and extraordinary. All that is necessary is to cease acquiescing in the public opinion of the past, now false and already defunct and only artificially induced by governments. It is only necessary for each individual to say what he really thinks and feels or at least to refrain from saying what he does not think.

If only men—even a few—would do that, the out-worn public opinion would at once and of itself fall away and a new, real, and vital public opinion would manifest itself. And with this change of public opinion all that inner fabric of men's lives which oppresses and torments them would change of its own accord. One is ashamed to say how little is needed to deliver all men from the calamities which now oppress them. It is only necessary to give up lying! Only let men reject the lie which is imposed upon them; only let them stop saying what they neither think nor feel, and at once such a change of the whole structure of our life will be accomplished as the revolutionaries would not achieve in centuries even if all power were in their hands.

If only men believed that strength lies not in might but in truth, and if they spoke that truth boldly, or at least did not go back on it in word or deed; if only they would cease saying what they do not think and doing what they regard as bad and stupid!

'What does it matter if one shouts: *"Vive la France"* or "Hurrah!" to some emperor, king, or conqueror, or puts on a uniform embroidered with a courtier's key and goes to wait in his antechamber, there to bow and address him by strange titles, and then impresses on all—especially on the young and the uneducated—that this is very praiseworthy? What does it matter if one writes an article in defence of the Franco-Russian Alliance or the tariff war, or in condemnation of the Germans, Russians, French, or English? What does it matter if one goes to patriotic festivities and drinks to the health of, and addresses laudatory speeches to, men one does not like and with whom one has nothing in common? What does it matter even, if in conversation one admits the value and

utility of treaties and alliances or remains silent when our
own people and State are praised while other races are ma-
ligned and abused, or when Catholicism, Orthodoxy, or Lutheranism is extolled, or heroes of war or rulers, such as Napoleon and Peter, or in our day Boulanger and Skobelev?'

All that may seem very unimportant. But yet in these apparently unimportant actions—in our indicating to the extent of our powers the unreasonableness of what we clearly
see to be irrational and refraining from taking part in it—lies
our great and irresistible power: the power which constitutes
that unconquerable force which makes up real genuine public opinion—that opinion which with its own advance moves
all humanity. Governments know this. They tremble before
that force and strive in every possible way to counteract and
overcome it.

They know that strength lies not in force but in the action
of the mind and in its clear expression. And they fear that expression of independent thought more than an army. So they
establish censorships, bribe newspapers, and seize control of
the Churches and schools. But the spiritual force which
moves the world eludes them. It is not in a book or a newspaper: it cannot be trapped but is always free, for it lies in
the depths of man's consciousness. This most powerful, elu-
sive, and free force shows itself in man's soul when he is alone
and reflects on the phenomena of the world and then involuntarily expresses his thoughts to his wife, his brother, his friend,
and to all from whom he accounts it a sin to conceal what he
considers to be the truth. No milliards of rubles, or millions of
troops, or any institutions, or wars, or revolutions, can or will
produce what a free man can produce by the simple expression of what he considers right, independently of what exists
and what is impressed upon him.

One free man says frankly what he thinks and feels in the
midst of thousands who by their actions and words maintain
just the opposite. It might be supposed that the man who
has frankly expressed his thoughts would remain isolated,
yet in most cases it happens that all, or the majority, of the
others have long thought and felt the same as he, only they

have not expressed it. And what yesterday was the novel opinion of one man becomes to-day the general opinion of the majority. And as soon as this opinion is established, at once by imperceptible degrees but irresistibly, the conduct of mankind begins to alter.

As it is each man, even if free, says to himself: 'What can I do alone against this ocean of evil and deception that overwhelms us? What is the use of expressing my opinion? Why indeed even form one? Better not think about these obscure and involved questions. Perhaps these contradictions are an inevitable condition of our existence. And why should I struggle alone with all the evil of the world? Is it not better to go with the stream that carries me along? If anything can be done it must be done in association with others and not alone.' And abandoning that mighty instrument of thought and its expression which moves the world, each individual man takes to the instrument of social activity, not noticing that all forms of social activity rest on the very foundations against which he ought to struggle, and that when entering on the social activity which exists in our world, every man is obliged at least to some extent to deviate from the truth and make concessions which destroy the force of the powerful weapon that has been given him. It is as though a man who has been given a blade with so keen an edge that it will cut through anything, should begin to use that edge to hammer nails.

We all complain of the senseless order of our life which is at variance with our whole being, and yet we neglect to use the unique and powerful instrument in our hands—the consciousness of truth and its expression. On the contrary, under pretext of struggling against evil we actually destroy that instrument and sacrifice it to the exigencies of an imaginary conflict with the existing order.

One man does not assert the truth he knows, because he feels himself bound to people with whom he is engaged; another because that truth might deprive him of a profitable position which enables him to support his family; a third because he wants to attain fame and power to be used afterwards in the service of mankind; a fourth because he does not wish to break with an ancient and sacred tradition; a fifth because he does not wish to offend people; and a sixth because the utterance of the truth would arouse persecution and interfere with some excellent social activity he is pursuing or intends to pursue.

One man serves as an emperor, a king, a minister, a government official, or an army officer, and assures himself and others that the deviations from truth that are unavoidable in his position are amply redeemed by the good he does. Another in the office of a spiritual pastor does not in the depth of his soul believe all he teaches, but permits himself a deviation from truth in consideration of the good he does. A third instructs men by means of literature, and despite the necessity of not telling the whole truth in order not to stir up the government and society against him, has no doubt that he is doing good. A fourth struggles openly with the existing order as a revolutionary or an anarchist, and is fully persuaded that the aims he pursues are so beneficial that the suppressing of the truth, or even the falsehoods necessary for the success of his activity, do not destroy the utility of his work.

That the order of life opposed to the conscience of men should be changed and replaced by one accordant with their consciences, it is necessary that the old outlived public opinion should be replaced by a new and living one.

And for the old, outlived public opinion to make way for the new and living one, it is necessary that men who recognize the new demands of life should express them clearly. Yet those who are conscious of these new demands, not only pass them over in silence—one for the sake of one thing, another for the sake of another—but both by word and deed attest their direct opposites. Only the truth and its free expression can establish that new public opinion which will reform the out-of-date and harmful order of life; and yet we not only fail to utter the truth we know but often give direct expression to what we ourselves regard as false.

If only free men would not rely on what has no power and

is never free, that is, external force; but would trust in what is always powerful and free, that is, the truth and its expression!

If only men would boldly and clearly express the truth already manifest to them (of the brotherhood of all nations and the crime of exclusive devotion to one's own) that defunct, false, public opinion on which rests the power of governments and all the evil they produce, would slough off of itself like a dead skin and reveal that new, living, public opinion which now only awaits the shedding of the old husk that has confined it, in order to announce its demands clearly and powerfully and establish new forms of existence in conformity with the conscience of mankind.

XVIII

Men have only to understand that what is given out to them as public opinion and is maintained by such complicated, strenuous, and artificial means, is not public opinion but a dead relic of what once was public opinion; they have only, above all, to believe in themselves—in the fact that what they are conscious of in the depths of their souls and what craves expression in each of them and remains unexpressed only because it runs counter to existing social opinion, is that force which transforms the world and to express which is man's vocation—they have only to believe that the truth lies not in what is said by the people around them but in what is said by their conscience, that is, by God—and the false and artificially maintained public opinion will instantly vanish and a true public opinion establish itself.

If only people would say what they think and refrain from saying what they do not think, all the superstitions bred by patriotism would fall away at once with all the evil feelings and acts of violence that are based upon them. The hatred and enmity of one country for another that is fanned by the governments would cease, and so would the glorification of warlike exploits, that is, of murder; and above all there would be an end of respect and subservience towards those

in power and of the surrender to them of men's labour—
for these things have no foundation but patriotism.

If that were done, the vast mass of weak people who are
always guided by outside influences would instantly pass over
to the side of the new public opinion. And a new public opinion would predominate in place of the old.

The governments may control the schools, the church, the
Press, milliards of rubles and millions of disciplined men made
into machines, but all that apparently terrible organization of
brute force is nothing before the recognition of the truth
which surges in the soul of each man who knows its power,
and from whom it is communicated to a second and a third,
as one candle can light an infinite number of others. That
light need only be kindled, and all that seemingly mighty
organization will melt away like wax before the fire and be
consumed.

If only men understood the mighty power given them in the
word which expresses truth; if only they would refuse to sell
their birthright for a mess of pottage, if only they would use
the power they possess, their rulers would not only not dare,
as now, to threaten at their caprice to plunge or not plunge
men into universal slaughter, but they would not even dare to
hold their reviews and manœuvres of disciplined murderers
before the eyes of a peaceful population. Nor would they
dare to arrange or upset tariff agreements in their own interest
and for the advantage of their assistants, and they would not
dare to take from the people the millions of rubles which
they distribute to their assistants and which they spend on
preparations for murder.

And so a change is not only possible but inevitable. That
such a change should not take place is as impossible as that a
dead tree should not decay and fall, and a young one grow
up.

*Peace I leave with you; my peace I give unto you. Let not
your heart be troubled, neither let it be afraid,* said Christ.
And that peace is already with us and it depends on us to
secure it.

If only the hearts of individual men would not be troubled

by the temptations which assail them every hour, and would not be frightened by the imaginary terrors that alarm them; if only men recognized in what their mighty and all-conquering power lies, the peace which they have always desired— not the peace obtained by diplomatic negotiations, by visits of emperors and kings from one town to another, by banquets, speeches, fortresses, artillery, dynamite and melinite, by exhausting the people by taxation or tearing the flower of the nation from toil and corrupting it, but the peace which is secured by the free advocacy of the truth by each individual man—would long since have been established among us.

[Moscow, March 17, 1894.]

PATRIOTISM AND GOVERNMENT

'The time is fast approaching when to call a man a
patriot will be the deepest insult you can offer him. Patriotism now means advocating plunder in the interests of the
privileged classes of the particular State system into which
we have happened to be born.'—E. BELFORT BAX.

I

I have already several times expressed the thought that in
our day the feeling of patriotism is an unnatural, irrational,
and harmful feeling, the cause of a great part of the ills from
which mankind is suffering, and that consequently this feeling should not be cultivated, as it now is, but should on the
contrary be suppressed and eradicated by all rational means.
Yet strange to say—though it is undeniable that the universal
armaments and destructive wars which are ruining the peoples result from that one feeling—all my arguments showing
the backwardness, anachronism, and harmfulness of patriotism have been and still are met either by silence, by intentional misinterpretation, or by a strange unvarying reply
to the effect that only bad patriotism (Jingoism, or Chauvinism) is evil, but that real, good patriotism is a very elevated
moral feeling to condemn which is not only irrational but
wicked.

What this real, good patriotism consists in, we are never
told. If anything is said about it we get declamatory, inflated

phrases, instead of explanation, or else some other conception is substituted—something which has nothing in common with the patriotism we all know and from the results of which we suffer so severely.

It is generally said that the real, good patriotism consists in desiring for one's own people or State such real benefits as do not infringe the well-being of other nations.

Talking recently to an Englishman about the present war,[1] I said to him that the real cause of the war was not avarice, as was generally said, but patriotism, as the whole temper of English society showed. The Englishman did not agree with me, and said that even were it so it merely showed that the patriotism at present inspiring Englishmen is a bad patriotism; but that good patriotism, such as he was imbued with, would cause his English compatriots to act well.

'Then do you wish only Englishmen to act well?' I asked.

'I wish all men to do so,' said he, indicating clearly by that reply the characteristic of true benefits whether moral, scientific, or even material and practical—which is that they spread out to all men. But to wish such benefits to everyone is evidently not only not patriotic but the reverse.

Neither do the peculiarities of each people constitute patriotism, though these things are purposely substituted for the conception of patriotism by its defenders. They say that the peculiarities of each people are an essential condition of human progress, and that patriotism, which seeks to maintain those peculiarities, is therefore a good and useful feeling. But is it not quite evident that if, once upon a time, these peculiarities of each people—these customs, creeds, languages— were conditions necessary for the life of humanity, in our time these same peculiarities form the chief obstacle to what is already recognized as an ideal—the brotherly union of the peoples? And therefore the maintenance and defence of any nationality—Russian, German, French, or Anglo-Saxon, provoking the corresponding maintenance and defence not only of Hungarian, Polish, and Irish nationalities, but also of

---

[1] The South African War of 1899-1902.—A. M.

Basque, Provençal, Mordvá,[2] Tchouvásh, and many other nationalities—serves not to harmonize and unite men but to estrange and divide them more and more from one another.

So that not the imaginary but the real patriotism which we all know, by which most people to-day are swayed and from which humanity suffers so severely, is not the wish for spiritual benefits for one's own people (it is impossible to desire spiritual benefits for one's own people only), but is a very definite feeling of preference for one's own people or State above all other peoples and States, and a consequent wish to get for that people or State the greatest advantages and power that can be got—things which are obtainable only at the expense of the advantages and power of other peoples or States.

It would therefore seem obvious that patriotism as a feeling is bad and harmful, and as a doctrine is stupid. For it is clear that if each people and each State considers itself the best of peoples and States, they all live in a gross and harmful delusion.

II

One would expect the harmfulness and irrationality of patriotism to be evident to everybody. But the surprising fact is that cultured and learned men not only do not themselves notice the harm and stupidity of patriotism, but resist every exposure of it with the greatest obstinacy and ardour (though without any rational grounds) and continue to belaud it as beneficent and elevating.

What does this mean?

Only one explanation of this amazing fact presents itself to me.

All human history from the earliest times to our own day may be considered as a movement of the consciousness both of individuals and of homogeneous groups from lower ideas to higher ones.

---

[2] The Mordvá (or Mordvinian) and Tchouvásh tribes are of Finnish origin, and inhabit chiefly the governments of the Middle Volga.—A. M.

The whole path travelled both by individuals and by homogeneous groups may be represented as a consecutive flight of steps from the lowest, on the level of animal life, to the highest attained by the consciousness of man at a given moment of history.

Each man, like each separate homogeneous group, nation, or State, always moved and moves up this ladder of ideas. Some portions of humanity are in front, others lag far behind, others again—the majority—move somewhere between the most advanced and the most backward. But all, whatever stage they may have reached, are inevitably and irresistibly moving from lower to higher ideas. And always, at any given moment, both the individuals and the separate groups of people—advanced, middle, or backward—stand in three different relations to the three stages of ideas amid which they move.

Always, both for the individual and for the separate groups of people, there are the ideas of the past, which are worn out and have become strange to them and to which they cannot revert: as for instance in our Christian world, the ideas of cannibalism, universal plunder, the rape of wives, and other customs of which only a record remains.

And there are the ideas of the present, instilled into men's minds by education, by example, and by the general activity of all around them; ideas under the power of which they live at a given time: for instance, in our own day, the ideas of property, State organization, trade, utilization of domestic animals, and so on.

And there are the ideas of the future, of which some are already approaching realization and are obliging people to change their way of life and to struggle against the former ways: such ideas in our world as those of freeing the labourers, of giving equality to women, of ceasing to use flesh food, and so on; while others, though already recognized, have not yet come into practical conflict with the old forms of life: such in our times are the ideas (which we call ideals) of the extermination of violence, the arrangement of a communal sys-

tem of property, of a universal religion, and of a general
brotherhood of men.

And therefore every man and every homogeneous group of
men, on whatever level they may stand, having behind them
the out-worn remembrances of the past and before them the
ideals of the future, are always in a state of struggle between
the moribund ideas of the present and the ideas of the future that are coming to life. It usually happens that when an
idea which has been useful and even necessary in the past
becomes superfluous, that idea, after a more or less prolonged struggle, yields its place to a new idea which was till
then an ideal, but which thus becomes a present idea.

But it does occur that an antiquated idea, already replaced
in people's consciousness by a higher one, is of such a kind
that its maintenance is profitable to those who have the greatest influence in their society. And then it happens that this
antiquated idea, though it is in sharp contradiction to the
whole surrounding form of life which has been altering in
other respects, continues to influence people and to sway their
actions. Such retention of antiquated ideas always has occurred, and still does occur, in the region of religion. And it
occurs because the priests, whose profitable positions are
bound up with the antiquated religious idea, purposely use
their power to hold people to this antiquated idea.

The same thing occurs in the political sphere, and for similar reasons, with reference to the patriotic idea on which all
arbitrary power is based. People to whom it is profitable to do
so maintain that idea by artificial means though it now lacks
both sense and utility. And as these people possess the most
powerful means of influencing others, they are able to achieve
their object.

In this, it seems to me, lies the explanation of the strange
contrast between the antiquated patriotic idea and that whole
drift of ideas making in a contrary direction which has already entered into the consciousness of the Christian world.

III

Patriotism as a feeling of exclusive love for one's own people and as a doctrine of the virtue of sacrificing one's tranquillity, one's property, and even one's life, in defence of one's own people from slaughter and outrage by their enemies, was the highest idea of the period when each nation considered it feasible and just for its own advantage to subject to slaughter and outrage the people of other nations.

But already some two thousand years ago humanity, in the person of the highest representatives of its wisdom, began to recognize the higher idea of a brotherhood of man; and that idea penetrating man's consciousness more and more, has in our time attained most varied forms of realization. Thanks to improved means of communication and to the unity of industry, of trade, of the arts, and of science, men are to-day so bound to one another that the danger of conquest, massacre, or outrage by a neighbouring people has quite disappeared, and all peoples (the peoples, but not the governments) live together in peaceful, mutually advantageous, and friendly commercial, industrial, artistic, and scientific relations, which they have no need and no desire to disturb. One would think therefore that the antiquated feeling of patriotism—being superfluous and incompatible with the consciousness we have reached of the existence of brotherhood among men of different nationalities—should dwindle more and more until it completely disappears. Yet the very opposite of this occurs: this harmful and antiquated feeling not only continues to exist, but burns more and more fiercely.

The peoples without any reasonable ground and contrary alike to their conception of right and to their own advantage, not only sympathize with governments in their attacks on other nations, in their seizures of foreign possessions and in defending by force what they have already stolen, but even themselves demand such attacks, seizures, and defences: are glad of them and take pride in them. The small oppressed nationalities which have fallen under the power of the great

States—the Poles, Irish, Bohemians, Finns, or Armenians—resenting the patriotism of their conquerors which is the cause of their oppression, catch from them the infection of this feeling of patriotism—which has ceased to be necessary and is now obsolete, unmeaning, and harmful—and catch it to such a degree that all their activity is concentrated upon it, and though they are themselves suffering from the patriotism of the stronger nations, they are ready for the sake of patriotism to perpetrate on other peoples the very same deeds that their oppressors have perpetrated and are perpetrating on them.

This occurs because the ruling classes (including not only the actual rulers with their officials but all the classes who enjoy an exceptionally advantageous position: the capitalists, journalists, and most of the artists and scientists) can retain their position—an exceptionally advantageous one in comparison with that of the labouring masses—thanks only to the government organization which rests on patriotism. They have in their hands all the most powerful means of influencing the people, and always sedulously support patriotic feelings in themselves and in others, more especially as those feelings which uphold the government's power are those that are always best rewarded by that power.

The more patriotic an official is, the more he prospers in his career. The war produced by patriotism gives the army man a chance of promotion.

Patriotism and its resulting wars give an enormous revenue to the newspaper trade and profits to many other trades. The more every writer, teacher, and professor preaches patriotism the more secure is he in his place. The more every emperor and king is addicted to patriotism the more fame he obtains.

The ruling classes have in their hands the army, the schools, the churches, the press, and money. In the schools they kindle patriotism in the children by means of histories describing their own people as the best of all peoples and always in the right. Among adults they kindle it by spectacles, jubilees, monuments, and by a lying patriotic press. Above all they inflame patriotism by perpetrating every kind of injustice and harshness against other nations, provoking in them enmity towards their own people, and then in turn exploit that enmity to embitter their people against the foreigner.

The intensification of this terrible feeling of patriotism has gone on among the European peoples in a rapidly increasing progression, and in our time has reached the utmost limits beyond which there is no room for it to extend.

IV

Within the memory of people not yet old an occurrence took place showing most obviously the amazing intoxication caused by patriotism among the people of Christendom.

The ruling classes of Germany excited the patriotism of the masses of their people to such a degree that, in the second half of the nineteenth century, a law was proposed in accordance with which all the men had to become soldiers: all the sons, husbands, fathers, learned men, and godly men, had to learn to murder, to become submissive slaves of those above them in military rank, and be absolutely ready to kill whomsoever they were ordered to kill; to kill men of oppressed nationalities, their own working men standing up for their rights, and even their own fathers and brothers—as was publicly proclaimed by that most impudent of potentates, William II.

That horrible measure, outraging all man's best feelings in the grossest manner, was acquiesced in without murmur by the people of Germany under the influence of patriotism. It resulted in their victory over the French. That victory excited the patriotism of Germany yet further, and by reaction that of France, Russia, and the other Powers; and the men of the European countries unresistingly submitted to the introduction of general military service—i.e., to a state of slavery involving a degree of humiliation and submission incomparably worse than any slavery of the ancient world. After this servile submission of the masses to the calls of patriotism, the audacity, cruelty, and insanity of the governments knew no bounds. A competition in the usurpation of other peoples' lands in Asia,

Africa, and America began—evoked partly by whim, partly by vanity, and partly by covetousness—and was accompanied by ever greater and greater distrust and enmity between the governments.

The destruction of the inhabitants of the lands seized was accepted as a quite natural proceeding. The only question was who should be first in seizing other peoples' land and destroying the inhabitants? All the governments not only most evidently infringed, and are infringing, the elementary demands of justice in relation to the conquered peoples and in relation to one another, but they were guilty, and continue to be guilty, of every kind of cheating, swindling, bribery, fraud, spying, robbery, and murder; and the peoples not only sympathized and still sympathize with them in all this, but rejoice when it is their own government and not another government that commits such crimes.

The mutual enmity between the different peoples and States has latterly reached such amazing dimensions that, notwithstanding the fact that there is no reason why one State should attack another, everyone knows that all the governments stand with their claws out and their teeth bared, and only waiting for someone to be in trouble or become weak, in order to tear him to pieces with as little risk as possible.

All the peoples of the so-called Christian world have been reduced by patriotism to such a state of brutality that not only those who are obliged to kill or be killed desire slaughter and rejoice in murder, but all the people of Europe and America, living peaceably in their homes exposed to no danger, are at each war—thanks to easy means of communication and to the press—in the position of the spectators in a Roman circus, and like them delight in the slaughter, and raise the bloodthirsty cry, *'Pollice verso.'* [3]

And not only adults, but children too, pure, wise children, rejoice, according to their nationality, when they hear that

---

[3] In the Roman amphitheatres the sign given by the spectators who wished a defeated gladiator to be slain was the turning out of thumbs (*pollice verso*).—A. M.

the number killed and lacerated by lyddite or other shells on some particular day was not seven hundred but a thousand Englishmen or Boers.

And parents (I know of such cases) encourage their children in such brutality.

But that is not all. Every increase in the army of one nation (and each nation, being in danger, seeks to increase its army for patriotic reasons) obliges its neighbours to increase their armies, also from patriotism, and this evokes a fresh increase by the first nation.

And the same thing occurs with fortifications and navies: one State has built ten ironclads, a neighbour builds eleven; then the first builds twelve, and so on to infinity.

'I'll pinch you.' 'And I'll punch your head.' 'And I'll stab you with a dagger.' 'And I'll bludgeon you.' 'And I'll shoot you.' . . . Only bad children, drunken men, or animals, quarrel or fight so, but yet it is just what is going on among the highest representatives of the most enlightened governments, the very men who undertake to direct the education and the morality of their subjects.

v

The position is becoming worse and worse, and there is no stopping this descent towards evident perdition.

The one way of escape believed in by credulous people has now been closed by recent events. I refer to the Hague Conference, and to the war between England and the Transvaal which immediately followed it.

If people who think little or only superficially were able to comfort themselves with the idea that international courts of arbitration would supersede wars and ever-increasing armaments, the Hague Conference and the war that followed it demonstrated in the most palpable manner the impossibility of finding a solution of the difficulty in that way. After the Hague Conference it became obvious that as long as governments with armies exist, the termination of armaments and of wars is impossible. That an agreement should become possible it is necessary that the parties to it should *trust* each other. And in order that the Powers should trust each other they must lay down their arms, as is done by the bearers of a flag of truce when they meet for a conference.

So long as governments continue to distrust one another, and instead of disbanding or decreasing their armies always increase them in correspondence with augmentations made by their neighbours, and by means of spies watch every movement of troops, knowing that each of the Powers will attack its neighbour as soon as it sees its way to do so, no agreement is possible, and every conference is either a stupidity, or a pastime, or a fraud, or an impertinence, or all of these together.

It was particularly becoming that the Russian rather than any other government should be the *enfant terrible* of the Hague Conference. No one at home being allowed to reply to all its evidently mendacious manifestoes and rescripts, the Russian Government is so spoilt that—having without the least scruple ruined its own people with armaments, strangled Poland, plundered Turkestan and China, and being specially engaged in suffocating Finland—it proposed disarmament to the governments in full assurance that it would be trusted!

But strange, unexpected, and indecent as such a proposal was—coming at the very time when it was preparing an increase of its own army—the words publicly uttered in the hearing of the people were such, that for the sake of appearances the governments of the other Powers could not decline the consultation, comical and evidently insincere as it was. The delegates met—knowing in advance that nothing would come of it—and for several weeks (during whch they drew good salaries) though laughing in their sleeves, they all conscientiously pretended to be much occupied in arranging peace among the nations.

The Hague Conference, followed up as it was by the terrible bloodshed of the Transvaal War which no one attempted or is now attempting to stop, was nevertheless of some use, though not at all in the way expected of it—it was useful because it showed in the most obvious manner that the evils from which the peoples are suffering cannot be cured by governments; that governments, even if they wished to, cannot terminate either armaments or wars.

To have a reason for existing, governments must defend their people from other people's attack. But not one people wishes to attack or does attack another. And therefore governments, far from wishing for peace, carefully excite the anger of other nations against themselves. And having excited other people's anger against themselves and stirred up the patriotism of their own people, each government then assures its people that it is in danger and must be defended.

And having the power in their hands the governments can both irritate other nations and excite patriotism at home, and they carefully do both the one and the other. Nor can they do otherwise, for their existence depends on their acting thus.

If in former times governments were necessary to defend their people from other people's attacks, now on the contrary governments artificially disturb the peace that exists between the nations and provoke enmity among them.

When it was necessary to plough in order to sow, ploughing was wise, but it is evidently absurd and harmful to go on ploughing after the seed has been sown. But this is just what the governments are obliging their people to do: to infringe the unity which exists and which nothing would infringe were it not for the governments.

VI

What really are these governments without which people think they could not exist?

There may have been a time when such governments were necessary, and when the evil of supporting a government was less than that of being defenceless against organized neighbours; but now such governments have become unnecessary and are a far greater evil than all the dangers with which they frighten their subjects.

Not only military governments but governments in general could be, I will not say useful but at least harmless, only if they consisted of immaculate, holy people, as is theoretically the case among the Chinese. But then, by the nature of their activity which consists in committing acts of violence,[4] governments are always composed of elements quite contrary to holiness—of the most audacious, unscrupulous, and perverted people.

A government therefore is the most dangerous organization possible, especially when it is entrusted with military power.

In the widest sense the government, including capitalists and the Press, is nothing but an organization which places the greater part of the people in the power of a smaller part who dominate them. That smaller part is subject to a yet smaller part, that again to a yet smaller, and so on, reaching at last a few people or one single man who by means of military force has power over all the rest. So that all this organization resembles a cone of which all the parts are completely in the power of those people, or that one person, who happen to be at the apex.

The apex of the cone is seized by those who are more cunning, audacious, and unscrupulous than the rest, or by someone who happens to be the heir of those who were audacious and unscrupulous.

To-day it may be Borís Godunóv,[5] and to-morrow Gregory Otrépyev.[6] To-day the licentious Catherine, who with her paramours has murdered her husband; to-morrow Pugachév;[7] then Paul the madman, Nicholas I, or Alexander III.

---

[4] The word *government* is frequently used in an indefinite sense as almost equivalent to management or direction; but in the sense in which the word is used in the present article, the characteristic feature of a government is that it claims a moral right to inflict physical penalties and by its decree to make murder a good action. —A. M.

[5] Borís Godunóv, brother-in-law of the weak Tsar Fëdor Ivánovich, succeeded in becoming Tsar, and reigned in Moscow from 1598 to 1605.—A. M.

[6] Gregory Otrépyev was a pretender, who passing himself off as Dmítri, son of Iván the Terrible, reigned in Moscow in 1605 and 1606.—A. M.

[7] Pugachév was the leader of a most formidable insurrection in 1773-5, and was executed in Moscow in 1775.—A. M.

To-day it may be Napoleon, to-morrow a Bourbon or an Orléans, a Boulanger or a Panama Company; to-day it may be Gladstone, to-morrow Salisbury, Chamberlain, or Rhodes.

And to such governments is allowed full power not only over property and lives, but even over the spiritual and moral development, the education, and the religious guidance of everybody.

People construct this terrible machine of power, they allow anyone to seize it who can (and the chances always are that it will be seized by the most morally worthless)—they slavishly submit to him, and are then surprised that evil comes of it. They are afraid of anarchists' bombs, and are not afraid of this terrible organization which is always threatening them with the greatest calamities.

People found it useful to tie themselves together in order to resist their enemies, as the Circassians[8] did when resisting attacks. And they still go on tying themselves together though the danger is quite past.

They carefully tie themselves up so that one man can have them all at his mercy. Then they throw away the end of the rope that ties them and leave it trailing for some rascal or fool to seize and to do them whatever harm he pleases.

And when people set up, submit to, and maintain an organized and military government, what are they doing but just that?

VII

To deliver men from the terrible and ever-increasing evils of armaments and wars, we want neither congresses nor conferences nor treaties nor courts of arbitration, but the destruction of those instruments of violence which are called governments and from which humanity's greatest evils flow.

---

[8] The Circassians, when surrounded, used to tie themselves together leg to leg, that all should die fighting and none escape. Instances of this kind occurred when their country was being annexed by Russia.—A. M.

To destroy governmental *violence* only one thing is needed: it is that people should understand that the feeling of patriotism which alone supports that instrument of violence is a rude, harmful, disgraceful, and bad feeling, and above all immoral. It is a rude feeling because it is natural only to people standing on the lowest level of morality and expecting from other nations such outrages as they themselves are ready to inflict. It is a harmful feeling because it disturbs advantageous and joyous peaceful relations with other peoples, and above all produces that governmental organization under which power may fall and does fall into the hands of the worst men. It is a disgraceful feeling because it turns man not merely into a slave but into a fighting cock, a bull, or a gladiator, who wastes his strength and his life for objects which are not his own but his government's. It is an immoral feeling because, instead of confessing himself a son of God (as Christianity teaches us) or even a free man guided by his own reason, each man under the influence of patriotism confesses himself the son of his fatherland and the slave of his government, and commits actions contrary to his reason and conscience.

It is only necessary that people should understand this, and the terrible bond called government by which we are chained together will fall to pieces of itself without a struggle, and with it the terrible and useless evils it produces will cease.

And people are already beginning to understand this. For instance, a citizen of the United States writes:

'We are farmers, mechanics, merchants, manufacturers, teachers, and all we ask is the privilege of attending to our own business. We own our homes, love our friends, are devoted to our families, and do not interfere with our neighbours—we have work to do and wish to work.

'Leave us alone!

'But they will not—these politicians. They insist on governing us and living off our labour. They tax us, eat our substance, conscript us, draft our boys into their wars. All the myriads of men who live on the government depend upon the government to tax us, and in order to tax us successfully standing armies are maintained. The plea that the army is needed for the protection of the country is pure fraud and pretence. The French Government frightens the people by telling them that the Germans are ready and anxious to fall upon them. The Russians fear the British. The British fear everybody. And now in America we are told we must increase our navy and add to our army because Europe may at any moment combine against us.

'This is fraud and untruth. The plain people in France, Germany, England, and America, are opposed to war. We only wish to be let alone. Men with wives, children, sweethearts, homes, aged parents, do not want to go off and fight someone. We are peaceable and we fear war. We hate it.

'We should like to obey the Golden Rule.

'War is the inevitable outcome of the existence of armed men. The country which maintains a large standing army will sooner or later have a war on hand. The man who prides himself on fisticuffs is going some day to meet a man who considers himself the better man, and they will fight. Germany and France have no issue save a desire to see which is the better man. They have fought many times—and they will fight again. Not that the people want to fight, but the superior class fan fright into fury and make men think they must fight to protect their homes.

'So the people who wish to follow the teachings of Christ are not allowed to do so, but are taxed, outraged, and deceived by governments.

'Christ taught humility, meekness, the forgiveness of one's enemies, and that to kill was wrong. The Bible teaches men not to swear; but the superior class make us swear on the Bible in which they do not believe.

'The question is: How are we to relieve ourselves of these cormorants who toil not, but who are clothed in broadcloth and blue, with brass buttons and many costly accoutrements —who feed upon our substance and for whom we delve and dig?

'Shall we fight them?

'No, we do not believe in bloodshed. Besides they have the guns and the money and can hold out longer than we.

'But who composes this army that they would order to fire upon us?

'Why, our neighbours and brothers—deceived into the idea that they are doing God's service by protecting their country from its enemies. When the fact is our country has no enemies save the superior class that pretends to look out for our interests if we will only obey and consent to be taxed.

'In this way they siphon our resources and turn our true brothers upon us to subdue and humiliate us. You cannot send a telegram to your wife, or an express package to your friend, or draw a cheque for your grocer, until you first pay the tax to maintain armed men who can quickly be used to kill you; and who will imprison you if you do not pay.

'The only relief lies in education. Educate men that it is wrong to kill. Teach them the Golden Rule, and yet again teach them the Golden Rule. Silently defy this superior class by refusing to bow down to their fetish of bullets. Cease supporting the preachers who cry for war and spout patriotism for a consideration. Let them go to work as we do. We believe in Christ—they do not. Christ spoke what He thought. They speak what they think will please the men in power—the superior class.

'We will not enlist. We will not shoot at their order. We will not "charge bayonet" upon a mild and gentle people. We will not fire upon shepherds and farmers fighting for their firesides, at the suggestion of Cecil Rhodes. Your false cry of "Wolf! wolf!" shall not alarm us. We pay your taxes only because we have to, and we will pay no longer than we have to. We will pay no pew-rents, no tithes to your sham charities, and we will speak our minds upon occasion.

'We will educate men.

'And all the time our silent influence will be making itself felt, and even the men who are conscripted will be half-hearted and refuse to fight. We will educate men into the thought that the Christ Life of Peace and Goodwill is better than the Life of Strife, Bloodshed, and War.

' "Peace on earth!"—it can only come when men do away with armies and are willing to do unto other men as they would be done by.'

So writes a citizen of the United States. And from various sides, in various forms, such voices are sounding.

This is what a German soldier writes:

'I went through two campaigns with the Prussian Guards (in 1866 and 1870), and I hate war from the bottom of my soul for it has made me inexpressibly unfortunate. We wounded soldiers generally receive such a miserable recompense that we have indeed to be ashamed of having once been patriots. I, for instance, get ninepence a day for my right arm which was shot through at the attack on St. Privat, August 18, 1870. Some hunting dogs are allowed more for their keep. And I have suffered for years from my twice wounded arm. Already in 1866 I took part in the war against Austria and fought at Trautenau and Königgrätz, and saw horrors enough. In 1870, being in the reserve, I was called out again, and as I have already said I was wounded in the attack at St. Privat: my right arm was twice shot through lengthwise. I had to leave a good place in a brewery and was unable afterwards to regain it. Since then I have never been able to get on my feet again. The intoxication soon passed and there was nothing left for the wounded invalid but to keep himself alive on a beggarly pittance eked out by charity. . . .

'In a world in which people run round like trained animals and are incapable of any other idea than that of overreaching one another for the sake of Mammon—in such a world let people think me a crank, but for all that I feel in myself the divine idea of peace which is so beautifully expressed in the Sermon on the Mount. My deepest conviction is that war is only trade on a larger scale—the ambitious and powerful trade with the happiness of the peoples.

'And what horrors do we not suffer from it! Never shall I forget the pitiful groans that pierced one to the marrow!

'People who never did each other any harm begin to slaughter one another like wild animals, and petty slavish souls implicate the good God, making Him their confederate in such deeds.

'My neighbour in the ranks had his jaw broken by a bullet. The poor wretch was mad with pain. He ran about like a lunatic and could not even get water to cool his horrible wound in the scorching summer heat. Our commander, the Crown Prince (who was afterwards the noble Emperor Frederick), wrote in his diary: "War is an irony on the Gospels." . . .'

People are beginning to understand the fraud of patriotism, in which all the governments take such pains to keep them involved.

VIII

'But,' it is usually asked, 'what will there be instead of governments?'

There will be nothing. Something that has long been useless and therefore superfluous and bad will be abolished. An organ that being unnecessary has become harmful will be abolished.

'But,' people generally say, 'if there is no government people will violate and kill each other.'

Why? Why should the abolition of the organization which arose in consequence of violence and which has been handed down from generation to generation to do violence—why should the abolition of such an organization, now devoid of use, cause people to outrage and kill one another? On the contrary, the presumption is that the abolition of the organ of violence would result in people ceasing to violate and kill one another.

Now some men are specially educated and trained to kill and to do violence to other people—there are men who are supposed to have a right to use violence, and who make use of an organization which exists for that purpose. Such deeds of violence and such killing are considered good and worthy deeds.

But then people will not be so brought up, and no one will have a right to use violence to others, and there will be no organization to do violence, and—as is natural to people of our time—violence and murder will always be considered bad actions no matter who commits them.

But should acts of violence continue to be committed even after the abolition of the governments, such acts will certainly be fewer than they are now when an organization specially devised to commit acts of violence exists, and we have a state of things in which acts of violence and murders are considered good and useful deeds.

The abolition of governments will merely rid us of an unnecessary organization which we have inherited from the past, an organization for the commission of violence and for its justification.

'But there will then be no laws, no property, no courts of justice, no police, no popular education', say people who intentionally confuse the use of violence by governments with various social activities.

The abolition of the organization of government formed to do violence does not at all involve the abolition of what is reasonable and good, and therefore not based on violence, in laws or law courts, or in property, or in police regulations, or in financial arrangements, or in popular education. On the contrary, the absence of the brutal power of government which is needed only for its own support, will facilitate a more just and reasonable social organization, needing no violence. Courts of justice, and public affairs, and popular education, will all exist to the extent to which they are really needed by the people, but in a form which will not involve the evils contained in the present form of government. Only that will be destroyed which was evil and hindered the free expression of the people's will.

But even if we assume that with the absence of governments there would be disturbances and civil strife, even then the position of the people would be better than it is at present. The position now is such that it is difficult to imagine anything worse. The people are ruined, and their ruin is becoming more and more complete. The men are all converted into war-slaves, and have from day to day to expect orders to go to kill and to be killed. What more? Are the ruined peoples to die of hunger? Even that is already beginning in Russia, in Italy, and in India. Or are the women as well as the men to go as soldiers? In the Transvaal even that has begun.

So that even if the absence of government really meant anarchy in the negative disorderly sense of that word—which is far from being the case—even then no anarchical disorder could be worse than the position to which governments have already led their peoples, and to which they are leading them.

And therefore emancipation from patriotism and the destruction of the despotism of government that rests upon it, cannot but be beneficial to mankind.

IX

Men, bethink yourselves! For the sake of your well-being, physical and spiritual, for the sake of your brothers and sisters, pause, consider, and think of what you are doing!

Reflect, and you will understand that your foes are not the Boers, or the English, or the French, or the Germans, or the Finns, or the Russians, but that your foes—your only foes—are you yourselves, who by your patriotism maintain the governments that oppress you and make you unhappy.

They have undertaken to protect you from danger and they have brought that pseudo-protection to such a point that you have all become soldiers—slaves—and are all ruined, or are being ruined more and more, and at any moment may and should expect that the tight-stretched cord will snap and a horrible slaughter of you and your children will commence.

And however great that slaughter may be and however that conflict may end the same state of things will continue. In the same way and with yet greater intensity, the governments will arm, and ruin, and pervert you and your children, and no one will help you to stop it or prevent it if you do not help yourselves.

There is only one kind of help possible—the abolition of that terrible cone of violence which enables the person or persons who succeed in seizing the apex to have power over all the rest, and to hold that power the more firmly the more cruel and inhuman they are, as we see by the cases of the Napoleons, Nicholas I, Bismarck, Chamberlain, Rhodes, and our Russian Dictators who rule the people in the Tsar's name.

There is only one way to destroy the binding together of this cone—it is by shaking off the hypnotism of patriotism.

Understand that you yourselves cause all the evils from which you suffer, by yielding to the suggestions by which emperors, kings, members of Parliament, governors, officers, capitalists, priests, authors, artists, and all who need this fraud of patriotism in order to live upon your labour, deceive you!

Whoever you may be—Frenchman, Russian, Pole, Englishman, Irishman, or Bohemian—understand that all your real human interests, whatever they may be—agricultural, industrial, commercial, artistic, or scientific—as well as your pleasures and joys, in no way run counter to the interests of other peoples or States, and that you are united with the folk of other lands by mutual co-operation, by interchange of services, by the joy of wide brotherly intercourse, and by the interchange not merely of goods but also of thoughts and feelings.

Understand that the question as to whether your government or another manages to seize Wei-hai-wei, Port Arthur, or Cuba does not affect you, or rather that every such seizure made by your government injures you by inevitably bringing in its train all sorts of pressure by your government to force you to take part in the robbery and violence by which alone such seizures are made, or can be retained when made. Understand that your life can in no way be bettered by Alsace becoming German or French and Ireland or Poland being free or enslaved—whoever holds them. You are free to live where you will, even if you be an Alsatian, an Irishman, or a Pole. Understand too, that by stirring up patriotism you will only make the case worse, for the subjection in which your people are kept has resulted simply from the struggle between patriotisms, and every manifestation of patriotism in one nation provokes a corresponding reaction in another. Understand that salvation from your woes is only possible when you free yourself from the obsolete idea of patriotism and from the obedience to governments that is based upon it, and when you boldly enter into the region of that higher idea, the brotherly union of the peoples, which has long since come to life and from all sides is calling you to itself.

If people would but understand that they are not the sons of some fatherland or other, nor of governments, but are sons of God and can therefore neither be slaves nor enemies one to another—those insane, unnecessary, worn-out, pernicious organizations called governments would cease, and with them all the sufferings, violations, humiliations, and crimes which they occasion.

[May 10, o.s., 1900.]

ADDRESS TO THE SWEDISH PEACE CONGRESS IN 1909

Dear Brothers:

We have met here to fight against war. War, the thing for the sake of which all the nations of the earth—millions and millions of people—place at the uncontrolled disposal of a few men or sometimes only one man, not merely milliards of rubles, talers, francs, or yen (representing a very large share of their labour), but also their very lives. And now we, a score of private people gathered from the various ends of the earth, possessed of no special privileges and above all having no power over anyone, intend to fight—and as we wish to fight we wish also to conquer—this immense power not of one government but of all the governments, which have at their disposal these milliards of money and millions of soldiers and who are well aware that the exceptional position of those who form the governments rests on the army alone: the army which has a meaning and purpose only if there is a war, the very war against which we wish to fight and which we wish to abolish.

For us to struggle, the forces being so unequal, must appear insane. But if we consider our opponents' means of strife and our own, it is not our intention to fight that will seem absurd but that the thing we mean to fight against can still exist. They have millions of money and millions of obedient soldiers; we have only one thing, but that is the most powerful thing in the world—Truth.

Therefore, insignificant as our forces may appear in comparison with those of our opponents, our victory is as sure as the victory of the light of the rising sun over the darkness of night.

Our victory is certain, but on one condition only—that when uttering the truth we utter it all, without compromise, concession, or modification. The truth is so simple, so clear, so evident, and so incumbent not only on Christians but on all reasonable men, that it is only necessary to speak it out completely in its full significance for it to be irresistible.

The truth in its full meaning lies in what was said thousands of years ago (in the law accepted among us as the Law of God) in four words: *Thou Shalt Not Kill.* The truth is that man may not and should not in any circumstances or under any pretext kill his fellow man.

That truth is so evident, so binding, and so generally acknowledged, that it is only necessary to put it clearly before men for the evil called war to become quite impossible.

And so I think that if we who are assembled here at this Peace Congress should, instead of clearly and definitely voicing this truth, address ourselves to the governments with various proposals for lessening the evils of war or gradually diminishing its frequency, we should be like men who having in their hand the key to a door, should try to break through walls they know to be too strong for them. Before us are millions of armed men, ever more and more efficiently armed and trained for more and more rapid slaughter. We know that these millions of people have no wish to kill their fellows and for the most part do not even know why they are forced to do that repulsive work, and that they are weary of their position of subjection and compulsion; we know that the murders committed from time to time by these men are committed by order of the governments; and we know that the existence of the governments depends on the armies. Can we, then, who desire the abolition of war, find nothing more conducive to our aim than to propose to the governments which exist only by the aid of armies and consequently by war—measures which would destroy war? Are we to propose to the governments that they should destroy themselves?

The governments will listen willingly to any speeches of

that kind, knowing that such discussions will neither destroy war nor undermine their own power, but will only conceal yet more effectually what must be concealed if wars and armies and themselves in control of armies are to continue to exist.

'But', I shall be told, 'this is anarchism; people never have lived without governments and States, and therefore governments and States and military forces defending them are necessary for the existence of the nations.'

But leaving aside the question of whether the life of Christian and other nations is possible without armies and wars to defend their governments and States, or even supposing it to be necessary for their welfare that they should slavishly submit to institutions called governments (consisting of people they do not personally know), and publish an appeal to all men, and especially to the Christian nations, in which we clearly and definitely express what everybody knows but hardly anyone says: namely that war is not—as most people now assume—a good and laudable affair, but that like all murder, it is a vile and criminal business not only for those who voluntarily choose a military career but for those who submit to it from avarice or fear of punishment.

With regard to those who voluntarily choose a military career, I would propose to state clearly and definitely in that appeal that notwithstanding all the pomp, glitter, and general approval with which it is surrounded, it is a criminal and shameful activity; and that the higher the position a man holds in the military profession the more criminal and shameful is his occupation. In the same way with regard to men of the people who are drawn into military service by bribes or by threats of punishments, I propose to speak clearly and definitely of the gross mistake they make—contrary to their faith, morality, and common sense—when they consent to enter the army; contrary to their faith, because by entering the ranks of murderers they infringe the Law of God which they acknowledge; contrary to morality, because for pay or from fear of punishment they agree to do what in their souls they know to be wrong; and contrary to common sense, because if they enter the army and war breaks out they risk having to suffer consequences as bad or worse than those they are threatened with if they refuse. Above all they act contrary to common sense in that they join that caste of people which deprives them of freedom and compels them to become soldiers.

With reference to both classes I propose in this appeal to express clearly the thought that for men of true enlightenment, who are therefore free from the superstition of military glory (and their number is growing every day) the military profession and calling, notwithstanding all the efforts to hide its real meaning, is as shameful a business as an executioner's and even more so. For the executioner only holds himself in readiness to kill those who have been adjudged harmful and criminal, while a soldier promises to kill all whom he is told to kill, even though they be those dearest to him or the best of men.

Humanity in general, and our Christian humanity in particular, has reached a stage of such acute contradiction between its moral demands and the existing social order, that a change has become inevitable, and a change not in society's moral demands which are immutable, but in the social order which can be altered. The demand for a different social order, evoked by that inner contradiction which is so clearly illustrated by our preparations for murder, becomes more and more insistent every year and every day. The tension which demands that alteration has reached such a degree that, just as sometimes only a slight shock is required to change a liquid into a solid body, so perhaps only a slight effort or even a single word may be needed to change the cruel and irrational life of our time—with its divisions, armaments, and armies—into a reasonable life in keeping with the consciousness of contemporary humanity. Every such effort, every such word, may be the shock which will instantly solidify the supercooled liquid. Why should not our gathering be that shock? In Andersen's fairy tale, when the King went in triumphal procession through the streets of the town and all the people were delighted with his beautiful new clothes, a word from a child who said what everybody knew but had not said, changed everything. He said: 'He has nothing on!' and the spell was broken and the King became ashamed and all those who had been assuring themselves that they saw him wearing beautiful new clothes perceived that he was naked! We must say the same. We must say what everybody knows but does not venture to say. We must say that by whatever name men may call murder—murder always remains murder and a criminal and shameful thing. And it is only necessary to say that clearly, definitely, and loudly, as we can say it here, and men will cease to see what they thought they saw and will see what is really before their eyes. They will cease to see the service of their country, the heroism of war, military glory, and patriotism, and will see what exists: the naked, criminal business of murder! And if people see that, the same thing will happen as in the fairy tale: those who do the criminal thing will feel ashamed, and those who assure themselves that they do not see the criminality of murder will perceive it and cease to be murderers.

But how will nations defend themselves against their enemies, how will they maintain internal order, and how can nations live without an army?

What form the life of men will take if they repudiate murder, we do not and cannot know; but one thing is certain: that it is more natural for men to be guided by the reason and conscience with which they are endowed, than to submit slavishly to people who arrange wholesale murders; and that therefore the form of social order assumed by the lives of those who are guided in their actions not by violence based on threats of murder but by reason and conscience, will in any case be no worse than that under which they now live.

That is all I want to say. I shall be very sorry if it offends or grieves anyone or evokes any ill feeling. But for me, a man eighty years old, expecting to die at any moment, it would be shameful and criminal not to speak out the whole truth as I understand it—the truth which, as I firmly believe, is alone capable of relieving mankind from the incalculable ills produced by war.

ON

MORAL,
POLITICAL,
AND
SOCIAL SUBJECTS

◇◇◇◇◇◇◇◇◇◇◇◇◇◇◇◇◇◇◇◇◇◇◇◇◇◇◇◇◇

WHY DO MEN STUPEFY THEMSELVES?

I

What is the explanation of the fact that people use things that stupefy them: vódka, wine, beer, hashish, opium, tobacco, and other things less common: ether, morphia, fly-agaric, &c.? Why did the practice begin? Why has it spread so rapidly, and why is it still spreading among all sorts of people, savage and civilized? How is it that where there is no vódka, wine or beer, we find opium, hashish, fly-agaric, and the like, and that tobacco is used everywhere?

Why do people wish to stupefy themselves?

Ask anyone why he began drinking wine and why he now drinks it. He will reply, 'Oh, I like it, and everybody drinks,' and he may add, 'it cheers me up.' Some—those who have never once taken the trouble to consider whether they do well or ill to drink wine—may add that wine is good for the health and adds to one's strength; that is to say, will make a statement long since proved baseless.

Ask a smoker why he began to use tobacco and why he now smokes, and he also will reply: 'To while away the time; everybody smokes.'

Similar answers would probably be given by those who use opium, hashish, morphia, or fly-agaric.

'To while away time, to cheer oneself up; everybody does it.' But it might be excusable to twiddle one's thumbs, to whistle, to hum tunes, to play a fife or to do something of that sort 'to while away the time,' 'to cheer oneself up,' or 'because everybody does it'—that is to say, it might be excusable to do something which does not involve wasting Nature's wealth, or spending what has cost great labour to produce, or doing what brings evident harm to oneself and to others. But to produce tobacco, wine, hashish, and opium, the labour of millions of men is spent, and millions and millions of acres of the best land (often amid a population that is short of land) are employed to grow potatoes, hemp, poppies, vines, and tobacco. Moreover, the use of these evidently harmful things produces terrible evils known and admitted by everyone, and destroys more people than all the wars and contagious diseases added together. And people know this, so that they cannot really use these things 'to while away time,' 'to cheer themselves up,' or because 'everybody does it.'

There must be some other reason. Continually and everywhere one meets people who love their children and are ready to make all kinds of sacrifices for them, but who yet spend on vódka, wine and beer, or on opium, hashish, or even tobacco, as much as would quite suffice to feed their hungry and poverty-stricken children, or at least as much as would suffice to save them from misery. Evidently if a man who has to choose between the want and sufferings of a family he loves on the one hand, and abstinence from stupefying things on the other, chooses the former—he must be induced thereto by something more potent than the consideration that everybody does it, or that it is pleasant. Evidently it is done not 'to while away time,' nor merely 'to cheer himself up.' He is actuated by some more powerful cause.

This cause—as far as I have detected it by reading about this subject and by observing other people, and particularly by observing my own case when I used to drink wine and smoke tobacco—this cause, I think, may be explained as follows:

When observing his own life, a man may often notice in himself two different beings: the one is blind and physical, the other sees and is spiritual. The blind animal being eats, drinks, rests, sleeps, propagates, and moves, like a wound-up machine. The seeing, spiritual being that is bound up with the animal does nothing of itself, but only appraises the activity of the animal being; coinciding with it when approving its activity, and diverging from it when disapproving.

This observing being may be compared to the needle of a compass, pointing with one end to the north and with the other to the south, but screened along its whole length by something not noticeable so long as it and the needle both point the same way; but which becomes obvious as soon as they point different ways.

In the same manner the seeing, spiritual being, whose manifestation we commonly call conscience, always points with one end towards right and with the other towards wrong, and we do not notice it while we follow the course it shows: the course from wrong to right. But one need only do something contrary to the indication of conscience to become aware of this spiritual being, which then shows how the animal activity has diverged from the direction indicated by conscience. And as a navigator conscious that he is on the wrong track cannot continue to work the oars, engine, or sails, till he has adjusted his course to the indications of the compass, or has obliterated his consciousness of this divergence —each man who has felt the duality of his animal activity and his conscience can continue his activity only by adjusting that activity to the demands of conscience, or by hiding from himself the indications conscience gives him of the wrongness of his animal life.

All human life, we may say, consists solely of these two activities: (1) bringing one's activities into harmony with conscience, or (2) hiding from oneself the indications of conscience in order to be able to continue to live as before.

Some do the first, others the second. To attain the first there is but one means: moral enlightenment—the increase of light in oneself and attention to what it shows. To attain the second—to hide from oneself the indications of conscience—there are two means: one external and the other internal. The external means consists in occupations that divert one's attention from the indications given by conscience; the internal method consists in darkening conscience itself.

As a man has two ways of avoiding seeing an object that

is before him: either by diverting his sight to other more striking objects, or by obstructing the sight of his own eyes —just so a man can hide from himself the indications of conscience in two ways: either by the external method of diverting his attention to various occupations, cares, amusements, or games; or by the internal method of obstructing the organ of attention itself. For people of dull, limited moral feeling, the external diversions are often quite sufficient to enable them not to perceive the indications conscience gives of the wrongness of their lives. But for morally sensitive people those means are often insufficient.

The external means do not quite divert attention from the consciousness of discord between one's life and the demands of conscience. This consciousness hampers one's life: and in order to be able to go on living as before people have recourse to the reliable, internal method, which is that of darkening conscience itself by poisoning the brain with stupefying substances.

One is not living as conscience demands, yet lacks the strength to reshape one's life in accord with its demands. The diversions which might distract attention from the consciousness of this discord are insufficient, or have become stale, and so—in order to be able to live on, disregarding the indications conscience gives of the wrongness of their life—people (by poisoning it temporarily) stop the activity of the organ through which conscience manifests itself, as a man by covering his eyes hides from himself what he does not wish to see.

II

The cause of the world-wide consumption of hashish, opium, wine, and tobacco, lies not in the taste, nor in any pleasure, recreation, or mirth they afford, but simply in man's need to hide from himself the demands of conscience.

I was going along the street one day, and passing some cabmen who were talking, I heard one of them say: 'Of course when a man's sober he's ashamed to do it!'

When a man is sober he is ashamed of what seems all right when he is drunk. In these words we have the essential underlying cause prompting men to resort to stupefiers. People resort to them either to escape feeling ashamed after having done something contrary to their consciences, or to bring themselves beforehand into a state in which they can commit actions contrary to conscience, but to which their animal nature prompts them.

A man when sober is ashamed to go after a prostitute, ashamed to steal, ashamed to kill. A drunken man is ashamed of none of these things, and therefore if a man wishes to do something his conscience condemns he stupefies himself.

I remember being struck by the evidence of a man-cook who was tried for murdering a relation of mine, an old lady in whose service he lived. He related that when he had sent away his paramour, the servant-girl, and the time had come to act, he wished to go into the bedroom with a knife, but felt that while sober he could not commit the deed he had planned . . . 'when a man's sober he's ashamed.' He turned back, drank two tumblers of vódka he had prepared beforehand, and only then felt himself ready, and committed the crime.

Nine-tenths of the crimes are committed in that way: 'Drink to keep up your courage.'

Half the women who fall do so under the influence of wine. Nearly all visits to disorderly houses are paid by men who are intoxicated. People know this capacity of wine to stifle the voice of conscience, and intentionally use it for that purpose.

Not only do people stupefy themselves to stifle their own consciences, but, knowing how wine acts, they intentionally stupefy others when they wish to make them commit actions contrary to conscience—that is, they arrange to stupefy people in order to deprive them of conscience. In war, soldiers are usually intoxicated before a hand-to-hand fight. All the French soldiers in the assaults on Sevastopol were drunk.

When a fortified place has been captured but the soldiers do not sack it and slay the defenceless old men and children, orders are often given to make them drunk and then they do what is expected of them.

Everyone knows people who have taken to drink in consequence of some wrong-doing that has tormented their conscience. Anyone can notice that those who lead immoral lives are more attracted than others by stupefying substances. Bands of robbers or thieves, and prostitutes, cannot live without intoxicants.

Everyone knows and admits that the use of stupefying substances is a consequence of the pangs of conscience, and that in certain immoral ways of life stupefying substances are employed to stifle conscience. Everyone knows and admits also that the use of stupefiers does stifle conscience: that a drunken man is capable of deeds of which when sober he would not think for a moment. Everyone agrees to this, but strange to say when the use of stupefiers does not result in such deeds as thefts, murders, violations, and so forth—when stupefiers are taken not after some terrible crimes, but by men following professions which we do not consider criminal, and when the substances are consumed not in large quantities at once but continually in moderate doses—then (for some reason) it is assumed that stupefying substances have no tendency to stifle conscience.

Thus it is supposed that a well-to-do Russian's glass of vódka before each meal and tumbler of wine with the meal, or a Frenchman's absinthe, or an Englishman's port wine and porter, or a German's lager-beer, or a well-to-do Chinaman's moderate dose of opium, and the smoking of tobacco with them—is done only for pleasure and has no effect whatever on these people's consciences.

It is supposed that if after this customary stupefaction no crime is committed—no theft or murder, but only customary bad and stupid actions—then these actions have occurred of themselves and are not evoked by the stupefaction. It is supposed that if these people have not committed offences against the criminal law they have no need to stifle the voice of conscience, and that the life led by people who habitually stupefy themselves is quite a good life, and would be precisely the same if they did not stupefy themselves. It is supposed that the constant use of stupefiers does not in the least darken their consciences.

Though everybody knows by experience that a man's frame of mind is altered by the use of wine or tobacco, that he is not ashamed of things which but for the stimulant he would be ashamed of, that after each twinge of conscience, however slight, he is inclined to have recourse to some stupefier, and that under the influence of stupefiers it is difficult to reflect on his life and position, and that the constant and regular use of stupefiers produces the same physiological effect as its occasional immoderate use does—yet in spite of all this it seems to men who drink and smoke moderately that they use stupefiers not at all to stifle conscience, but only for the flavour or for pleasure.

But one need only think of the matter seriously and impartially—not trying to excuse oneself—to understand, first, that if the use of stupefiers in large occasional doses stifles man's conscience, their regular use must have a like effect (always first intensifying and then dulling the activity of the brain) whether they are taken in large or small doses. Secondly, that all stupefiers have the quality of stifling conscience, and have this always—both when under their influence murders, robberies, and violations are committed, and when under their influence words are spoken which would not have been spoken, or things are thought and felt which but for them would not have been thought and felt; and, thirdly, that if the use of stupefiers is needed to pacify and stifle the consciences of thieves, robbers, and prostitutes, it is also wanted by people engaged in occupations condemned by their own consciences, even though these occupations may be considered proper and honourable by other people.

In a word, it is impossible to avoid understanding that the use of stupefiers, in large or small amounts, occasionally or regularly, in the higher or lower circles of society, is evoked by one and the same cause, the need to stifle the voice of conscience in order not to be aware of the discord existing between one's way of life and the demands of one's conscience.

III

In that alone lies the reason of the widespread use of all stupefying substances, and among the rest of tobacco—probably the most generally used and most harmful.

It is supposed that tobacco cheers one up, clears the thoughts, and attracts one merely like any other habit—without at all producing the deadening of conscience produced by wine. But you need only observe attentively the conditions under which a special desire to smoke arises, and you will be convinced that stupefying with tobacco acts on the conscience as wine does, and that people consciously have recourse to this method of stupefactions just when they require it for that purpose. If tobacco merely cleared the thoughts and cheered one up there would not be such a passionate craving for it, a craving showing itself just on certain definite occasions. People would not say that they would rather go without bread than without tobacco, and would not often actually prefer tobacco to food.

That man-cook who murdered his mistress said that when he entered the bedroom and had gashed her throat with his knife and she had fallen with a rattle in her throat and the blood had gushed out in a torrent—he lost his courage. 'I could not finish her off,' he said, 'but I went back from the bedroom to the sitting-room and sat down there and smoked a cigarette.' Only after stupefying himself with tobacco was he able to return to the bedroom, finish cutting the old lady's throat, and begin examining her things.

Evidently the desire to smoke at that moment was evoked in him, not by a wish to clear his thoughts or be merry, but by the need to stifle something that prevented him from completing what he had planned to do.

Any smoker may detect in himself the same definite desire to stupefy himself with tobacco at certain specially difficult moments. I look back at the days when I used to smoke: when was it that I felt a special need of tobacco? It was always at moments when I did not wish to remember certain things that presented themselves to my recollection, when I wished to forget—not to think. I sit by myself doing nothing and know I ought to set to work, but I don't feel inclined to, so I smoke and go on sitting. I have promised to be at someone's house by five o'clock, but I have stayed too long somewhere else. I remember that I have missed the appointment, but I do not like to remember it, so I smoke. I get vexed and say unpleasant things to someone, and know I am doing wrong and see that I ought to stop, but I want to give vent to my irritability—so I smoke and continue to be irritable. I play at cards and lose more than I intended to risk—so I smoke. I have placed myself in an awkward position, have acted badly, have made a mistake, and ought to acknowledge the mess I am in and thus escape from it, but I do not like to acknowledge it, so I accuse others—and smoke. I write something and am not quite satisfied with what I have written. I ought to abandon it, but I wish to finish what I have planned to do—so I smoke. I dispute, and see that my opponent and I do not understand and cannot understand one another, but I wish to express my opinion, so I continue to talk—and I smoke.

What distinguishes tobacco from most other stupefiers, besides the ease with which one can stupefy oneself with it and its apparent harmlessness, is its portability and the possibility of applying it to meet small, isolated occurrences that disturb one. Not to mention that the use of opium, wine, and hashish involves the use of certain appliances not always at hand, while one can always carry tobacco and paper with one; and that the opium-smoker and the drunkard evoke horror while a tobacco-smoker does not seem at all repulsive —the advantage of tobacco over other stupefiers is, that the stupefaction of opium, hashish, or wine extends to all the sensations and acts received or produced during a certain somewhat extended period of time—while the stupefaction from tobacco can be directed to any separate occurrence.

You wish to do what you ought not to, so you smoke a cigarette and stupefy yourself sufficiently to enable you to do what should not be done, and then you are all right again, and can think and speak clearly; or you feel you have done what you should not—again you smoke a cigarette and the unpleasant consciousness of the wrong or awkward action is obliterated, and you can occupy yourself with other things and forget it.

But apart from individual cases in which every smoker has recourse to smoking, not to satisfy a habit or while away time but as a means of stifling his conscience with reference to acts he is about to commit or has already committed, is it not quite evident that there is a strict and definite relation between men's way of life and their passion for smoking?

When do lads begin to smoke? Usually when they lose their childish innocence. How is it that smokers can abandon smoking when they come among more moral conditions of life, and again start smoking as soon as they fall among a depraved set? Why do gamblers almost all smoke? Why among women do those who lead a regular life smoke least? Why do prostitutes and madmen *all* smoke? Habit is habit, but evidently smoking stands in some definite connexion with the craving to stifle conscience, and achieves the end required of it.

One may observe in the case of almost every smoker to what an extent smoking drowns the voice of conscience. Every smoker when yielding to his desire forgets, or sets at naught, the very first demands of social life—demands he expects others to observe, and which he observes in all other cases until his conscience is stifled by tobacco. Everyone of average education considers it inadmissible, ill-bred, and inhumane to infringe the peace, comfort, and still more the health of others for his own pleasure. No one would allow himself to wet a room in which people are sitting, or to make a noise, shout, let in cold, hot, or ill-smelling air, or commit acts that incommode or harm others. But out of a thousand smokers not one will shrink from producing unwholesome smoke in a room where the air is breathed by non-smoking women and children.

If smokers do usually say to those present: 'You don't object?' everyone knows that the customary answer is: 'Not at all' (although it cannot be pleasant to a non-smoker to breathe tainted air, and to find stinking cigar-ends in glasses and cups or on plates and candlesticks, or even in ashpans).[1] But even if non-smoking adults did not object to tobacco-smoke, it could not be pleasant or good for the children whose consent no one asks. Yet people who are honourable and humane in all other respects smoke in the presence of children at dinner in small rooms, vitiating the air with tobacco-smoke, without feeling the slightest twinge of conscience.

It is usually said (and I used to say) that smoking facilitates mental work. And that is undoubtedly true if one considers only the quantity of one's mental output. To a man who smokes, and who consequently ceases strictly to appraise and weigh his thoughts, it seems as if he suddenly had many thoughts. But this is not because he really has many thoughts, but only because he has lost control of his thoughts.

When a man works he is always conscious of two beings in himself: the one works, the other appraises the work. The stricter the appraisement the slower and the better is the work; and vice versa, when the appraiser is under the influence of something that stupefies him, more work gets done, but its quality is poorer.

'If I do not smoke I cannot write. I cannot get on; I begin and cannot continue,' is what is usually said, and what I used to say. What does it really mean? It means either that you have nothing to write, or that what you wish to write has not yet matured in your consciousness but is only beginning dimly to present itself to you, and the appraising critic within, when not stupefied with tobacco, tells you so. If you did not

---

[1] In the matters alluded to the Russian customs are worse than the English, partly perhaps because in Russia the smell of stale tobacco in the rooms is less offensive than in England owing to a drier climate.—A. M.

smoke you would either abandon what you have begun, or you would wait until your thought has cleared itself in your mind; you would try to penetrate into what presents itself dimly to you, would consider the objections that offer themselves, and would turn all your attention to the elucidation of the thought. But you smoke, the critic within you is stupefied, and the hindrance to your work is removed. What seemed insignificant to you when not inebriated by tobacco, again seems important; what seemed obscure no longer seems so; the objections that presented themselves vanish and you continue to write, and write much and rapidly.

IV

But can such a small—such a trifling—alteration as the slight intoxication produced by the moderate use of wine or tobacco produce important consequences? 'If a man smokes opium or hashish, or intoxicates himself with wine till he falls down and loses his senses, of course the consequences may be very serious; but it surely cannot have any serious consequences if a man merely comes slightly under the influence of hops or tobacco,' is what is usually said. It seems to people that a slight stupefaction, a little darkening of the judgement, cannot have any important influence. But to think so is like supposing that it may harm a watch to be struck against a stone, but that a little dirt introduced into it cannot be harmful.

Remember, however, that the chief work actuating man's whole life is not done by his hands, his feet, or his back, but by his consciousness. Before a man can do anything with his feet or hands, a certain alteration has first to take place in his consciousness. And this alteration defines all the subsequent movements of the man. Yet these alterations are always minute and almost imperceptible.

Bryullóv[2] one day corrected a pupil's study. The pupil, having glanced at the altered drawing, exclaimed: 'Why, you

---

[2] K. P. Bryullóv, a celebrated Russian painter (1799-1852).—A. M.

only touched it a tiny bit, but it is quite another thing.'
Bryullóv replied: 'Art begins where the tiny bit begins.'

That saying is strikingly true not only of art but of all life.
One may say that true life begins where the tiny bit begins—
where what seem to us minute and infinitely small alterations
take place. True life is not lived where great external changes
take place—where people move about, clash, fight, and slay
one another—it is lived only where these tiny, tiny, infinitesi-
mally small changes occur.

Raskólnikov[3] did not live his true life when he murdered
the old woman or her sister. When murdering the old woman
herself, and still more when murdering her sister, he did not
live his true life, but acted like a machine, doing what he
could not help doing—discharging the cartridge with which
he had long been loaded. One old woman was killed, another
stood before him, the axe was in his hand.

Raskólnikov lived his true life not when he met the old
woman's sister, but at the time when he had not yet killed
any old woman, nor entered a stranger's lodging with intent
to kill, nor held the axe in his hand, nor had the loop in his
overcoat by which the axe hung. He lived his true life when
he was lying on the sofa in his room, deliberating not at all
about the old woman, nor even as to whether it is or is not
permissible at the will of one man to wipe from the face of
the earth another, unnecessary and harmful, man, but
whether he ought to live in Petersburg or not, whether he
ought to accept money from his mother or not, and on other
questions not at all relating to the old woman. And then—in
that region quite independent of animal activities—the question whether he would or would not kill the old woman was
decided. That question was decided—not when, having
killed one old woman, he stood before another, axe in hand
—but when he was doing nothing and was only thinking,
when only his consciousness was active: and in that consciousness tiny, tiny alterations were taking place. It is at such
times that one needs the greatest clearness to decide cor-

---

[3] The hero of Dostoévsky's novel, *Crime and Punishment.*—A. M.

rectly the questions that have arisen, and it is just then that one glass of beer, or one cigarette, may prevent the solution of the question, may postpone the decision, stifle the voice of conscience and prompt a decision of the question in favour of the lower, animal nature—as was the case with Raskólnikov.

Tiny, tiny alterations—but on them depend the most immense and terrible consequences. Many material changes may result from what happens when a man has taken a decision and begun to act: houses, riches, and people's bodies may perish, but nothing more important can happen than what was hidden in the man's consciousness. The limits of what can happen are set by consciousness.

And boundless results of unimaginable importance may follow from most minute alterations occurring in the domain of consciousness.

Do not let it be supposed that what I am saying has anything to do with the question of free will or determinism. Discussion on that question is superfluous for my purpose, or for any other for that matter. Without deciding the question whether a man can, or cannot, act as he wishes (a question in my opinion not correctly stated), I am merely saying that since human activity is conditioned by infinitesimal alterations in consciousness, it follows (no matter whether we admit the existence of free will or not) that we must pay particular attention to the condition in which these minute alterations take place, just as one must be specially attentive to the condition of scales on which other things are to be weighed. We must, as far as it depends on us, try to put ourselves and others in conditions which will not disturb the clearness and delicacy of thought necessary for the correct working of conscience, and must not act in the contrary manner—trying to hinder and confuse the work of conscience by the use of stupefying substances.

For man is a spiritual as well as an animal being. He may be moved by things that influence his spiritual nature, or by things that influence his animal nature, as a clock may be moved by its hands or by its main wheel. And just as it is best to regulate the movement of a clock by means of its inner mechanism, so a man—oneself or another—is best regulated by means of his consciousness. And as with a clock one has to take special care of that part by means of which one can best move the inner mechanism, so with a man one must take special care of the cleanness and clearness of consciousness which is the thing that best moves the whole man. To doubt this is impossible; everyone knows it. But a need to deceive oneself arises. People are not as anxious that consciousness should work correctly as they are that it should seem to them that what they are doing is right, and they deliberately make use of substances that disturb the proper working of their consciousness.

V

People drink and smoke, not casually, not from dulness, not to cheer themselves up, not because it is pleasant, but in order to drown the voice of conscience in themselves. And in that case, how terrible must be the consequences! Think what a building would be like erected by people who did not use a straight plumb-rule to get the walls perpendicular, nor right-angled squares to get the corners correct, but used a soft rule which would bend to suit all irregularities in the walls, and a square that expanded to fit any angle, acute or obtuse.

Yet, thanks to self-stupefaction, that is just what is being done in life. Life does not accord with conscience, so conscience is made to bend to life.

This is done in the life of individuals, and it is done in the life of humanity as a whole, which consists of the lives of individuals.

To grasp the full significance of such stupefying of one's consciousness, let each one carefully recall the spiritual conditions he has passed through at each period of his life. Everyone will find that at each period of his life certain moral questions confronted him which he ought to solve, and on the solution of which the whole welfare of his life depended. For

the solution of these questions great concentration of attention was needful. Such concentration of attention is a labour.
In every labour, especially at the beginning, there is a time
when the work seems difficult and painful, and when human
weakness prompts a desire to abandon it. Physical work
seems painful at first; mental work still more so. As Lessing
says: people are inclined to cease to think at the point at
which thought begins to be difficult; but it is just there, I
would add, that thinking begins to be fruitful. A man feels
that to decide the questions confronting him needs labour
—often painful labour—and he wishes to evade this. If he
had no means of stupefying his faculties he could not expel
from his consciousness the questions that confront him, and
the necessity of solving them would be forced upon him. But
man finds that there exists a means to drive off these questions
whenever they present themselves—and he uses it. As soon as
the questions awaiting solution begin to torment him he has
recourse to these means, and avoids the disquietude evoked
by the troublesome questions. Consciousness ceases to demand their solution, and the unsolved questions remain unsolved till his next period of enlightenment. But when that
period comes the same thing is repeated, and the man goes
on for months, years, or even for his whole life, standing before those same moral questions and not moving a step towards their solution. Yet it is in the solution of moral questions that life's whole movement consists.

What occurs is as if a man who needs to see to the bottom
of some muddy water to obtain a precious pearl, but who
dislikes entering the water, should stir it up each time it begins to settle and become clear. Many a man continues to
stupefy himself all his life long, and remains immovable at
the same once-accepted, obscure, self-contradictory view of
life—pressing, as each period of enlightenment approaches,
ever at one and the same wall against which he pressed ten or
twenty years ago, and which he cannot break through because he intentionally blunts that sharp point of thought
which alone could pierce it.

Let each man remember himself as he has been during

the years of his drinking or smoking, and let him test the matter in his experience of other people, and everyone will see a definite constant line dividing those who are addicted to stupefiers from those who are free from them. The more a man stupefies himself the more he is morally immovable.

VI

Terrible, as they are described to us, are the consequences of opium and hashish on individuals; terrible, as we know them, are the consequences of alcohol to flagrant drunkards; but incomparably more terrible to our whole society are the consequences of what is considered the harmless, moderate use of spirits, wine, beer, and tobacco, to which the majority of men, and especially our so-called cultured classes, are addicted.

The consequences must naturally be terrible, admitting the fact, which must be admitted, that the guiding activities of society—political, official, scientific, literary, and artistic— are carried on for the most part by people in an abnormal state: by people who are drunk.

It is generally supposed that a man who, like most people of our well-to-do classes, takes alcoholic drink almost every time he eats, is in a perfectly normal and sober condition next day, during working hours. But this is quite an error. A man who drank a bottle of wine, a glass of spirits, or two glasses of ale, yesterday, is now in the usual state of drowsiness or depression which follows excitement, and is therefore in a condition of mental prostration, which is increased by smoking. For a man who habitually smokes and drinks in moderation, to bring his brain into a normal condition would require at least a week or more of abstinence from wine and tobacco. But that hardly ever occurs.[4]

---

[4] But how is it that people who do not drink or smoke are often morally on an incomparably lower plane than others who drink and smoke? And why do people who drink and smoke often manifest very high qualities both mentally and morally?

The answer is, first, that we do not know the height that those

So that most of what goes on among us, whether done by people who rule and teach others, or by those who are ruled and taught, is done when the doers are not sober.

And let not this be taken as a joke or an exaggeration. The confusion, and above all the imbecility, of our lives, arises chiefly from the constant state of intoxication in which most people live. Could people who are not drunk possibly do all that is being done around us—from building the Eiffel Tower to accepting military service?

Without any need whatever, a company is formed, capital collected, men labour, make calculations, and draw plans; millions of working days and thousands of tons of iron are spent to build a tower; and millions of people consider it their duty to climb up it, stop awhile on it, and then climb down again; and the building and visiting of this tower evoke no other reflection than a wish and intention to build other towers, in other places, still bigger. Could sober people act like that? Or take another case. For dozens of years past, all the European peoples have been busy devising the very best ways of killing people, and teaching as many young men as possible, as soon as they reach manhood, how to murder. Everyone knows that there can be no invasion by barbarians, but that these preparations made by the different civilized and Christian nations are directed against one another; everyone knows that this is burdensome, painful, inconvenient, ruinous, immoral, impious, and irrational—but everyone con-

---

who drink and smoke would have attained had they not drunk and smoked. And secondly, from the fact that morally gifted people achieve great things in spite of the deteriorating effect of stupefying substances, we can but conclude that they would have produced yet greater things had they not stupefied themselves. It is very probable, as a friend remarked to me, that Kant's works would not have been written in such a curious and bad style had he not smoked so much. Lastly, the lower a man's mental and moral plane the less does he feel the discord between his conscience and his life, and therefore the less does he feel a craving to stupefy himself; and on the other hand a parallel reason explains why the most sensitive natures—those which immediately and morbidly feel the discord between life and conscience—so often indulge in narcotics and perish by them.—L. T.

tinues to prepare for mutual murder. Some devise political combinations to decide who is to kill whom and with what allies, others direct those who are being taught to murder, and others again yield—against their will, against their conscience, against their reason—to these preparations for murder. Could sober people do these things? Only drunkards who never reach a state of sobriety could do them and live on in the horrible state of discord between life and conscience in which, not only in this but in all other respects, the people of our society are now living.

Never before, I suppose, have people lived with the demands of their conscience so evidently in contradiction to their actions.

Humanity to-day has as it were stuck fast. It is as though some external cause hindered it from occupying a position in natural accord with its perceptions. And the cause—if not the only one, then certainly the greatest—is this physical condition of stupefaction induced by wine and tobacco to which the great majority of people in our society reduce themselves.

Emancipation from this terrible evil will be an epoch in the life of humanity; and that epoch seems to be at hand. The evil is recognized. An alteration has already taken place in our perception concerning the use of stupefying substances. People have understood the terrible harm of these things and are beginning to point them out, and this almost unnoticed alteration in perception will inevitably bring about the emancipation of men from the use of stupefying things—will enable them to open their eyes to the demands of their consciences, and they will begin to order their lives in accord with their perceptions.

And this seems to be already beginning. But as always it is beginning among the upper classes only after all the lower classes have already been infected.

[June 10, o.s., 1890.]

The above essay was written by Leo Tolstóy as a preface to a book on *Drunkenness* written by my brother-in-law, Dr. P. S. Alexéyev.—A. M.

THE FIRST STEP

I

If a man is working in order to accomplish whatever he has in hand and not merely making a pretence of work, his actions will necessarily follow one another in a certain sequence determined by the nature of the work. If he postpones to a later time what from the nature of the work should be done first, or if he altogether omits some essential part, he is certainly not working seriously but only pretending. This rule holds unalterably true whether the work be physical or not. As a man seriously wishing to bake bread first kneads the flour and then heats the brick-oven, sweeps out the ashes, and so on, so also a man seriously wishing to lead a good life adopts a certain order of succession in the attainment of the necessary qualities.

This rule is especially important in regard to right living; for whereas in the case of physical work, such as making bread, it is easy to discover by the result whether a man is seriously engaged in work or only pretending, no such verification is possible in regard to goodness of life. If without kneading the dough or heating the oven people merely pretend to make bread—as they do in the theatre—then the absence of bread makes it obvious that they were only pretending; but when a man pretends to be leading a good life we have no such direct indications that he is not striving seriously but only pretending, for not only are the results of a good life not always evident and palpable to those around, but very often such results even appear to them harmful. Respect for a man's activity and the acknowledgement of its utility and pleasantness by his contemporaries, furnish no proof of the real goodness of his life.

Therefore, to distinguish the reality from the mere appearance of a good life, the indication given by a regular order of succession in the acquirement of the essential qualities is especially valuable. And this indication is valuable, not so much to enable us to discover the seriousness of other men's strivings after goodness as to test this sincerity in ourselves, for in this respect we are liable to deceive ourselves even more than we deceive others.

A correct order of succession in the attainment of virtues is an indispensable condition of advance towards a good life, and consequently the teachers of mankind have always prescribed a certain invariable order for their attainment.

All moral teachings set up that ladder which, as the Chinese wisdom has it, reaches from earth to heaven, and the ascent of which can only be accomplished by starting from the lowest step. As in the teaching of the Brahmins, Buddhists, Confucians, so also in the teaching of the Greek sages, steps were fixed, and a superior step could not be attained without the lower one having been previously taken. All the moral teachers of mankind, religious and non-religious alike, have admitted the necessity of a definite order of succession in the attainment of the qualities essential to a righteous life. The necessity for this sequence lies in the very essence of things, and therefore, it would seem, ought to be recognized by everyone.

But, strange to say, from the time to time Church-Christianity spread widely, the consciousness of this necessary order appears to have been more and more lost, and is now retained only among ascetics and monks. Among worldly Christians it is taken for granted that the higher virtues may be attained not only in the absence of the lower ones, which are a necessary condition of the higher, but even in company with the greatest vices; and consequently the very conception of what constitutes a good life has reached a state of the greatest confusion in the minds of the majority of worldly people to-day.

II

In our times people have quite lost consciousness of the necessity of a sequence in the qualities a man must have to enable him to live a good life, and in consequence have lost the very conception of what constitutes a good life. This it seems to me has come about in the following way.

When Christianity replaced paganism it put forth moral demands superior to the heathen ones, and at the same time (as was also the case with pagan morality) it necessarily laid down an indispensable order for the attainment of virtues— certain steps to the attainment of a righteous life.

Plato's virtues, beginning with self-control, advanced through courage and wisdom to justice; the Christian virtues, commencing with self-renunciation, rise, through devotion to the will of God, to love.

Those who accepted Christianity seriously and strove to live righteous Christian lives, understood Christianity in this way, and always began living rightly by renouncing their lusts; which renunciation included the self-control of the pagans.

But let it not be supposed that Christianity in this matter was only echoing the teachings of paganism; let me not be accused of degrading Christianity from its lofty place to the level of heathenism. Such an accusation would be unjust, for I regard the Christian teaching as the highest the world has known, and as quite different from heathenism. Christian teaching replaced pagan teaching simply because the former was different from and superior to the latter. But both Christian and pagan teaching alike lead men toward truth and goodness; and as these are always the same, the way to them must also be the same, and the *first steps* on this way must inevitably be the same for Christian as for heathen.

The difference between the Christian and pagan teaching of goodness lies in this: that the heathen teaching is one of final perfection, while the Christian is one of infinite perfecting. Every heathen, non-Christian, teaching sets before men a model of final perfection; but the Christian teaching sets before them a model of infinite perfection. Plato, for instance, makes justice the model of perfection, whereas Christ's model is the infinite perfection of love. *'Be ye perfect, even as your Father in heaven is perfect.'* In this lies the difference, and from this results the different relation of pagan and Christian teaching towards different grades of virtue. According to the former the attainment of the highest virtue was possible, and each step towards this attainment had its comparative merit —the higher the step the greater the merit; so that from the pagan point of view men may be divided into moral and immoral, into more or less immoral—whereas according to the Christian teaching, which sets up the ideal of infinite perfection, this division is impossible. There can be neither higher nor lower grades. In the Christian teaching, which shows the infinity of perfection, all steps are equal in relation to the infinite ideal.

Among the pagans the plane of virtue attained by a man constituted his merit; in Christianity merit consists only in the process of attaining, in the greater or lesser speed of attainment. From the pagan point of view a man who possessed the virtue of reasonableness stood morally higher than one deficient in that virtue, a man who in addition to reasonableness possessed courage stood higher still, a man who to reasonableness and courage added justice stood yet higher. But one Christian cannot be regarded as morally either higher or lower than another. A man is more or less of a Christian only in proportion to the speed with which he advances towards infinite perfection, irrespective of the stage he may have reached at a given moment. Hence the stationary righteousness of the Pharisee was worth less than the progress of the repentant thief on the cross.

Such is the difference between the Christian and the pagan teachings. Consequently the stages of virtue, as for instance self-control and courage, which in paganism constitute merit, constitute none whatever in Christianity. In this respect the teachings differ. But with regard to the fact that there can be no advance towards virtue, towards perfection, except by mounting the lowest steps, paganism and Christianity are alike: here there can be no difference.

The Christian, like the pagan, must commence the work of perfecting himself from the beginning—at the same step at which the heathen begins it, namely, self-control; just as a man who wishes to ascend a flight of stairs cannot avoid beginning at the first step. The only difference is that for the pagan, self-control itself constitutes a virtue; whereas for the Christian it is only part of that self-abnegation which is itself but an indispensable condition of all aspiration after perfection. Therefore the manifestation of true Christianity could not but follow the same path that had been indicated and followed by paganism.

But not all men have understood Christianity as an aspiration towards the perfection of the heavenly Father. The majority of people have regarded it as a teaching about salvation —that is, deliverance from sin by grace transmitted through the Church according to the Catholics and Greek Orthodox; by faith in the Redemption according to the Protestants, the Reformed Church, and the Calvinists; or by means of the two combined according to others.

And it is precisely this teaching that has destroyed the sincerity and seriousness of men's relation to the moral teaching of Christianity. However much the representatives of these faiths may preach that these means of salvation do not hinder man in his aspiration after a righteous life but on the contrary contribute towards it—still, from certain assertions certain deductions necessarily follow, and no arguments can prevent men from making these deductions when once they have accepted the assertions from which they flow. If a man believes that he can be saved through grace transmitted by the Church, or through the sacrifice of the Redemption, it is natural for him to think that efforts of his own to live a right life are unnecessary—the more so when he is told that even the hope that his efforts will make him better is a sin. Consequently a man who believes that there are means other than personal effort by which he may escape sin or its results, cannot strive with the same energy and seriousness as the man who knows no other means. And not striving with perfect seriousness, and knowing of other means besides personal effort, a man will inevitably neglect the unalterable order of succession for the attainment of the good qualities necessary to a good life. And this has happened with the majority of those who profess Christianity.

III

The doctrine that personal effort is not necessary for the attainment of spiritual perfection by man, but that there are other means of acquiring it, caused a relaxation of efforts to live a good life and a neglect of the consecutiveness indispensable for such a life.

The great mass of those who accepted Christianity, accepting it only externally, took advantage of the substitution of Christianity for paganism to free themselves from the demands of the heathen virtues—no longer imposed on them as Christians—and to free themselves from all conflict with their animal nature.

The same thing happens with those who cease to believe in the teaching of the Church. They are like the believers just mentioned, only—instead of grace bestowed by the Church or through Redemption—they put forward some imaginary good work approved of by the majority of men, such as the service of science, art, or humanity; and in the name of this imaginary good work they liberate themselves from the consecutive attainment of the qualities necessary for a good life, and are satisfied with pretending, like men on the stage, to live a good life.

Those who fell away from paganism without embracing Christianity in its true significance, began to preach love for God and man apart from self-renunciation, and justice without self-control; that is to say, they preached the higher virtues while omitting the lower ones: they preached not the virtues themselves, but their semblance.

Some preach love of God and man without self-renunciation, and others preach humaneness—the service of humanity

—without self-control. And as this teaching, while pretending to introduce man into higher moral regions, encourages his animal nature by liberating him from the most elementary demands of morality—long ago acknowledged by the heathens and not only not rejected but strengthened by true Christianity—it was readily accepted both by believers and unbelievers.

Only the other day the Pope's Encyclical[1] on Socialism was published, in which, after a pretended refutation of the Socialist view of the wrongfulness of private property, it was plainly said: *'No one is commanded to distribute to others that which is required for his own necessities and those of his household; nor even to give away what is reasonably required to keep up becomingly his condition in life; for no one ought to live unbecomingly.'* (This is from St. Thomas Aquinas, who says, *Nullus enim inconvenienter vivere debet.*) *'But when necessity has been fairly supplied, and one's position fairly considered, it is a duty to give to the indigent out of that which is over. That which remaineth give alms.'*

Thus now preaches the head of the most widespread Church. Thus have preached all the Church teachers who considered salvation by works as insufficient. And together with this teaching of selfishness, which prescribes that you shall give to your neighbours only what you do not want yourself, they preach love, and recall with pathos Paul's celebrated words about love in the thirteenth chapter of the First Epistle to the Corinthians.

Notwithstanding that the Gospels overflow with demands for self-renunciation, with indications that self-renunciation is the first condition of Christian perfection; notwithstanding such clear expressions as: 'Whosoever will not take up his cross . . .' 'Whosoever hath not forsaken father and mother . . .' 'Whosoever shall lose his life . . .'—people assure themselves and others that it is possible to love men without re-

---

[1] This refers to the Encyclical of Pope Leo XIII. In the passage quoted the official English translation of the Encyclical has been followed. See the *Tablet*, 1891.—A. M.

nouncing that to which one is accustomed, or even what one pleases to consider becoming for oneself.

So speak the Church people; and Freethinkers who reject not only the Church but also the Christian teaching, think, speak, write, and act, in just the same way. These men assure themselves and others that they can serve mankind and lead a good life without in the least diminishing their needs and without overcoming their lusts.

Men have thrown aside the pagan sequence of virtues; but, not assimilating the Christian teaching in its true significance, they have not accepted the Christian sequence and are left quite without guidance.

IV

In olden times, when there was no Christian teaching, all the teachers of life, beginning with Socrates, regarded self-control—ἐγκράτεια or σωφροσύνη—as the first virtue of life; and it was understood that every virtue must begin with and pass through this one. It was clear that a man who had no self-control, who had developed an immense number of desires and had yielded himself up to them, could not lead a good life. It was evident that before a man could even think of disinterestedness and justice—to say nothing of generosity or love—he must learn to exercise control over himself. According to our present ideas nothing of the sort is necessary. We are convinced that a man who has developed his desires to the climax reached in our society, a man who cannot live without satisfying the hundred unnecessary habits that enslave him, can yet lead an altogether moral and good life. Looked at from any point of view: the lowest, utilitarian; the higher, pagan, which demands justice; and especially the highest, Christian, which demands love—it should surely be clear to everyone that a man who uses for his own pleasure (which he might easily forgo) the labour, often the painful labour, of others, behaves wrongly; and that this is the very first wrong he must cease to commit if he wishes to live a good life.

From the utilitarian point of view such conduct is bad, because as long as he forces others to work for him a man is always in an unstable position; he accustoms himself to the satisfaction of his desires and becomes enslaved by them, while those who work for him do so with hatred and envy and only await an opportunity to free themselves from the necessity of so working. Consequently such a man is always in danger of being left with deeply rooted habits which create demands he cannot satisfy.

From the point of view of justice such conduct is bad, because it is not well to employ for one's own pleasure the labour of other men who themselves cannot afford a hundredth part of the pleasures enjoyed by him for whom they labour.

From the point of view of Christian love it can hardly be necessary to prove that a man who loves others will give them his own labour rather than take the fruit of their labour from them for his own pleasure.

But these demands of utility, justice, and love, are altogether ignored by our modern society. With us the effort to limit our desires is regarded as neither the first nor even the last condition of a good life, but as altogether unnecessary.

On the contrary, according to the prevailing and most widely spread teaching of life to-day, the augmentation of one's wants is regarded as a desirable condition; as a sign of development, civilization, culture, and perfection. So-called educated people regard habits of comfort, that is, of effeminacy, as not only harmless but even good, indicating a certain moral elevation—as almost a virtue.

It is thought that the more the wants, and the more refined these wants, the better.

This is shown very clearly by the descriptive poetry, and even more so by the novels, of the last two centuries.

How are the heroes and heroines who represent the ideals of virtue portrayed?

In most cases the men who are meant to represent something noble and lofty—from Childe Harold down to the latest heroes of Feuillet, Trollope, or Maupassant—are sim-

ply depraved sluggards, consuming in luxury the labour of
thousands, and themselves doing nothing useful for anybody. The heroines—the mistresses who in one way or another afford more or less delight to these men—are as idle as
they, and are equally ready to consume the labour of others
by their luxury.

I do not refer to the representations of really abstemious
and industrious people one occasionally meets with in literature. I am speaking of the usual type that serves as an ideal
to the masses: of the character that the majority of men and
women are trying to resemble. I remember the difficulty
(inexplicable to me at the time) that I experienced when I
wrote novels, a difficulty with which I contended and with
which I know all novelists now contend who have even the
dimmest conception of what constitutes real moral beauty—
the difficulty of portraying a type taken from the upper
classes as ideally good and kind, and at the same time true
to life. To be true to life, a description of a man or woman
of the upper, educated classes must show him in his usual
surroundings—that is, in luxury, physical idleness, and demanding much. From a moral point of view such a person is
undoubtedly objectionable. But it is necessary to represent
this person in such a way that he may appear attractive.
And novelists try to do so. I also tried. And, strange to say,
such a representation, making an immoral fornicator and
murderer (duellist or soldier), an utterly useless, idly drift-
ing, fashionable buffoon, appear attractive, does not require
much art or effort. The readers of novels are for the most
part exactly such men, and therefore readily believe that these
Childe Harolds, Onégins, Messieurs de Camors,[2] &c., are very
excellent people.

V

Clear proof that the men of our time really do not admit
pagan self-control and Christian self-renunciation to be good

[2] Onégin is the hero of a famous Russian poem by Púshkin. M. de
Camors is the hero of a French novel by Octave Feuillet.—A. M.

and desirable qualities, but on the contrary regard the augmentation of wants as good and elevated, is to be found in
the education given to the vast majority of children in our
society. Not only are they not trained to self-control, as among
the pagans, or to the self-renunciation proper to Christians,
but they are deliberately inoculated with habits of effeminacy,
physical idleness, and luxury.

I have long wished to write a fairy tale of this kind: A
woman, wishing to revenge herself on one who has injured
her, carries off her enemy's child, and going to a sorcerer asks
him to teach her how she can most cruelly wreak her vengeance on the stolen infant, the only child of her enemy. The
sorcerer bids her carry the child to a place he indicates, and
assures her that a most terrible vengeance will result. The
wicked woman follows his advice; but, keeping an eye upon
the child, is astonished to see that it is found and adopted by
a wealthy, childless man. She goes to the sorcerer and re-
proaches him, but he bids her wait. The child grows up in
luxury and effeminacy. The woman is perplexed, but again
the sorcerer bids her wait. And at length the time comes when
the wicked woman is not only satisfied but has even to pity
her victim. He grows up in the effeminacy and dissoluteness
of wealth, and owing to his good nature is ruined. Then begins a sequence of physical sufferings, poverty, and humiliation, to which he is especially sensitive and against which he
knows not how to contend. Aspirations towards a moral life—
and the weakness of his effeminate body accustomed to
luxury and idleness; vain struggles; lower and still lower decline; drunkenness to drown thought, then crime and insanity
or suicide.

And, indeed, one cannot regard without terror the education of the children of the wealthy class in our day. Only the
cruellest foe could, one would think, inoculate a child with
those defects and vices which are now instilled into him by
his parents, especially by mothers. One is awestruck at the
sight, and still more at the results of this, if only one knows
how to discern what is taking place in the souls of the best of
these children, so carefully ruined by their parents. Habits of

effeminacy are instilled into them at a time when they do not yet understand their moral significance. Not only is the habit of temperance and self-control neglected, but, contrary to the educational practice of Sparta and of the ancient world in general, this quality is altogether atrophied. Not only is man not trained to work, and to all the qualities essential to fruit-ful labour—concentration of mind, strenuousness, endur-ance, enthusiasm for work, ability to repair what is spoiled, familiarity with fatigue, joy in attainment—but he is habitu-ated to idleness and to contempt for all the products of la-bour: is taught to spoil, throw away, and again procure for money anything he fancies, without a thought of how things are made. Man is deprived of the power of acquiring the primary virtue of reasonableness, indispensable for the attain-ment of all the others, and is let loose in a world where peo-ple preach and praise the lofty virtues of justice, the service of man, and love.

It is well if the youth be endowed with a morally feeble and obtuse nature, which does not detect the difference be-tween make-believe and genuine goodness of life, and is sat-isfied with the prevailing mutual deception. If this be the case all goes apparently well, and such a man will sometimes quietly live on with his moral consciousness unawakened till death.

But it is not always thus, especially of late, now that the consciousness of the immorality of such life fills the air and penetrates the heart unsought. Frequently, and ever more frequently, it happens that there awakens a demand for real, unfeigned morality; and then begin a painful inner struggle and suffering which end but rarely in the triumph of the moral sentiment.

A man feels that his life is bad, that he must reform it from the very roots, and he tries to do so; but he is then attacked on all sides by those who have passed through a similar strug-gle and have been vanquished. They endeavour by every means to convince him that this reform is quite unnecessary: that goodness does not at all depend upon self-control and self-renunciation, that it is possible while addicting himself to gluttony, personal adornment, physical idleness, and even fornication, to be a perfectly good and useful man. And the struggle in most cases terminates lamentably. Either the man, overcome by his weakness, yields to the general opinion, stifles the voice of conscience, distorts his reason to justify himself, and continues to lead the old dissipated life, assuring himself that it is redeemed by faith in the Redemption or the Sacraments, or by service to science, to the State, or to art; or else he struggles, suffers, and finally becomes insane or shoots himself.

It seldom happens, amid all the temptations that surround him, that a man of our society understands what was thousands of years ago, and still is, an elementary truth for all reasonable people: namely, that for the attainment of a good life it is necessary first of all to cease to live an evil life; that for the attainment of the higher virtues it is needful first of all to acquire the virtue of abstinence or self-control as the pagans called it, or of self-renunciation as Christianity has it, and therefore it seldom happens that he succeeds in attaining this primary virtue by gradual efforts.

VI

I have just been reading the letters of one of our highly educated and advanced men of the eighteen-forties, the exile Ogaryëv, to another yet more highly educated and gifted man, Herzen. In these letters Ogaryëv gives expression to his sincere thoughts and highest aspirations, and one cannot fail to see that—as was natural to a young man—he rather shows off before his friend. He talks of self-perfecting, of sacred friendship, love, the service of science, of humanity, and the like. And at the same time he calmly writes that he often irritates the companion of his life by 'returning home in an unsober state, or disappearing for many hours with a fallen, but dear creature. . . .' as he expresses it.

Evidently it never even occurred to this remarkably kind-hearted, talented, and well-educated man that there was anything at all objectionable in the fact that he, a married man awaiting the confinement of his wife (in his next letter he writes that his wife has given birth to a child), returned home intoxicated and disappeared with dissolute women. It did not enter his head that until he had commenced the struggle and had at least to some extent conquered his inclination to drunkenness and fornication, he could not think of friendship and love and still less of serving anyone or anything. But he not only did not struggle against these vices— he evidently thought there was something very nice in them, and that they did not in the least hinder the struggle for perfection; and therefore instead of hiding them from the friend in whose eyes he wishes to appear in a good light, he exhibits them.

Thus it was half a century ago. I was contemporary with such men. I knew Ogaryëv and Herzen themselves, and others of that stamp, and men educated in the same traditions. There was a remarkable absence of consistency in the lives of all these men. Together with a sincere and ardent wish for good there was an utter looseness of personal desire, which they thought could not hinder the living of a good life nor the performance of good and even great deeds. They put unkneaded loaves into a cold oven and believed that bread would be baked. And then, when with advancing years they began to notice that the bread did not bake—i.e. that no good came of their lives—they saw in this something peculiarly tragic.

And the tragedy of such lives is indeed terrible. And this same tragedy apparent in the lives of Herzen, Ogaryëv, and others of their time, exists to-day in the lives of very many so-called educated people who hold the same views. A man desires to lead a good life, but the consecutiveness which is indispensable for this is lost in the society in which he lives. The majority of men of the present day, like Ogaryëv, Herzen and others fifty years ago, are persuaded that to lead an effeminate life, to eat sweet and rich foods, to delight themselves in every way and satisfy all their desires, does not hinder them from living a good life. But as it is evident that a good life in their case does not result, they give themselves up to pessimism, and say, 'Such is the tragedy of human life.'

It is strange too that these people, who know that the distribution of pleasures among men is unequal and regard this inequality as an evil and wish to correct it, yet do not cease to strive to augment their own pleasures—that is, to augment inequality in the distribution of pleasures. In acting thus, these people are like men who being the first to enter an orchard hasten to gather all the fruit they can lay their hands on, and while professing a wish to organize a more equal distribution of the fruit of the orchard between themselves and later comers, continue to pluck all they can reach.

VII

The delusion that men while addicting themselves to their desires and regarding this life of desire as good, can yet lead a good, useful, just, and loving life, is so astonishing that men of later generations will, I should think, simply fail to understand what the men of our time meant by the words 'good life', when they said that the gluttons—the effeminate, lustful sluggards—of our wealthy classes led good lives. Indeed, one need only put aside for a moment the customary view of the life of our wealthy classes, and look at it, I do not say from the Christian point of view, but from the pagan standpoint, from the standpoint of the very lowest demands of justice, to be convinced that, living amidst the violation of the plainest laws of justice or fairness, such as even children in their games think it wrong to violate, we men of the wealthy classes have no right even to talk about a good life.

Any man of our society who would, I do not say begin a good life but even begin to make some little approach towards it, must first of all cease to lead a bad life, must begin to destroy those conditions of an evil life with which he finds himself surrounded.

How often one hears, as an excuse for not reforming our lives, the argument that any act that is contrary to the usual mode of life would be unnatural, ludicrous—would look like a desire to show off, and would therefore not be a good action. This argument seems expressly framed to prevent people from ever changing their evil lives. If all our life were good, just, kind, then and only then would an action in conformity with the usual mode of life be good. If half our life were good and the other half bad, then there would be as much chance of an action not in conformity with the usual mode of life being good as of its being bad. But when life is altogether bad and wrong, as is the case of our upper classes, then a man cannot perform a single good action without disturbing the usual current of life. He can do a bad action without disturbing this current, but not a good one.

A man accustomed to the life of our well-to-do classes cannot lead a righteous life without first coming out of those conditions of evil in which he is immersed—he cannot begin to do good until he has ceased to do evil. It is impossible for a man living in luxury to lead a righteous life. All his efforts after goodness will be in vain until he changes his life, until he performs that work which stands first in sequence before him. A good life according to the pagan view, and still more according to the Christian view, is, and can be, measured in no other way than by the mathematical relation between love of self and love of others. The less there is of love of self with all the ensuing care about self and the selfish demands made upon the labour of others, and the more there is of love of others with the resultant care for and labour bestowed upon others, the better is the life.

Thus has goodness of life been understood by all the sages of the world and by all true Christians, and in exactly the same way do all plain men understand it now. The more a man gives to others and the less he demands for himself, the better he is: the less he gives to others and the more he demands for himself, the worse he is.

And not only does a man become morally better the more love he has for others and the less for himself, but the less he loves himself the easier it becomes for him to be better, and contrariwise. The more a man loves himself, and consequently the more he demands labour from others, the less possibility is there for him to love and to work for others; less not only by as much as the increase of his love for himself, but less in an enormously greater degree—just as when we move the fulcrum of a lever from the long end towards the short end, we not only increase the long arm but also reduce the short one. Therefore if a man possessing a certain faculty (love) augments his love and care for himself, he thereby diminishes his power of loving and caring for others not only in proportion to the love he has transferred to himself but in a much greater degree. Instead of feeding others a man eats too much himself; by so doing he not only diminishes the possibility of giving away the surplus, but by overeating deprives himself of power to help others.

In order to love others in reality and not in word only, one must cease to love oneself also in reality and not merely in word. In most cases it happens thus: we think we love others, we assure ourselves and others that it is so, but we love them only in words while we love ourselves in reality. We forget to feed and put others to bed, ourselves—never. Therefore, in order really to love others in deed, we must learn not to love ourselves in deed, learn to forget to feed ourselves and put ourselves to bed, exactly as we forget to do these things for others.

We say of a self-indulgent person accustomed to lead a luxurious life, that he is a 'good man' and 'leads a good life'. But such a person—whether man or woman—although he may possess the most amiable traits of character, meekness, good nature, &c., cannot be good and lead a good life, any more than a knife of the very best workmanship and steel can be sharp and cut well unless it is sharpened. To be good and lead a good life means to give to others more than one takes from them. But a self-indulgent man accustomed to a luxurious life cannot do this, first because he himself always needs a great deal (and this not because he is selfish, but because he is accustomed to luxury and finds it painful to be deprived of that to which he is accustomed); and secondly, because by consuming all that he receives from others he weakens himself and renders himself unfit for labour, and therefore unfit to serve others. A self-indulgent man who sleeps long upon a soft bed and consumes an abundance of rich, sweet food, who always wears clean clothes and such as are suited to the temperature, who has never accustomed himself to the effort of laborious work, can do very little.

We are so accustomed to our own lies and the lies of others, and it is so convenient for us not to see through the lies of others that they may not see through ours, that we are not in the least astonished at, and do not doubt the truth of, the assertion of the virtue, sometimes even the sanctity, of people who are leading a perfectly unrestrained life.

A person, man or woman, sleeps on a spring bed with two mattresses, two smooth clean sheets, and feather pillows in pillow-cases. By the bedside is a rug that the feet may not get cold on stepping out of bed, though slippers also lie near. Here also are the necessary utensils so that he need not leave the house—whatever uncleanliness he may produce will be carried away and all made tidy. The windows are covered with curtains that the daylight may not awaken him, and he sleeps as long as he is inclined. Besides all this, measures are taken that the room may be warm in winter and cool in summer, and that he may not be disturbed by the noise of flies or other insects. While he sleeps hot and cold water for his ablutions, and sometimes baths and preparations for shaving, are provided. Tea and coffee are also prepared, stimulating drinks to be taken immediately upon rising. Boots, shoes, galoshes— several pairs dirtied the previous day—are already being cleaned, freed from every speck of dust, and made to shine like glass. Other various garments soiled on the preceding day are similarly cleaned, and these differ in texture to suit not only summer and winter, but also spring, autumn, rainy, damp, and warm weather. Clean linen, washed, starched, and ironed, is being made ready, with studs, shirt buttons, and buttonholes, all carefully inspected by specially appointed people.

If the person be active he rises early—at seven o'clock— but still a couple of hours later than those who are making all these preparations for him. And besides clothes for the day and covering for the night there is also a special costume and footgear for him while he is dressing—dressing-gown and slippers. And now he undertakes his washing, cleaning, brushing, for which several kinds of brushes are used as well as soap and a great quantity of water. (Many English men and women, for some reason or other, are specially proud of using a great deal of soap and pouring a large quantity of water over themselves.) Then he dresses, brushes his hair before a special kind of looking-glass (different from those that hang in almost every room in the house), takes the things he needs, such as spectacles or eyeglasses, and then distributes in different pockets a clean pocket-handkerchief to blow his nose on; a watch with a chain, though in almost every room he goes to there will be a clock; money of various kinds, small change (often in a specially contrived case which saves him the trouble of looking for the required coin) and bank-notes; also visiting cards on which his name is printed (saving him the trouble of saying or writing it); pocket-book and pencil. In the case of women, the toilet is still more complicated: corsets, arranging of long hair, adornments, laces, elastics, ribbons, ties, hairpins, pins, brooches.

But at last all is complete and the day commences, generally with eating: tea and coffee are drunk with a great quantity of sugar; bread made of the finest white flour is eaten with large quantities of butter, and sometimes the flesh of pigs. The men for the most part smoke cigars or cigarettes meanwhile, and read fresh papers which have just been brought. Then, leaving to others the task of setting right the soiled and disordered room, they go to their office or business, or drive in carriages produced specially to move such people about. Then comes a luncheon of slain beasts, birds, and fish, followed by a dinner consisting, if it be very modest, of three courses, dessert, and coffee. Then playing at cards and playing music—or the theatre, reading, and conversation in soft spring armchairs by the intensified and shaded light of candles, gas, or electricity. After this, more tea, more eating— supper—and to bed again, the bed shaken up and prepared with clean linen, and the utensils washed to be made foul again.

Thus pass the days of a man of modest life, of whom, if he

is good-natured and does not possess any habits specially ob-
noxious to those about him, it is said that he leads a good
and virtuous life.

But a good life is the life of a man who does good to others; and can a man accustomed to live thus do good to others?
Before he can do good to men he must cease to do evil.
Reckon up all the harm such a man, often unconsciously, does
to others, and you will see that he is far indeed from doing
good. He would have to perform many acts of heroism to redeem the evil he commits, but he is too much enfeebled by
his self-created needs to perform any such acts. He might
sleep with more advantage, both physical and moral, lying on
the floor wrapped in his cloak as Marcus Aurelius did; thus
saving all the labour and trouble involved in the manufacture of mattresses, springs, and pillows, as well as the daily
labour of the laundress—one of the weaker sex burdened by
the bearing and nursing of children—who washes linen for
this strong man. By going to bed earlier and getting up earlier
he might save window-curtains and the evening lamp. He
might sleep in the same shirt he wears during the day,
might step barefooted upon the floor, and go out into the
yard; he might wash at the pump. In a word, he might live
like those who work for him, and thus save all this work
that is done for him. He might save all the labour expended
upon his clothing, his refined food, his recreations. And he
knows under what conditions all these labours are performed:
how men perish and suffer in performing them, and how
they often hate those who take advantage of their poverty to
force them to do it.

How then can such a man do good to others and lead a
righteous life, without abandoning this self-indulgence and
luxury?

But we need not speak of how other people appear in our
eyes—everyone must see and feel this concerning himself.

I cannot but repeat this same thing again and again, notwithstanding the cold and hostile silence with which my
words are received. A moral man, living a life of comfort, a
man even of the middle class (I will not speak of the upper

classes, who daily consume the results of hundreds of working days to satisfy their caprices), cannot live quietly, knowing that all he is using is produced by the labour of working people whose lives are crushed, who are dying without hope —ignorant, drunken, dissolute, semi-savage creatures employed in mines, factories, and in agricultural labour, producing the things that he uses.

At the present moment I who am writing this and you who will read it, whoever you may be—have wholesome, sufficient, perhaps abundant and luxurious food, pure warm air to breathe, winter and summer clothing, various recreations, and, most important of all, leisure by day and undisturbed repose at night. And here by our side live the working people, who have neither wholesome food nor healthy lodgings nor sufficient clothing nor recreations, and who above all are deprived not only of leisure but even of rest: old men, children, women, worn out by labour, by sleepless nights, by disease, who spend their whole lives providing for us those articles of comfort and luxury which they do not possess, and which are for us not necessities but superfluities. Therefore a moral man (I do not say a Christian, but simply a man professing humane views or merely esteeming justice) cannot but wish to change his life and to cease to use articles of luxury produced under such conditions.

If a man really pities those who manufacture tobacco, then the first thing he will naturally do will be to cease smoking, because by continuing to buy and smoke tobacco he encourages the preparation of tobacco by which men's health is destroyed. And so with every other article of luxury. If a man can still continue to eat bread notwithstanding the hard work by which it is produced, this is because he cannot forgo what is indispensable while waiting for the present conditions of labour to be altered. But with regard to things which are not only unnecessary but are even superfluous there can be no other conclusion than this: that if I pity men engaged in the manufacture of certain articles, then I must on no account accustom myself to require such articles.

But nowadays men argue otherwise. They invent the most

varied and intricate arguments, but never say what naturally occurs to every plain man. According to them, it is not at all necessary to abstain from luxuries. One can sympathize with the condition of the working men, deliver speeches and write books on their behalf, and at the same time continue to profit by the labour that one sees to be ruinous to them.

According to one argument, I may profit by labour that is harmful to the workers because if I do not another will. Which is something like the argument that I must drink wine that is injurious to me because it has been bought and if I do not drink it others will.

According to another argument, it is even beneficial to the workers to be allowed to produce luxuries, for in this way we provide them with money—that is with the means of subsistence: as if we could not provide them with the means of subsistence in any other way than by making them produce articles injurious to them and superfluous to us.

But according to a third argument, now most popular, it seems that, since there is such a thing as division of labour, any work upon which a man is engaged—whether he be a Government official, priest, landowner, manufacturer, or merchant—is so useful that it fully compensates for the labour of the working classes by which he profits. One serves the State, another the Church, a third science, a fourth art, and a fifth serves those who serve the State, science, and art; and all are firmly convinced that what they give to mankind certainly compensates for all they take. And it is astonishing how, while continually augmenting their luxurious requirements without increasing their activity, these people continue to be certain that their activity compensates for all they consume.

Whereas if you listen to these people's judgement of one another it appears that each individual is far from being worth what he consumes. Government officials say that the work of the landlords is not worth what they spend, landlords say the same about merchants, and merchants about Government officials, and so on. But this does not disconcert them, and they continue to assure people that they (each of them) profit by the labours of others exactly in proportion to

the service they render to others. So that the payment is not
determined by the work, but the value of the imaginary work
is determined by the payment. Thus they assure one another,
but they know perfectly well in the depth of their souls that
all their arguments do not justify them; that they are not necessary to the working men, and that they profit by the labour
of those men not on account of any division of labour but
simply because they have the power to do so, and because
they are so spoiled that they cannot do without it.

And all this arises from people imagining that it is possible
to lead a good life without first acquiring the primary quality
necessary for a good life.

And that first quality is self-control.

VIII

There never has been and cannot be a good life without
self-control. Apart from self-control no good life is imaginable.
The attainment of goodness must begin with that.

There is a scale of virtues, and if one would mount the
higher steps it is necessary to begin with the lowest; and the
first virtue a man must acquire if he wishes to acquire the
others is that which the ancients called ἐγκράτεια or σωφροσύνη
—that is, self-control or moderation.

If in the Christian teaching self-control was included in
the conception of self-renunciation, still the order of succession remained the same, and the acquirement of any Christian virtue is impossible without self-control—and this not
because such a rule has been invented, but because it is the
essential nature of the case.

But even self-control, the first step in every righteous life, is
not attainable all at once but only by degrees.

Self-control is the liberation of man from desires—their
subordination to moderation, σωφροσύνη. But a man's desires
are many and various, and in order to contend with them
successfully he must begin with the fundamental ones—
those upon which the more complex ones have grown up—
and not with those complex lusts which have grown up

upon the fundamental ones. There are complex lusts like that of the adornment of the body, sports, amusements, idle talk, inquisitiveness, and many others; and there are also fundamental lusts—gluttony, idleness, sexual love. And one must begin to contend with these lusts from the beginning; not with the complex but with the fundamental ones, and that also in a definite order. And this order is determined both by the nature of things and by the tradition of human wisdom.

A man who eats too much cannot strive against laziness, while a gluttonous and idle man will never be able to contend with sexual lust. Therefore, according to all moral teachings, the effort towards self-control commences with a struggle against the lust of gluttony—commences with fasting. In our time, however, every serious relation to the attainment of a good life has been so long and so completely lost that not only is the very first virtue—self-control—without which the others are unattainable, regarded as superfluous, but the order of succession necessary for the attainment of this first virtue is also disregarded, and fasting is quite forgotten, or is looked upon as a silly superstition, utterly unnecessary.

And yet, just as the first condition of a good life is self-control, so the first condition of a life of self-control is fasting.

One may wish to be good, one may dream of goodness, without fasting; but to *be* good without fasting is as impossible as it is to advance without getting up on one's feet.

Fasting is an indispensable condition of a good life, whereas gluttony is and always has been the first sign of the opposite; and unfortunately this vice is in the highest degree characteristic of the life of the majority of the men of our time.

Look at the faces and figures of the men of our circle and day. On all those faces with pendent cheeks and chins, those corpulent limbs and prominent stomachs, lies the indelible seal of a dissolute life. Nor can it be otherwise. Consider our life and the actuating motive of the majority of men in our society, and then ask yourself, What is the chief interest of this majority? And, strange as it may appear to us who are accustomed to hide our real interests and to profess false, artificial ones, you will find that the chief interest of their life is the satisfaction of the palate, the pleasure of eating— gluttony. From the poorest to the richest, eating is, I think, the chief aim, the chief pleasure, of our life. Poor working people form an exception, but only inasmuch as want prevents their addicting themselves to this passion. No sooner have they the time and the means, than, in imitation of the higher classes, they procure rich and tasty foods, and eat and drink as much as they can. The more they eat the more do they deem themselves not only happy, but also strong and healthy. And in this conviction they are encouraged by the upper classes, who regard food in precisely the same way. The educated classes (following the medical men who assure them that the most expensive food, flesh, is the most wholesome) imagine that happiness and health consist in tasty, nourishing, easily digested food—in gorging—though they try to conceal this.

Look at rich people's lives, listen to their conversation. What lofty subjects seem to occupy them: philosophy, science, art, poetry, the distribution of wealth, the welfare of the people, and the education of the young! But all this is, for the immense majority, a sham. All this occupies them only in the intervals of business, real business: in the intervals, that is, between lunch and dinner, while the stomach is full and it is impossible to eat more. The only real living interest of the majority both of men and women, especially after early youth, is eating— How to eat, what to eat, where to eat, and when to eat.

No solemnity, no rejoicing, no consecration, on opening of anything, can dispense with eating.

Watch people travelling. In their case the thing is specially evident. 'Museums, libraries, Parliament—how very interesting! But where shall we dine? Where is one best fed?' Look at people when they come together for dinner, dressed up, perfumed, around a table decorated with flowers—how joyfully they rub their hands and smile!

If we could look into the hearts of the majority of people what should we find they most desire? Appetite for breakfast and for dinner. What is the severest punishment from infancy upwards? To be put on bread and water. What artisans get the highest wages? Cooks. What is the chief interest of the mistress of the house? To what subject does the conversation of middle-class housewives generally tend? If the conversation of the members of the higher classes does not tend in the same direction it is not because they are better educated or are occupied with higher interests, but simply because they have a housekeeper or a steward who relieves them of all anxiety about their dinner. But once deprive them of this convenience and you will see what causes them most anxiety. It all comes round to the subject of eating: the price of grouse, the best way of making coffee, of baking sweet cakes, and so on. People come together whatever the occasion —a christening, a funeral, a wedding, the consecration of a church, the departure or arrival of a friend, the consecration of regimental colours, the celebration of a memorable day, the death or birth of a great scientist, philosopher, or teacher of morality—men come together as if occupied by the most lofty interests. But it is only a pretence: they all know that there will be eating—good tasty food—and drinking, and it is chiefly this that brings them together. To this end, for several days before, animals have been slaughtered, baskets of provisions brought from gastronomic shops, cooks and their helpers, kitchen boys and maids, specially attired in clean, starched frocks and caps, have been 'at work'. Chefs, receiving £50 a month and more, have been occupied in giving directions. Cooks have been chopping, kneading, roasting, arranging, adorning. With like solemnity and importance a master of the ceremonies has been working, calculating, pondering, adjusting, with his eye, like an artist. A gardener has been employed upon the flowers. Scullery-maids. . . . An army of men has been at work, the result of thousands of working days are being swallowed up, and all this that people may come together to talk about some great teacher of science or morality, or recall the memory of a deceased friend, or to greet a young couple just entering upon a new life.

In the middle and lower classes it is perfectly evident that every festivity, every funeral or wedding, means gluttony. There the matter is so understood. To such an extent is gluttony the motive of the assembly that in Greek and in French the same word means both 'wedding' and 'feast'. But in the upper classes of the rich, especially among the refined who have long possessed wealth, great skill is used to conceal this and to make it appear that eating is a secondary matter necessary only for appearance. And this pretence is easy, for in the majority of cases the guests are satiated in the true sense of the word—they are never hungry.

They pretend that dinner, eating, is not necessary to them, is even a burden; but this is a lie. Try giving them—instead of the refined dishes they expect—I do not say bread and water, but porridge or gruel or something of that kind, and see what a storm it will call forth and how evident will become the real truth, namely, that the chief interest of the assembly is not the ostensible one but—gluttony.

Look at what men sell. Go through a town and see what men buy—articles of adornment and things to devour. And indeed this must be so, it cannot be otherwise. It is only possible not to think about eating, to keep this lust under control, when a man does not eat except in obedience to necessity. If a man *ceases* to eat only in obedience to necessity—if, that is, he eats when the stomach is full—then the state of things cannot but be what it actually is. If men love the pleasure of eating, if they allow themselves to love this pleasure, if they find it good (as in the case with the vast majority of men in our time, and with educated men quite as much as with uneducated, though they pretend that it is not so), there is no limit to the augmentation of this pleasure, no limit beyond which it may not grow. The satisfaction of a *need* has limits, but pleasure has none. For the satisfaction of our needs it is necessary and sufficient to eat bread, porridge, or rice; for the augmentation of a pleasure there is no end to the possible flavourings and seasonings.

Bread is a necessary and sufficient food. (This is proved by the millions of men who are strong, active, healthy, and hard-working on rye bread alone.) But it is pleasanter to eat bread with some flavouring. It is well to soak the bread in water boiled with meat. Still better to put into this water some vegetable or, even better, several vegetables. It is well to eat flesh. And flesh is better not stewed, but roasted. It is better still with butter, and underdone, and choosing out certain special parts of the meat. But add to this vegetables and mustard. And drink wine with it, red wine for preference. One does not need any more, but one can still eat some fish if it is well flavoured with sauces and swallowed down with white wine. It would seem as if one could get through nothing more, either rich or tasty, but a sweet dish can still be managed; in summer ices, in winter stewed fruits, preserves, and the like. And thus we have a dinner, a modest dinner. The pleasure of such a dinner can be greatly augmented. And it is augmented, and there is no limit to this augmentation: stimulating snacks, *hors-d'œuvres* before dinner, and *entremets* and desserts, and various combinations of tasty things, and flowers and decorations and music during dinner.

And strange to say, men who daily overeat themselves at such dinners—in comparison with which the feast of Belshazzar that evoked the prophetic warning was nothing—are naïvely persuaded that they may yet be leading a moral life.

IX

Fasting is an indispensable condition of a good life; but in fasting, as in self-control in general, the question arises, what shall we begin with?— How to fast, how often to eat, what to eat, what to avoid eating? And as we can do no

work seriously without regarding the necessary order of sequence, so also we cannot fast without knowing where to
begin—with what to commence self-control in food.

Fasting! And even an analysis of how to fast and where
to begin! The notion seems ridiculous and wild to the majority of men.

I remember how an Evangelical preacher who was attacking monastic asceticism once said to me with pride at his
own originality, 'Ours is not a Christianity of fasting and
privations, but of beefsteaks.' Christianity, or virtue in general—and beefsteaks!

During a long period of darkness and lack of all guidance,
Pagan or Christian, so many wild, immoral ideas have made
their way into our life (especially into that lower region of
the first steps towards a good life—our relation to food to
which no one paid any attention), that it is difficult for us
in our days even to understand the audacity and senselessness of upholding Christianity or virtue with beefsteaks.

We are not horrified by this association simply because a
strange thing has befallen us. We look and see not; listen
and hear not. There is no bad odour, no sound, no mon-
strosity, to which man cannot become so accustomed that he
ceases to remark what would strike a man unaccustomed to
it. And it is precisely the same in the moral region. Christianity and morality with beefsteaks!

A few days ago I visited the slaughter-house in our town
of Túla. It is built on the new and improved system practised in large towns, with a view to causing the animals as
little suffering as possible. It was on a Friday, two days before Trinity Sunday. There were many cattle there.

Long before this, when reading that excellent book, *The
Ethics of Diet*, I had wished to visit a slaughter-house in
order to see with my own eyes the reality of the question
raised when vegetarianism is discussed. But at first I felt
ashamed to do so, as one is always ashamed of going to look
at suffering which one knows is about to take place but
which one cannot avert; and so I kept putting off my visit.

But a little while ago I met on the road a butcher returning to Túla after a visit to his home. He is not yet an experienced butcher, and his duty is to stab with a knife. I asked him whether he did not feel sorry for the animals that he killed. He gave me the usual answer: 'Why should I feel sorry? It is necessary.' But when I told him that eating flesh is not necessary, but is only a luxury, he agreed; and then he admitted that he was sorry for the animals. 'But what can I do?' he said, 'I must earn my bread. At first I was *afraid* to kill. My father, he never even killed a chicken in all his life.' The majority of Russians cannot kill; they feel pity, and express the feeling by the word '*fear*'. This man had also been 'afraid', but he was so no longer. He told me that most of the work was done on Fridays, when it continues until the evening.

Not long ago I also had a talk with a retired soldier, a butcher, and he too was surprised at my assertion that it was a pity to kill, and said the usual things about its being ordained. But afterwards he agreed with me: 'Especially when they are quiet, tame cattle. They come, poor things! trusting you. It is very pitiful.'

This is dreadful! Not the suffering and death of the animals, but that man suppresses in himself, unnecessarily, the highest spiritual capacity—that of sympathy and pity towards living creatures like himself—and by violating his own feelings becomes cruel. And how deeply seated in the human heart is the injunction not to take life!

Once, when walking from Moscow,[3] I was offered a lift by some carters who were going from Sérpukhov to a neighbouring forest to fetch wood. It was the Thursday before Easter. I was seated in the first cart with a strong, red, coarse carman, who evidently drank. On entering a village we saw a well-fed, naked, pink pig being dragged out of the first yard to be slaughtered. It squealed in a dreadful voice, resembling the shriek of a man. Just as we were passing they began to

---

[3] When returning to Yásnaya Polyána in spring after his winter's residence in Moscow, Tolstóy repeatedly chose to walk the distance (something over 130 miles) instead of going by rail. Sérpukhov is a town he had to pass on the way.—A. M.

kill it. A man gashed its throat with a knife. The pig squealed still more loudly and piercingly, broke away from the men, and ran off covered with blood. Being near-sighted I did not see all the details. I saw only the human-looking pink body of the pig and heard its desperate squeal, but the carter saw all the details and watched closely. They caught the pig, knocked it down, and finished cutting its throat. When its squeals ceased the carter sighed heavily. 'Do men really not have to answer for such things?' he said.

So strong is man's aversion to all killing. But by example, by encouraging greediness, by the assertion that God has allowed it, and above all by habit, people entirely lose this natural feeling.

On Friday I decided to go to Túla, and, meeting a meek, kind acquaintance of mine, I invited him to accompany me.

'Yes, I have heard that the arrangements are good, and have been wishing to go and see it; but if they are slaughtering I will not go in.'

'Why not? That's just what I want to see! If we eat flesh it must be killed.'

'No, no, I cannot!'

It is worth remarking that this man is a sportsman and himself kills animals and birds.

So we went to the slaughter-house. Even at the entrance one noticed the heavy, disgusting, fetid smell, as of carpenter's glue, or paint on glue. The nearer we approached the stronger became the smell. The building is of red brick, very large, with vaults and high chimneys. We entered the gates. To the right was a spacious enclosed yard, three-quarters of an acre in extent—twice a week cattle are driven in here for sale—and adjoining this enclosure was the porter's lodge. To the left were the chambers, as they are called —i.e. rooms with arched entrances, sloping asphalt floors, and contrivances for moving and hanging up the carcasses. On a bench against the wall of the porter's lodge were seated half a dozen butchers, in aprons covered with blood, their tucked-up sleeves disclosing their muscular arms also besmeared with blood. They had finished their work half an hour before, so that day we could only see the empty chambers. Though these chambers were open on both sides, there was an oppressive smell of warm blood; the floor was brown and shining, with congealed black blood in the cavities.

One of the butchers described the process of slaughtering, and showed us the place where it was done. I did not quite understand him, and formed a wrong, but very horrible, idea of the way the animals are slaughtered; and I fancied that, as is often the case, the reality would very likely produce upon me a weaker impression than the imagination. But in this I was mistaken.

The next time I visited the slaughter-house I went in good time. It was the Friday before Trinity—a warm day in June. The smell of glue and blood was even stronger and more penetrating than on my first visit. The work was at its height. The dusty yard was full of cattle, and animals had been driven into all the enclosures beside the chambers.

In the street before the entrance stood carts to which oxen, calves, and cows were tied. Other carts drawn by good horses and filled with live calves, whose heads hung down and swayed about, drew up and were unloaded; and similar carts containing the carcasses of oxen, with trembling legs sticking out, with heads and bright red lungs and brown livers, drove away from the slaughter-house. By the fence stood the cattle-dealers' horses. The dealers themselves, in their long coats, with their whips and knouts in their hands, were walking about the yard, either marking with tar cattle belonging to the same owner, or bargaining, or else guiding oxen and bulls from the great yard into the enclosures which lead into the chambers. These men were evidently all preoccupied with money matters and calculations, and any thought as to whether it was right or wrong to kill these animals was as far from their minds as were questions about the chemical composition of the blood that covered the floor of the chambers.

No butchers were to be seen in the yard; they were all in the chambers at work. That day about a hundred head of cattle were slaughtered. I was on the point of entering one of the chambers, but stopped short at the door. I stopped both because the chamber was crowded with carcasses which were being moved about, and also because blood was flowing on the floor and dripping from above. All the butchers present were besmeared with blood, and had I entered I, too, should certainly have been covered with it. One suspended carcass was being taken down, another was being moved towards the door, a third, a slaughtered ox, was lying with its white legs raised, while a butcher with strong hand was ripping up its tight-stretched hide.

Through the door opposite the one at which I was standing, a big, red, well-fed ox was led in. Two men were dragging it, and hardly had it entered when I saw a butcher raise a knife above its neck and stab it. The ox, as if all four legs had suddenly given way, fell heavily on its belly, immediately turned over on one side, and began to work its legs and its whole hind-quarters. Another butcher at once threw himself upon the ox from the side opposite to the twitching legs, caught its horns and twisted its head down to the ground, while another butcher cut its throat with a knife. From beneath the head there flowed a stream of blackish-red blood, which a besmeared boy caught in a tin basin. All the time this was going on the ox kept incessantly twitching its head as if trying to get up, and waved its four legs in the air. The basin was quickly filling, but the ox still lived, and, its stomach heaving heavily, both hind and fore legs worked so violently that the butchers held aloof. When one basin was full the boy carried it away on his head to the albumen factory, while another boy placed a fresh basin, which also soon began to fill up. But still the ox heaved its body and worked its hind legs.

When the blood ceased to flow the butcher raised the animal's head and began to skin it. The ox continued to writhe. The head, stripped of its skin, showed red with white veins, and kept the position given it by the butcher; the skin hung on both sides. Still the animal did not cease to writhe. Then another butcher caught hold of one of the legs, broke it, and cut it off. In the remaining legs and the stomach the convulsions still continued. The other legs were cut off and thrown aside, together with those of other oxen belonging to the same owner. Then the carcass was dragged to the hoist and hung up and the convulsions were over.

Thus I looked on from the door at the second, third, and fourth ox. It was the same with each: the same cutting off of the head with bitten tongue, and the same convulsive members. The only difference was that the butcher did not always strike at once so as to cause the animal's fall. Sometimes he missed his aim, whereupon the ox tried to escape. But then his head was pulled under a bar, struck a second time, and he fell.

I afterwards entered by the door at which the oxen were led in. Here I saw the same thing, only nearer, and therefore more plainly. But chiefly I saw here, what I had not seen before, how the oxen were forced to enter this door. Each time an ox was seized in the enclosure and pulled forward by a rope tied to its horns, the animal, smelling blood, refused to advance, and sometimes bellowed and drew back. It would have been beyond the strength of two men to drag it in by force, so one of the butchers went round each time, grasped the animal's tail, and twisted it so violently that the gristle crackled, and the ox advanced.

When they had finished with the cattle of one owner they brought in those of another. The first animal of this next lot was not an ox but a bull—a fine, well-bred creature, black, with white spots on its legs, young, muscular, full of energy. He was dragged forward, but he lowered his head and resisted sturdily. Then the butcher who followed behind seized the tail like an engine-driver grasping the handle of a whistle, twisted it, the gristle crackled, and the bull rushed forward, upsetting the men who held the rope. Then it stopped, looking sideways with its black eyes, the whites of which had filled with blood. But again the tail crackled, and the bull sprang forward and reached the required spot. The striker approached, took aim, and struck. But the blow missed the mark. The bull leaped up, shook his head, bellowed, and, covered with blood, broke free and rushed back. The men at the doorway all sprang aside; but the experienced butchers, with the dash of men inured to danger, quickly caught the rope; again the tail operation was repeated, and again the bull was in the chamber, where he was dragged under the bar, from which he did not again escape. The striker quickly took aim at the spot where the hair divides like a star, and, notwithstanding the blood, found it, struck, and the fine animal, full of life, collapsed, its head and legs writhing while it was bled and the head skinned.

'There, the cursèd devil hasn't even fallen the right way!' grumbled the butcher as he cut the skin from the head.

Five minutes later the head was stuck up, red instead of black, without skin; the eyes that had shone with such splendid colour five minutes before, fixed and glassy.

Afterwards I went into the compartment where small animals are slaughtered—a very large chamber with asphalt floor, and tables with backs, on which sheep and calves are killed. Here the work was already finished; in the long room, impregnated with the smell of blood, were only two butchers. One was blowing into the leg of a dead lamb and patting the swollen stomach with his hand; the other, a young fellow in an apron besmeared with blood, was smoking a bent cigarette. There was no one else in the long dark chamber, filled with a heavy smell. After me there entered a man, apparently an ex-soldier, bringing in a young yearling ram, black with a white mark on its neck, and its legs tied. This animal he placed upon one of the tables as if upon a bed. The old soldier greeted the butchers, with whom he was evidently acquainted, and began to ask when their master allowed them leave. The fellow with the cigarette approached with a knife, sharpened it on the edge of the table, and answered that they were free on holidays. The live ram was lying as quietly as the dead inflated one, except that it was briskly wagging its short little tail and its sides were heaving more quickly than usual. The soldier pressed down its uplifted head gently, without effort; the butcher, still continuing the conversation, grasped with his left hand the head of the ram and cut its throat. The ram quivered, and the little tail stiffened and ceased to wave. The fellow, while waiting for the blood to flow, began to relight his cigarette which had gone out. The blood flowed and the ram began to writhe. The conversation continued without the slightest interruption. It was horribly revolting.

And how about those hens and chickens which daily, in thousands of kitchens, with heads cut off and streaming with blood, comically, dreadfully, flop about, jerking their wings?

And see, a kind, refined lady will devour the carcasses of these animals with full assurance that she is doing right, at the same time asserting two contradictory propositions:

First, that she is, as her doctor assures her, so delicate that she cannot be sustained by vegetable food alone and that for her feeble organism flesh is indispensable; and secondly, that she is so sensitive that she is unable, not only herself to inflict suffering on animals, but even to bear the sight of suffering.

Whereas the poor lady is weak precisely because she has been taught to live upon food unnatural to man; and she cannot avoid causing suffering to animals—for she eats them.

X

We cannot pretend that we do not know this. We are not ostriches, and cannot believe that if we refuse to look at what we do not wish to see, it will not exist. This is especially the case when what we do not wish to see is what we wish to eat. If it were really indispensable, or if not indispensable, at least in some way useful! But it is quite unnecessary,[4] and only serves to develop animal feelings, to excite desire, and

---

[4] Let those who doubt this read the numerous books upon the subject, written by scientists and doctors, in which it is proved that flesh is not necessary for the nourishment of man. And let them not listen to those old-fashioned doctors who defend the assertion that flesh is necessary, merely because it has long been so regarded by their predecessors and by themselves; and who defend their opinion with tenacity and malevolence, as all that is old and traditional always is defended.—L. T.

to promote fornication and drunkenness. And this is continually being confirmed by the fact that young, kind, undepraved people—especially women and girls—without knowing how it logically follows, feel that virtue is incompatible with beefsteaks, and, as soon as they wish to be good, give up eating flesh.

What, then, do I wish to say? That in order to be moral people must cease to eat meat? Not at all.

I only wish to say that for a good life a certain order of good actions is indispensable; that if a man's aspirations towards right living be serious they will inevitably follow one definite sequence; and that in this sequence the first virtue a man will strive after will be self-control, self-restraint. And in seeking for self-control a man will inevitably follow one definite sequence, and in this sequence the first thing will be self-control in food—fasting. And in fasting, if he be really and seriously seeking to live a good life, the first thing from which he will abstain will always be the use of animal food, because, to say nothing of the excitation of the passions caused by such food, its use is simply immoral, as it involves the performance of an act which is contrary to moral feeling—killing; and is called forth only by greediness and the desire for tasty food.

The precise reason why abstinence from animal food will be the first act of fasting and of a moral life is admirably explained in the book, *The Ethics of Diet;* and not by one man only, but by all mankind in the persons of its best representatives during all the conscious life of humanity.

But why, if the wrongfulness—i.e. the immorality—of animal food was known to humanity so long ago, have people not yet come to acknowledge this law? will be asked by those who are accustomed to be led by public opinion rather than by reason.

The answer to this question is that the moral progress of humanity—which is the foundation of every other kind of progress—is always slow; but that the sign of true, not casual, progress is its uninterruptedness and its continual acceleration.

And the progress of vegetarianism is of this kind. That progress is expressed both in the words of the writers cited in the above-mentioned book and in the actual life of mankind, which from many causes is involuntarily passing more and more from carnivorous habits to vegetable food, and is also deliberately following the same path in a movement which shows evident strength, and which is growing larger and larger—viz. vegetarianism. That movement has during the last ten years advanced more and more rapidly. More and more books and periodicals on this subject appear every year; one meets more and more people who have given up meat; and abroad, especially in Germany, England, and America, the number of vegetarian hotels and restaurants increases year by year.

This movement should cause especial joy to those whose life lies in the effort to bring about the kingdom of God on earth, not because vegetarianism is in itself an important step towards that kingdom (all true steps are both important and unimportant), but because it is a sign that the aspiration of mankind towards moral perfection is serious and sincere, for it has taken the one unalterable order of succession natural to it, beginning with the first step.

One cannot fail to rejoice at this, as people could not fail to rejoice, who, after striving to reach the upper story of a house by trying vainly and at random to climb the walls from different points, should at last assemble at the first step of the staircase and crowd towards it, convinced that there can be no way up except by mounting this first step of the stairs.

[1892.]

The above essay was written as a Preface to a Russian translation of Hovard William's *The Ethics of Diet.*

CONCLUSION: *THE KINGDOM OF GOD IS WITHIN YOU*

Repent ye, for the Kingdom of Heaven is at hand.

1

I was just finishing this two years' work when on September 9th [1892] I had to go by rail to the district in Túla and Ryazán provinces where the peasants suffered from famine last year and are suffering still more this year. At one of the local stations we encountered a special train conveying troops commanded by the Governor of the province and armed with rifles, ammunition, and rods to flog and kill those starving peasants.

Despite the fact that corporal punishment was abolished by law thirty years ago, the flogging of men with rods in execution of decrees issued by the authorities has of late been practised more and more frequently in Russia.

I had heard of this and had even read in the papers about the terrible floggings of which Baránov, the Governor of Nízhni-Nóvgorod, seemed to boast, and of those that took place in Chernýgov, Tambóv, Sarátov, Astrakhán, and Orël. But I had never before happened to see men engaged on inflicting such punishments.

Now I saw with my own eyes kindly Russians imbued with the Christian spirit, travelling with rifles and rods to kill and torture their starving brothers.

The cause of their going was this:

On one of the estates of a wealthy landowner the peasants had grown (that is, had tended during its growth) a wood on land they held in common with the landowner. They had always made use of it, and therefore considered it theirs or at least as held in common, but the landowner, having appropriated that wood, began to cut down the trees. The peasants lodged a complaint. The judge in the first instance, unjustly (I say 'unjustly' on the word of the public prosecutor and the Governor, who should know) decided the case in favour of the landowner. All the higher courts, including the Senate, though they could see that the matter had been decided wrongly, confirmed this decision, and the wood was awarded to the landowner. He again began cutting down the trees, but the peasants, unable to believe that such an evident injustice could be done them by the higher authorities, did not submit to the decision and drove away the workmen sent to fell the trees, declaring that the wood belonged to them and that they would carry the matter to the Tsar but would not let the trees be cut down.

The matter was reported to Petersburg, and from there the Governor received instructions to carry into effect the decision of the court. He asked for troops. And now the soldiers, armed with rifles and bayonets and ball-cartridges as well as a supply of rods expressly prepared for the purpose and heaped up on one of the trucks, were on their way to carry out this decision of the higher authorities.

Decisions of the higher authorities are enforced by the murder and torture of men, or by threats of one or the other, according to whether resistance is offered or not.

In the first case, if the peasants offer resistance, the following course is pursued in Russia (and everywhere where a State organization and private property exist): the commanding officer makes a speech and demands submission. The excited crowd, usually deluded by their leaders, understanding nothing of what the representative of authority has said in official, bookish language, continue to be turbulent. Then the Governor announces that if they do not submit and disperse, he will be obliged to have recourse to force. And if the crowd does not then submit and disperse he gives orders to load rifles and fire over the people's heads. If they still do not disperse he gives the order to fire into their midst. The soldiers fire, and the killed and wounded people fall in the street. Then the crowd usually runs away, and the soldiers, at the Governor's command, seize those who seem to him to be the ringleaders and lead them away under escort.

After that they gather up the bloodstained, dying, maimed, killed and wounded men, sometimes with women and children also among them. The dead they bury and the maimed are sent to hospital. Those they consider to be ringleaders are taken to town and are there tried by a special military court. And if on their side any violence has been committed they are sentenced to be hanged. And then a gallows is set up and several defenceless people are throttled with cords, as has been done repeatedly in Russia and is and must be done wherever the social order is based on violence. This is what happens in cases of resistance.

In the second case, when the peasants submit, something strange and peculiarly Russian takes place. The Governor, having arrived on the scene of action, makes a speech to the people rebuking them for their lack of obedience, and either quarters troops on the houses of the village (where they sometimes remain for a month, their keep ruining the peasants), or contenting himself with threats graciously pardons the people and departs, or as most frequently happens announces that the ringleaders must be punished, and arbitrarily and without trial selects a certain number of men considered to be ringleaders and has them flogged in his presence.

To give an idea of how these things are done I will describe one that took place in Orël and was approved of by the higher authorities.

What happened in Orël was this. Here, just as in Túla province, a landowner wanted to deprive the peasants of some property, and the peasants opposed him in just the same way. The landowner, without the consent of the peasants,

wanted to keep the water in his mill-pond at so high a level
that it flooded their meadows. The peasants resisted and the
landowner laid a complaint before the district commissary,
who illegally (as was recognized later by the Court) decided the case in the landowner's favour and granted him
permission to raise the level of the water. The peasants were
indignant at this unjust decision and when the landowner
sent workmen to dam up the canal through which the water
flowed down, they sent their womenfolk to prevent its being
done. The women went to the dam, overturned the workmen's
carts, and drove the men away. The landowner lodged a
complaint against the women for thus taking the law into
their own hands, and the district commissary issued an order
to lock up one woman from every homestead in the village.
The order was not one that could well be executed for
there were several women in each homestead and it was
impossible to know which of them was to be arrested. Consequently the police did not carry it out. The landowner then
complained to the Governor of the inactivity of the police,
and the Governor without looking into the matter gave the
chief of rural police strict orders to carry out the commissary's decision. In obedience to his superior the rural chief of
police went to the village, and with a disregard for other
people characteristic of Russian officials, ordered his men to
seize one woman from each house. But since there was more
than one woman in each house and no way of knowing which
was to be incarcerated, altercations and resistance arose. In
spite of this the rural chief gave orders that some one woman
should be seized in each homestead and put into confinement. The peasants began to defend their wives and mothers
and would not give them up, and incidentally beat the rural
chief of police and his men. This was a fresh and terrible
crime—resistance to authority—and a report of the new offence was sent to the town. Then the Governor went by special
train to the scene of action (just as the Túla Governor was
now doing) taking a battalion of soldiers equipped with
rifles and rods, utilizing the telegraph and telephones and

railways, and taking also a learned doctor whose duty it was to supervise the hygiene of the floggings—fully personifying the Genghis Khan with telegraphs foretold by Herzen.

Near the house of the rural communal administration stood the soldiers, a detachment of gendarmes with revolvers slung on red cords, the village functionaries, and the accused. Around stood a crowd of a thousand or more. The Governor, having driven up, alighted from his carriage, made an introductory speech, and called for the culprits and a bench. The latter demand was not at first understood. But a gendarme the Governor always took about with him and whose business it was to attend to the preparation of the torture—which had been enacted in the province more than once before—explained that what was required was a bench for flogging. A bench was brought, the rods were produced, and the executioners were summoned. (They had been previously chosen from among horse-thieves of that village, as the soldiers had refused to perform the duty.)

When all was ready the commander ordered the first of the twelve men whom the landowner pointed out as specially culpable, to come forward. He was the father of a family, a man of forty, who had always stood up manfully for the rights of the community and therefore enjoyed the respect of all the villagers. He was led to the bench, stripped, and ordered to lie down.

The man attempted to beg for mercy, but seeing that this was useless, crossed himself and lay down. Two gendarmes rushed forward to hold him. The learned doctor stood by ready to render scientific medical assistance when necessary. The horse-thieves, having spat on their hands, swung their rods and began to flog. It happened, however, that the bench was too narrow, and it was difficult to keep on it the writhing man they were torturing. Then the Governor ordered them to bring another bench and to lay a plank across the two. And men, raising their hands to their caps and saying: 'Yes, your Excellency!' hastened to execute the order. Meanwhile the tortured man, half-naked, pale, and scowling, stood waiting, his eyes fixed on the ground, his teeth chattering and his naked legs trembling. When another bench had been brought they again laid him down, and the horse-thieves again began to flog him. The back, buttocks, thighs, and even the sides of the victim became more and more covered with weals and bruises, and at every blow came dull sounds he was unable to repress. From the crowd standing around arose the wails of the wives, mothers, children, and families of the tortured man and of all the others who had been picked out for punishment.

The miserable Governor, intoxicated by power, and to whom it appeared that he could not act otherwise, counted the blows, bending his fingers as he did so, and smoked cigarettes incessantly—several officious persons hastening to hand him a lighted match at every opportunity. When more than fifty strokes had been given, the peasant ceased to cry out or writhe, and the doctor—educated in a crown establishment to serve his Tsar and his fatherland by his scientific knowledge—went up to the victim, felt his pulse, listened to his heart, and informed the representative of authority that the man had lost consciousness and that, according to the data of science, it might endanger his life to continue the punishment. But the miserable Governor, now completely intoxicated by the sight of blood, ordered them to continue, and the torture continued up to seventy strokes—the number that for some reason seemed necessary to the Governor. When the seventieth stroke had been given, he said: 'Enough! Next one!' And the mutilated victim with his swollen back was carried away in a swoon and another was led up. The sobs and groans of the crowd grew louder, but the representative of the State continued the torture.

They flogged each of the twelve victims in the same way. Each of them received seventy strokes, and each of them begged for mercy, shrieked, and groaned. The sobs and groans of the crowd of women grew louder and more heart-rending, and the men's faces became more and more gloomy. But they were surrounded by troops, and the torture did not cease till it had reached the full measure decided on by the caprice of the miserable, half-intoxicated, and deluded creature they called the Governor.

The officials, officers, and soldiers were not merely present, but by their presence shared in this State action and prevented its being interfered with by the crowd.

When I asked a certain Governor why such tortures were inflicted on people who had already submitted and when troops were already in the village, he replied, with the imposing air of one familiar with all the subtleties of statecraft, that it was done because experience proves that if the peasants are not subjected to torture they soon resist the orders of the authorities again, but that the torture of a few ensures respect for the authorities' orders for ever.

So now the Governor of Túla accompanied by officials, officers, and soldiers, was going to perpetrate an act of this kind! The decision of the highest authority was to be carried out in just the same way by murder or torture. And this decision decreed that a young landowner who had an income of a hundred thousand rubles a year, was to get three thousand rubles more, for timber he had taken by fraud from a whole commune of peasants who were dying of cold and hunger. He might squander that money in two or three weeks in the saloons of Moscow, Petersburg, or Paris.

That was the business the men I met were engaged on.

After my thoughts had been fixed for two years in one and the same direction, fate seemed to have brought me for the first time in my life expressly in contact with an occurrence which plainly showed in practise what had long been clear to me in theory, namely, that the whole order of our lives rests not on principles of jurisprudence (as people occupying advantageous positions are pleased to imagine) but on the simplest, coarsest violence—on the murder and torture of men.

Those who own large estates and fortunes, or who receive large incomes drawn from working people who go short even of necessities; and those who, like tradesmen, doctors, artists, clerks, scientists, cooks, writers, valets, and lawyers, live by serving those rich people, like to believe that the advantages they enjoy result not from violence, but from an absolutely free and proper exchange of services. They like to believe that their advantages—far from being gained by beatings and murders such as took place in Orël and in many other parts of Russia this summer, and that occur continually all over Europe and America—have no kind of connexion with such violence. They like to believe that their privileges exist of themselves, and result from voluntary agreement among people, and that the violence enacted also exists of itself, and results from some general, higher juridical, political, or economic laws. They try not to see that they enjoy their advantages as a result of the very thing which forces the peasants who have tended the wood and are in great need of the timber to yield it up to a wealthy landowner, who took no part in tending it during its growth and is in no need of it—that is, the knowledge that if they do not give it up they will be flogged or killed.

Yet it is clear that the mill in Orël was able to yield its owner a larger profit, and that the wood planted by the peasants became the property of the landowner, only in consequence of floggings and murders or the threat of them. And in the same way it should be clear that all the other exceptional rights the rich enjoy, depriving the poor of necessities, rest on the same basis. If peasants who need land to maintain their families may not plough the land around their homes, but that land, to an extent sufficient to feed a thousand families, is at the disposal of a single man—a Russian, English, Austrian or any other great landowner, who never works on it or cultivates it himself, and if a merchant who has bought grain from the workers when they were in need can keep it safely in his barns amid starving people, and sell it at three times its cost to the same cultivators from whom he bought it—then this, too, rests on the same basis. And if no one may buy cheap goods from beyond a certain conventional line called a frontier without paying customs duties to men who had no share in their production, and if people are obliged to give up their last cow for taxes which the

Government distributes among its officials and spends on the maintenance of soldiers who may have to kill those very tax-payers—it would seem obvious that this, too, has certainly not come about because of any abstract rights, but because of the thing that happened in Orël and may now happen in the province of Túla, the thing that periodically happens in one form or another the world over, wherever there is a governmental organization and wherever there are rich and poor.

As however torture and murder are not employed in all cases of oppression, those who enjoy the exceptional advantages of the ruling classes assure themselves and others that their privileges are not based on torture and murder but on some mysterious general causes, abstract rights, and so on. Yet it would seem clear that if men consider it unjust (as all the working classes now consider it) to yield the chief part of the produce of their labour to a capitalist or landowner, or to pay taxes knowing that a bad use is made of them, they do these things primarily not from recognition of some abstract rights of which they have never heard, but simply because they know that they will be beaten or killed if they refuse to do them.

And if there is no need to imprison, beat, or kill men when the landowners collect rent, or a man in need of corn pays a triple price to a swindling dealer, or a factory-hand puts up with pay that is proportionately only half of what his employer takes, or when a poor man pays his last ruble in customs-dues and taxes—this is only because so many men have been beaten and killed for trying to resist what was demanded of them, that the others firmly remember it.

A trained tiger in a cage who does not eat the meat put under his nose and who jumps over a stick at the word of command, does this not because he wishes to, but because he remembers the red-hot irons or the hunger from which he suffered every time he did not obey. And in the same way men who submit to what is disadvantageous and even ruinous to them and that they consider unjust, do so because they remember what happened to them when they resisted.

But those who profit by the privileges resulting from previous violence often forget, and are pleased to forget, how those advantages were obtained. Yet we need only think of history—not the history of the triumphs of various dynasties and rulers—but real history, the history of the oppression of the majority by a small minority—to see that the advantages of the rich over the poor have originated from nothing but rods, prisons, convict-settlements, and murder.[1]

One need but consider the unceasing and persistent struggle to increase material prosperity that guides everybody in our times, to be convinced that the advantages of the rich over the poor could not and cannot be maintained by anything but violence.

There may be cases where oppressions, beatings, prisons, and executions, are not inflicted to secure the advantages of the propertied classes (though such cases are rare). But one may confidently say that in our society (where for every well-to-do man living in comfort there are ten who are exhausted by labour, envious, covetous, and whose whole families are often suffering) all the advantages of the rich, all their luxuries and superfluities, all that is beyond what an average workman possesses, is obtained and maintained by tortures, imprisonments, and executions.

2

The special train I met on September 9th, going with soldiers, rifles, ball-cartridges, and rods, to secure to the rich landowner the small wood he did not need, and which he had taken from hungry peasants who needed it very badly, showed in a striking way to what a degree men have developed a capacity to commit deeds contrary to their convictions without seeing that they are doing so.

The special train I encountered consisted of one first-class

---

[1] This indictment could to-day be illustrated by reference to the behaviour of the rulers to the ruled in the U.S.S.R. or in Germany, quite as strikingly as by the references Tolstóy was able to use.— A. M.

carriage for the Governor, officials, and officers, and several luggage-vans crowded with soldiers.

The brisk young soldiers in their clean new uniforms were standing about in groups, or sitting with their legs dangling from the wide-open doors of the trucks. Some were smoking, others nudging one another, joking, grinning, and laughing. Others were cracking sunflower seeds, self-confidently spitting out the husks. Some of them ran along the platform to the water-butt for a drink, and when they met an officer, slackened their pace and made their stupid gesture of salute, raising their hands to their foreheads with serious faces as if they were doing something not only reasonable but very important. They kept their eyes on the officer till they had passed him, and then ran on still more merrily, stamping along the planks of the platform, laughing and chattering, as is natural to healthy, good-natured young fellows travelling from one place to another in lively company.

They went to the murder of their hungry fathers and grandfathers just as if they were going to some gay, or at any rate quite ordinary, business.

A similar impression was produced by the smart officials and officers scattered about the platform and in the first-class refreshment-room. At a table set out with bottles sat the Governor, the chief of the whole expedition, in a semi-military uniform, eating something and speaking calmly about the weather with some acquaintance he had met, as though his errand were so simple and ordinary that it could not ruffle his composure or interfere with his interest in the change of the weather.

At a little distance from the table and not eating anything sat a chief of gendarmes whose impenetrable face wore an air of boredom, as though he were weary of the tedious formality that had to be enacted. On all sides officers in their handsome gold-braided uniforms moved about and chatted. One, sitting at the table, was finishing a bottle of beer; another, standing at the buffet, munched a savoury patty, brushing the crumbs from the breast of his uniform and with a self-confident air throwing down a coin; another, dragging his feet, sauntered in front of the carriages of our train, staring at the women.

All these men, on their way to murder or torture the hungry and defenceless creatures who provided them with sustenance, had an air of being firmly convinced that they were doing their duty. They were even rather proud of themselves—'swaggering' about it.

How is this?

All these men are within half-an-hour's journey of the place where—in order to ensure that a rich young man should have three thousand rubles he had taken from a whole commune of famishing peasants—they may be obliged, as in Orël, to commit the most terrible things that can be conceived, to murder or torture innocent beings, their fellow men. And they are quite serene as they approach the place where this is to be done and the time draws near to begin it.

To say that these men—all these officials, officers, and soldiers—do not know what is before them and what they are going for, is impossible, for they have prepared for it. The Governor must have given instructions, and the officials must have purchased those birch switches, bargained for them, and entered the item in their accounts. The officers must have received, issued, and executed, the orders about the ball-cartridges. They all know that they are going to torture, perhaps to kill, their brother men who are exhausted by hunger, and that they must set to work on it perhaps within an hour.

To say, as is usually said and as they themselves repeat, that they do this from conviction of the necessity of maintaining the State system, would be mistaken. For these people have hardly ever even thought about the State system and its necessity, they cannot possibly be convinced that the act they are taking part in will tend to support, and not to destroy, the State, and in practice most if not all of them, far from sacrificing their tranquillity or pleasure to support the State, never miss an opportunity of furthering their own interest at its expense. So they are not moved by belief in the abstract principle of the State.

What then?

You see, I know all these men. If I do not know each of them personally I know their characters pretty well, their past, and their way of thinking. They all have had mothers, and some of them have wives and children. They are for the most part mild, kindly, even tender-hearted men who hate all cruelty. Not to speak of the killing of men, many of them would not even kill or torture an animal. Moreover all of them profess Christianity, and regard the use of violence against defenceless people as an abject and abominable action. Not one of them in ordinary life would be capable, for his own petty personal profit, of doing a one-hundredth part of what the Orël Governor did. Each one of them would be insulted at the suggestion that he was capable of anything of the kind in private life.

And yet here they are within half-an-hour's journey of the place where they may unavoidably be forced to do it.

What does it mean?

How could, not only these men travelling by this train and prepared to murder and torture, but those who began the whole business: the landowner, his steward, the judges, and those in Petersburg who gave the order and are responsible for it—the minister, and the Tsar, who are also good men professing Christianity—how could they devise and prescribe such a plan, knowing the consequences? How could the spectators even who took no part in the affair—men who are indignant at any case of violence in private life—how could they allow such a horrible deed to be perpetrated? How was it they did not rise in indignation and stand across the road crying out: 'No, we won't allow you to kill and flog starving men because they won't let their last possessions be taken from them by fraud!'? But not only did no one do that; on the contrary the majority, even the initiators of the affair (the steward, the landowner, the judges, and those who took part in making the peasants yield and arranged it

—the Governor, the minister, and the Emperor) are perfectly tranquil and do not even feel a prick of conscience.
And all these men who are travelling by train to perform
this crime are apparently equally tranquil.

The spectators it seemed were quite unmoved, and for the
most part looked on with sympathy rather than with disapproval at all those who were preparing to do this infamous
thing. In the carriage with me was a lumber-dealer of peasant
origin, and he plainly and openly expressed sympathy with
the treatment that awaited the peasants: 'They must not
disobey the authorities,' said he. 'That's what the authorities
are for. Wait a bit and they'll have their fleas driven from
them! They'll learn not to riot, no fear! They're getting their
deserts!'

Why is this?

It is impossible to say that all these people—those who
instigated and participated in and tolerated this affair—
were such wretches that for a salary, for profit, or from fear
of punishment, they did an action contrary to their convictions, knowing all the loathsomeness of what they were doing.
All of them in certain circumstances are capable of standing
up for their convictions. Not one of those officials would steal
a purse, read another man's letter, or put up with an affront
without demanding satisfaction. Not one of those officers
would allow himself to cheat at cards, omit to pay a card
debt, betray a comrade, run away from the field of battle,
or abandon his flag. Not one of these soldiers would spit
out the holy sacrament, or even eat meat on Good Friday.
All these men are ready to face any kind of privation, suffering, and danger, rather than consent to do what they consider wrong. And therefore they have the strength to resist
doing what is against their principles.

It is still more impossible to say that all these men are such
brutes that it is not painful for them to do such deeds, but
natural. One need only talk to them to see that they all—
landowner, judges, minister, Emperor, Governor, officers, and
soldiers—in the depth of their souls not only disapprove of

such things, but suffer from the consciousness of their own participation in them when they are reminded of what they imply.

They only try not to think about it.

One need only talk to any of those who are taking part in the affair—from the landowner to the least of the gendarmes or soldiers—to see that in the depths of their souls they all know that it is a wicked thing it would be better to have nothing to do with, and that they suffer on this account.

A lady of liberal tendencies who was travelling in the same train with us, seeing the Governor and the officers in the first-class refreshment-room and learning the object of the expedition, began to abuse the existing order of things, intentionally raising her voice so that the men who were taking part in this affair should hear her. Everyone felt awkward. No one knew where to look. No one contradicted her, however. They assumed an air of not condescending to answer such empty remarks. But it was evident by their faces and their averted eyes that they all felt ashamed. I noticed that it was the same with the soldiers. They, too, knew that what they were being sent to do was a shameful thing, but they did not want to think about it.

When the timber-merchant (and he it seemed to me insincerely and only to show his culture) began to speak of the necessity of such measures, the soldiers who heard him all turned away scowling and pretended not to hear.

All these men, both those who, like the landowner, his steward, the minister, and the Emperor, were responsible for this act, as well as those who were now to execute it, and even those who were mere spectators, knew that it was a bad business and were ashamed of their part in it.

Why then did they do it? Why are they still doing it? And why do they allow it to be done?

Ask those who, like the landowner, started the business, and those who, like the judges, gave a decision which though legal in form was evidently unjust, and those who decreed the execution of the decision, and those who, like the soldiers, gendarmes, and peasants, themselves carry it out and flog and

kill their brothers—and they who have devised, abetted, executed, or tolerated these crimes will all say essentially one
and the same thing.

Those in authority who have initiated and abetted and directed the affair will say that they act as they do because
such things are necessary for the maintenance of the existing
order and the maintenance of the existing order is necessary
for the welfare of the country, for humanity, and for the possibility of social existence and human progress.

Men of the lower orders—the peasants and soldiers who
have to execute this violence with their own hands—will say
that they do so because it is ordered by the higher authorities and the higher authorities know what they are doing.
And it appears to them an indubitable truth that the right
people constitute authority, and that they know what they
are doing. If they admit the possibility of mistakes or errors
they do so only in regard to officials of lower rank. The highest
power, on whom everything depends, seems to them unquestionably infallible.

Both those in authority and their subordinates, though they
explain the motives of their conduct differently, agree that
they act as they do because the existing order is just the order
that must and should exist at the present time, and that to
support it is therefore each man's sacred duty.

On this acceptance of the necessity and therefore the immutability of the existing order rests also the argument by
which those who take part in governmental violence always
justify themselves. They say that as the existing order is immutable, the refusal of some one individual to fulfil the duties
laid upon him has no real influence on things, but only means
that his place will be taken by someone else who may do
worse than he; that is, may exercise more cruelty and do more
harm to the victims.

It is this conviction that the existing order is a necessary
and therefore immutable order, to support which is the sacred duty of every man, that makes it possible for good
men, of high principles in private life, to take part with more
or less untroubled conscience in affairs such as that commit-

ted in Orël, and that which the men in the Túla train were going to perpetrate.

But on what is this conviction based?

It is understandable that a landowner should find it agreeable to believe that the existing order is necessary and immutable, because this existing order secures him the income he receives from his hundreds and thousands of acres, thanks to which he leads his customary idle and luxurious life.

It is also understandable that the judge readily believes in the necessity of that order as a result of which he receives fifty times as much as the most industrious labourer earns. And the same applies to the judges of the higher Court who receive a salary of six thousand rubles or more, and to all the higher officials. Only under the existing order can Governors, public prosecutors, senators, and members of various councils, receive this salary of several thousand rubles a year without which they and their families would immediately perish, since except in those particular posts they could not, with their capacity, industry, and knowledge, get a one-thousandth part of that sum. The minister, the Emperor, and every one of the higher authorities, is in the same position; only with this difference, that the higher and more exceptional their position the more necessary it is for them to believe that the existing order of things is the only possible order. For without it they would not only be unable to get an equally good position but would have to stand much lower than the rest of mankind. A man who voluntarily enters the police force at a wage of ten rubles a month, which he could easily earn in any other position, stands in little need of the preservation of the existing régime, and can therefore get along without believing in its immutability. But a king or an emperor, receiving millions in that office and knowing that around him there are thousands of people who would like to thrust him aside and take his place, knowing also that in no other position would he receive such an income or such honours, knowing even (in the majority of cases of more or less despotic rule) that if he is thrown out he will be tried for all his abuse of power—a king or emperor cannot but believe in the immutability and sanctity of the existing order. The higher the position a man occupies, the more advantageous and therefore the more unstable it is, and the more terrible and dangerous his fall, the more does such a man believe in the immutability of the existing order, and therefore for the maintenance of that order (and not as it were for himself) he is able to perpetrate most cruel and wicked deeds with a tranquil conscience.

This is the case with all those—from the lowest police-officers to the highest authorities—who occupy more advantageous positions than they could hold but for the existence of the present régime. All these people believe more or less in the immutability of the existing order, chiefly because it is advantageous for them.

But what makes the peasants and soldiers (who stand on the lowest rung of the ladder and can have no advantage from the present régime, under which indeed they are in a position of the utmost subjection and humiliation) believe that the existing order is the one that ought to exist and which they ought to support even by doing evil deeds contrary to their conscience?

What makes these men hold the false opinion that the existing order is immutable and that they must therefore support it, when that order is obviously only immutable because they support it?

What causes these men (taken only yesterday from the plough and dressed in these indecorous and unseemly clothes with light blue collars and gilt buttons) to go with guns and sabres to murder their famishing fathers and brothers? They gain no advantage by so doing, nor have they any desirable position to lose, for their present position is worse than that from which they were taken.

People of the higher classes: kings, landowners, merchants, judges, senators, governors, ministers and officers, taking part in such affairs support the existing order because it is advantageous for them. Moreover these (in many cases good and kindly) people are enabled to take part in such affairs by the fact that their participation is limited to instigations, decisions, and the issuing of orders. They do not themselves do what they instigate, decide on, or order to be done. For the most part they do not even see how the terrible deeds they have instigated and authorized are carried out.

But the unfortunate people of the lower orders who gain no advantage from the existing régime, being on the contrary held in the greatest contempt as a result of it, tear people from their families, bind them, confine them in prisons, drive them into exile, keep guard on them, and shoot them with their own hands for the maintenance of that order. Why do they do it?

What forces them to believe that the existing order is immutable and should be maintained?

All actual physical violence rests on these men who beat, bind, imprison, and kill, with their own hands. If it were not for them—these soldiers and policemen and armed men in general, ready to do violence and to kill all whom they are ordered to—not one of those who sign sentences of death, imprisonment, and exile for life, would ever hang, imprison, or torture a one-thousandth part of those whom they now, quietly sitting at their desks, order to be hanged or tortured in all sorts of ways simply because they do not see it and it is done not by them but by servile tools somewhere far off.

All the injustices and cruelties customary in present-day life have become habitual only because there are men always ready to carry out these injustices and cruelties. If it were not for them there would not only be no one to wreak violence on those immense masses of oppressed people, but those who issue the orders would never venture to do so, and would not even dare to dream of the sentences they now confidently pass.

Were it not for these men ready to torture or kill anyone they are commanded to, no one would dare to claim what is confidently claimed by all the non-working landowners, namely that land surrounded by men who are suffering for lack of land, is the property of a man who does not work on it, or that stores of grain collected by trickery ought to be preserved untouched in the midst of a population dying of hunger, because the merchant wants to make a profit. But for the existence of these people, ready at the will of the authorities to torture and kill anyone they are told to, it could never enter the head of a landowner to deprive the peasants of a wood they had grown, or of the officials to consider it proper to receive salaries taken from the famishing people for oppressing them, not to mention executing, imprisoning, or evicting people for exposing falsehood and preaching the truth.[2] In fact all this is demanded and done only because the authorities are all fully convinced that they have always at hand servile people ready to carry out all their demands by means of tortures and killings.

Only because of that are such deeds committed as are perpetrated by all tyrants, from Napoleon to the most insignificant of company commanders who fires on a crowd. The power supplied by the obedient people standing behind them, ready to carry out whatever order may be given, stupefies them. All power therefore depends on those who with their own hands execute the deeds of violence—that is, on the soldiers and police, chiefly the soldiers, for the police can only do their work because they have the army behind them.

What brings these good people—obliged to do all these terrible things with their own hands and reaping no advantage from it—to the amazing delusion that the existing unprofitable, ruinous order, tormenting to them as it is, is the very order that ought to exist?

Who has given them this amazing delusion?

They have not persuaded themselves that they ought to do what is tormenting, disadvantageous, and ruinous for them and their whole class (constituting nine-tenths of the population) and is also contrary to their conscience.

I have often asked different soldiers: 'How can you kill people when the law of God says "Thou shalt not kill"?', and my question has always caused the man uneasiness and confusion by reminding him of what he would like to forget. He

---

[2] This last allusion refers to the religious persecutions of nonconformist peasants, which engaged much of Tolstóy's attention at that time and subsequently.—A. M.

knew that there is an obligatory law of God: 'Thou shalt not kill', he knew too that there is an obligatory military service, but he had never considered the contradiction between the two. The drift of the timid replies I received to that question was always approximately this: that to kill in war and to execute criminals on the order of the Government is not included in the general prohibition of murder. When I said that this limitation is not made in the law of God, and reminded them of the teaching of brotherhood, forgiveness of injuries, and love—which cannot be reconciled with killing—they usually agreed, but in their turn set me a question. 'Why is it', they asked, 'that the Government' (which according to their precepts cannot do wrong) 'sends the army to war when necessary, and orders the execution of offenders?' When I replied that the Government does wrong when it acts so, they were thrown into still greater confusion and either broke off the conversation or grew angry with me.

'They must have found such a law, and I expect the bishops know better than we do,' one of them said to me. And by saying this he evidently set his mind at rest and felt fully convinced that his spiritual guides had discovered the law under which his forefathers had to serve the Tsars and the Tsars' heirs and which compelled him and millions of other men to serve. He felt that what I had said to him was a jest—some sort of subtle conundrum or hoax.

Everyone in our Christian world is firmly convinced by tradition, by revelation, and by the irrefutable voice of conscience, that murder is one of the most fearful crimes a man can commit, as the Gospel tells us; and that the sin of murder cannot be limited to certain people—so that it should be a sin for some people to murder but not a sin for others to do so. Everyone knows that if murder is a sin, it is always a sin whoever may be murdered, just as it is with the sins of adultery, robbery, or anything else. Yet at the same time, from their childhood and youth up, people see that murder is not only permitted but even blessed by those whom they are accustomed to regard as their spiritual guides, appointed by God. They see their civil leaders, too, organizing murder with assurance, carrying instruments of murder themselves and being proud of them, and in the name of the law of the country, and even of God, demanding participation in murder from everybody. Men see that there is some contradiction here, but being unable to unravel it involuntarily assume that this contradiction is only the result of their own ignorance. The very grossness and obviousness of the contradiction confirms them in this conviction.

They cannot imagine that the learned men who instruct them could so confidently preach two propositions so obviously contradictory as the law of Christ and murder. An unperverted child or youth cannot imagine that those who stand so high in his estimation, and whom he regards as holy and learned men, could mislead him so shamefully for any purpose whatever. But that is just what has been and is constantly being done. It is done, first, by instilling by example and by direct instruction from childhood to old age into all the working people who have not time to examine moral and religious questions themselves, that torture and murder are compatible with Christianity, and that for certain purposes of State they are not only allowable but even necessary; and, secondly, by instilling into certain people—enlisted, conscripted, or hired—that the perpetration of torture and murder with their own hands is a sacred duty, and even a glorious exploit worthy of praise and reward.

The general deception, diffused among all the people and stated in all the catechisms and the books which nowadays replace them in the compulsory education of children, is this: that violence (that is, torture, imprisonments, and executions, as well as murder in civil or foreign war for the maintenance and defence of the existing government—whatever it may be —an autocracy, a monarchy, a convention, a consulate, an empire of the First or Third Napoleon or of a Boulanger, a constitutional monarchy, a commune, or a republic) is absolutely lawful and does not conflict either with morality or with Christianity.

This is stated in all catechisms and books used in schools. And men are so persuaded of it that they grow up, live, and die in that conviction without ever doubting it.

That is one form of deception, a general deception instilled into everyone. But there is another special deception practised on the soldiers and police (selected by one means or another) who carry out the tortures and murders necessary for the maintenance and defence of the existing order.

The military regulations all contain, in these or other words, what the Russian military code says:

(Article 87) 'To fulfil accurately and unquestioningly the orders of a superior officer. To obey his order precisely, without considering whether it is good or not, or whether it is possible to execute it. The superior officer himself answers for the consequences of the orders he gives.'

(Article 88) 'The subordinate must always obey the orders of his superior officer except when he sees clearly that by executing them he . . .' (one naturally expects the following words to be '. . . when he sees clearly that by executing them he will violate the law of God', but nothing of the kind!) '. . . when he sees clearly that by executing them he would violate his oath of fidelity and allegiance to the Emperor.'

It says that a man who is a soldier can and should obey *all* his superiors' orders without exception. And as for a soldier these consist chiefly of murder, it follows that he should break all laws, human and divine, but not his fidelity and allegiance to whoever happens at the given moment to be in possession of power.

So it is expressed in the Russian military instructions, and in just the same way, though in different words, it is said in all manuals of military instructions. Nor can it be otherwise, for the whole power of the army and the State is based essentially on that deception, which releases men from their duty to God and their conscience and substitutes the duty of obedience to the officer who happens to be in command.

On that is founded the terrible assurance of the lower classes that the existing régime, which is pernicious for them, is the régime which ought to exist and which they therefore should support even by torture and murder.

That conviction is based on a conscious deception practised on them by the higher orders.

Nor can it be otherwise. To compel the lower classes, which are the most numerous, to ill-treat themselves by committing actions opposed to their conscience it was necessary to deceive them. And that is what has been done.

A few days ago I once more saw this shameless deception being openly practised, and once more marvelled at the unopposed and impudent way in which it was done.

Early in November, as I was passing through Túla, I once again saw the familiar sight of a dense crowd of people at the gates of the County Council Office, and heard both drunken shouts and the pitiful wailing of mothers and wives. This was a levy of recruits.

As always happens, I could not pass by that spectacle. It drew me to itself as by some evil spell. I again went among the crowd, stood there, looked about, inquired, and was once again amazed at the way in which this hideous crime is perpetrated unopposed and in broad daylight in the midst of a large town.

As in former years on November 1st the village elders in all the hamlets and villages of the hundred-millions of Russians had called up the young men entered on their lists (often including sons of their own) and had taken them to town.

On the road the recruits had drunk all the time and the elders had not hindered them, feeling that to go on such an insane errand, abandoning their wives and mothers and renouncing all that is sacred only to become senseless instruments of murder, would be too agonizing if they did not stupefy themselves with drink.

And so they had driven along, drinking, swearing, singing, fighting, and maiming themselves. They had spent the night in taverns. In the morning they had had another nip and were now gathered at the County Council Office.

Some of them, in new sheepskin coats, with knitted scarves round their necks and with moist, drunken eyes, kept up

wild cries of bravado, while some awaited their turn quietly
and despondently, squeezing around the gates among the
weeping mothers and wives. (I happened to be there on the
day of the actual enrolment—that is, the examination of those
taken to the office.) Others meanwhile were crowding into
the waiting-room.

In the office itself work is proceeding busily. The door is
opened and the guard calls up Peter Sídorov. Peter Sídorov
starts, crosses himself, and goes into a small room with a glass
door where the conscripts have to undress. A comrade of his,
who has just been passed for service and has come out of the
examination room naked, is hurriedly dressing with chattering
teeth. Peter Sídorov has already heard and sees by his face
that his comrade has been taken. He wants to question him,
but is hurried on and ordered to undress. He throws off his
sheepskin coat, draws the long boot from each leg with the
other foot, takes off his waistcoat and draws his shirt over his
head, and naked, with protruding ribs, trembling all over
and exhaling an odour of spirits, tobacco, and sweat, he goes
barefoot into the revision office not knowing what to do with
his brawny bare arms.

In the revision office, straight in front of him in a great gold
frame hangs a portrait of the Tsar in a uniform with a sash. In
the corner is a small picture of Christ in a shirt and crown of
thorns. In the middle of the room is a table covered with
green cloth on which papers are spread, and there is also a
three-cornered ornament surmounted by an eagle, called a
'mirror of justice'. Around the room sit the recruiting officers,
looking quite confident and tranquil. One is smoking a cigarette, another turns over the papers. As soon as Sídorov
comes in a guard goes up to him and places him under the
measuring scale, pushing up his chin and putting his feet
straight. The man with a cigarette comes up—this is the doctor—not looking at the recruit's face but somewhere beyond
it. He feels Sídorov's body with an air of disgust, measures
him, pinches him, and orders the guard to make the man
open his mouth. He tells him to breathe and to say something.
Someone notes something down. At last, without having once

looked him in the face, the doctor says: 'He'll do. Next one!' and with a weary air re-seats himself at the table. Again the soldiers hustle and hurry the young fellow. He somehow hurriedly pulls on his shirt, fumbling for the sleeves, pulls on his breeches, wraps his leg-bands round his legs, puts on his boots, looks for his scarf and cap, and catches up his sheepskin coat under his arm. And they lead him into the main hall, where he is fenced off by a bench. Behind that bench those who have been conscripted are waiting. Another village lad like himself, but from a distant province, who is already a soldier with a rifle and a sharp fixed bayonet, stands guard over him ready to stab him should he attempt to run away.

Meanwhile the crowd of fathers, mothers, and wives, jostled by the police, press together at the doors to learn who has been taken and who rejected. One lad who has been turned down comes out and announces that Petrúka has been taken, and Petrúka's young wife, for whom the word 'taken' means separation for four or five years and the dissolute life of a soldier's wife in service as a cook, screams aloud.

But now along the street drives a man with long hair and in a peculiar dress distinguishing him from everybody else, and he gets down from his dróshky and goes up to the County Council Office. The police clear a path for him through the crowd. The reverend Father has come to administer the oath. And now this 'father', who has been persuaded that he is a special and exceptional servant of Christ, and who in most cases is blind to the deception under which he labours, goes into the hall where the conscripts are waiting. He puts on a garment of gold brocade, releases his long hair from under it, opens the Gospel (in which it is forbidden to swear), takes the cross (the cross on which Christ was crucified because he would not do what this pseudo-servant of his is telling men to do) and places them on a lectern, and all those unhappy, defenceless, and deluded lads repeat after him the falsehood which he from habit pronounces so boldly.

He reads and they repeat: 'I promise and swear by Almighty God, upon His holy Gospel', &c., 'to defend', &c.— that is, to murder all those I am ordered to, and to do everything I am ordered to do by men I know nothing of and to whom I am only necessary that I may commit the evil deeds by which they are kept in their position and that oppress my brothers. All the conscripts senselessly repeat these ferocious words, and then the so-called 'father' drives away with a sense of having done his duty efficiently and conscientiously. And all these deluded lads consider that those nonsensical and to them unintelligible words which they have just uttered have freed them from their duties as men for the whole period of their service and bound them by new and more obligatory duties as soldiers.

And this crime is committed publicly, and no one cries out to the deceivers and the deceived: 'Bethink yourselves, and go away! This is a most odious and cunning lie and destroys not only your bodies but also your souls.'

No one does that. On the contrary, when all the recruits have been enrolled and it is necessary to let them out again, the military commander (as though to mock them) goes into the hall where the deceived and drunken lads are confined, and with a self-confidently majestic manner shouts to them in a bold military voice: 'Your health, lads! I congratulate you on entering the Tsar's service.' And the poor fellows (someone has already instructed them) mutter indistinctly in half-tipsy voices something to the effect that they, too, are glad.

Meanwhile the crowd of fathers, mothers, and wives, stand outside waiting; the women with tearful eyes fixed on the door. And now it opens and the conscripts come out staggering and swaggering, Petrúka and Vanúkha and Makár, trying not to look at their own folk and not to see them. The wailing of mothers and wives is heard. Some embrace each other and weep, others try to look brave, others again comfort one another.

The mothers and wives lament and wail aloud, knowing that for three or four years they will, like orphans, remain without their breadwinners. The fathers say little. They regretfully click their tongues and sigh, knowing that they will see no more the helpers they have reared and trained, who will come back not the quiet hard-working labourers they were before, but for the most part depraved and swaggering soldiers unaccustomed to a simple life.

And now all the crowd get into their sledges and move off down the street to the inns and taverns. And songs, sobbing, drunken shouts, the wailing laments of mothers and wives, sounds of accordions, and words of abuse are heard, interrupting one another and growing louder. They all make their way to the pot-houses and taverns which yield revenue to the government, and are overcome by drunkenness that stifles their sense of the wrong which is being done to them.

For two or three weeks they go on living at home, and for the most part make holiday—that is, drink.

On the appointed day they are assembled, driven like cattle to one place, and begin to drill and learn soldierly ways. This is taught them by men like themselves, but deceived and brutalized two or three years earlier. The methods of instruction are: deception, stupefaction, blows, and vódka. Before a year passes, these good, intelligent, healthy-minded lads will become brutalized beings just like their instructors.

'And suppose your own father were a prisoner and he tried to run away?' I asked a young soldier.

'I should stab him with my bayonet,' he replied in a peculiar, unintelligent, soldierly voice. 'And if he made off I should have to shoot him,' he added, evidently proud of knowing what must be done if his father tried to escape.

And when a kindly young man has been brought to this condition, lower than a brute, he is just what is needed by those who use him as an instrument of violence. He is then ready. The man has been destroyed, and a new instrument of violence has been produced.

And all this is done each year, every autumn, everywhere all over Russia in broad daylight and in large towns where all may see it; and the deception is so artful, so cunning, that though everyone sees it and in the depth of his soul knows all its horror and all its terrible consequences, he cannot free himself from it.

3

When a man's eyes are opened to this awful deception perpetrated on men, he is astonished that preachers of the Christian religion and of morality, instructors of youth, or even the good-hearted intelligent parents to be found everywhere, can teach any kind of morality in a society in which it is openly admitted by all the churches and governments that torture and murder form a necessary condition of the life of the community and that there must always be special men prepared to kill their fellows, and that any one of us may have to become such a man.

How can children, youths, and people in general, be taught any kind of morality (to say nothing of enlightening them in the spirit of Christianity) side by side with the doctrine that murder is necessary for the public (and consequently our own) welfare, and is therefore legitimate; and that there are people—of whom any one of us may have to be one—whose duty it is to torture and murder their neighbours and commit all kinds of crime at the will of those who possess power? If men may and should torture, kill, and commit every sort of crime at the will of those in power, there is and can be no moral law, but only a recognition of the right of the strong. And so it is. In reality that is the doctrine, theoretically justified for some men by the theory of the struggle for existence, which prevails in our society.

Indeed what moral teaching can there be under which murder, for any purpose whatever, can be sanctioned? It is as impossible as a theory of mathematics which admits the possibility of 2 being equal to 3.

There may be a semblance of mathematics which admits that 2 equals 3, but there can be no real mathematical knowledge. There may also be a semblance of morality which admits of murder in the form of executions, wars, or self-defence, but there can be no real morality. The recognition of the sanctity of the life of every man is the first and only basis of all morality.

The doctrine of an eye for an eye, a tooth for a tooth, and a life for a life, was abrogated by Chrstianity because that teaching is a justification of immorality and has no real meaning, but is a mere semblance of equity. Life is a quantity having neither weight nor measure and incommensurable with any other, so that the destruction of one life for another can have no sense. Besides, every social law aims at the amelioration of man's life, and how can the destruction of one man's life ameliorate the life of another? The destruction of life is not an act ameliorating life, but a suicidal act.

To destroy another life for the sake of justice, is as though a man having lost one hand should seek to remedy that misfortune by cutting off the other.

To say nothing of the sin of deluding men into regarding the most terrible crime as their duty, of the terrible sin of employing the name and authority of Christ to sanction what he most condemned (as is done in the administration of the oath of allegiance), or the offence by means of which they destroy not only the bodies but the souls of 'these little ones' —not to speak of all that, how can people who value their own way of life and their progress, tolerate among them, even for the sake of their own personal safety, that terrible, senseless, cruel and ruinous force presented by every organized government that rests on its army? The most cruel and terrible band of robbers is not so much to be dreaded as such a State organization. The authority of a robber chief is to a certain degree limited by members of his band who retain some degree of human liberty and can refuse to commit actions contrary to their conscience. But there are no limits for men who form part of a regularly organized government with an army under such discipline as prevails to-day. There are no crimes so revolting that men forming part of a government will not commit them at the wish of the man (Boulanger, Pugachëv, or Napoleon) who may chance to stand at its head.

Often when I see not only the levies of recruits, the military exercises and the manœuvres, but also the policemen with loaded revolvers and the sentries with rifles and fixed bayonets, when for whole days at a time I hear (as I do in the Khamóvniki where I live) the whistling and rattle of bullets as they hit the target; and when I see in the city (where any attempt at violence in self-defence is suppressed, where the sale of drugs and ammunition is prohibited, and where rapid driving and treatment by an unlicenced doctor is forbidden) thousands of disciplined men trained to murder and subject to one man's will, I ask myself: How can people who value their safety quietly allow and put up with this? Apart from its harmfulness and immorality, nothing can be more dangerous. What are men—I do not speak of Christians, ministers of religion, humanitarians, and moralists, but simply men who value their own lives, safety, and welfare—what are they thinking about? For this organization will act in the same way in whosoever's hands it may be. To-day, let us say, the power is in the hands of a tolerable ruler, but to-morrow it may be seized by a Biron,[3] an Elizabeth,[4] a Catherine,[5] a Pugachëv, a Napoleon I [6] or a Napoleon III. And the man in whose hands the power lies may be tolerable to-day but to-morrow may become a beast, or he may be succeeded by

---

[3] E. J. de Biron (1690-1772), son of Bühren, a Courland proprietor. Peter the Great's niece, Anna Ivánovna, became his mistress and when she came to the throne of Russia he assumed the name and arms of the French dukes de Biron, and ruled Russia in her name. He had more than a thousand people executed, and when the Empress died assumed the regency. Three weeks later a group of conspirators arrested him and banished him to Siberia.—A. M.

[4] Elizabeth (1709-62) was the pre-nuptial daughter of Peter the Great and Catherine I. She seized the throne by a *coup d'état* in 1741.—A. M.

[5] Catherine (the Great) (1729-96) was concerned in the imprisonment and assassination of her husband Peter III and of the young Prince Iván. In her reign Pugachëv revolted and for a while held several provinces in the Volga district.—A. M.

[6] Tolstóy's opinion of Napoleon I is known to readers of *War and Peace*, and his dislike of Napoleon III, in whose reign he witnessed the guillotining of a man in Paris, was hardly less pronounced.—A. M.

a mad or crazy heir—like the King of Bavaria,[7] or our Paul I.[8]

And terrible misdeeds can be committed not only by the highest rulers but by all the little satraps who are scattered about everywhere—the various Baránovs, police masters, or even the village police officers, company commanders, and police officials, before there is time for them to be dismissed. And this constantly occurs.

One involuntarily asks oneself how men can tolerate such things, not from higher political considerations alone, but out of consideration for their own safety.

And the reply to that question is that not everybody does tolerate it. The majority of men are deluded and submissive and have no choice but to tolerate anything. But there are those who can occupy advantageous positions only under such an organization, and they tolerate it because the risk of suffering from an irrational or cruel man being at the head of the government or the army, is for them always less than the disadvantages they would be exposed to by the abolition of the organization itself.

A judge, a policeman, a governor, or an officer, can keep his position just the same under Boulanger, Pugachëv, Catherine, or a republic. But should the existing order which secures him his advantageous position collapse, he would certainly lose that position. And so these people are none of them alarmed as to who will be at the head of the organization of violence—they can adapt themselves to anyone. They only fear the abolition of the organization itself, and that is the reason—though sometimes an unconscious one—why they maintain it.

One often wonders why independent people who are in no

---

[7] Louis II of Bavaria (1845-86) came to the throne in 1864. He spent extravagant sums on patronizing Wagner and his music, was subsequently declared insane, and drowned himself and his physician in a lake.—A. M.

[8] Paul I (1754-1801), who was mad, was killed by his own officers, with the connivance of his son, Alexander I.—A. M.

way compelled to do so—the so-called flower of society—
enter the army in Russia, England, Germany, Austria, and
even in France, and seek opportunities to become murderers.
Why do parents, even moral parents, send their boys to col-
leges to prepare them for a military career? Why do mothers
buy their children helmets, guns, and swords, as their fa-
vourite toys? (Peasant children never play at soldiers.) Why
do good men and even women, quite unconnected with military matters, go into raptures over the various exploits of
Skóbelev[9] and other generals, and vie with one another in
glorifying them? Why do men under no obligation to do so
and receiving no salary for it (the Marshals of Nobility in
Russia, for instance) assiduously devote whole months to the
physically disagreeable and morally distressing work of en-
rolling conscripts? Why do all the emperors and kings go
about in military dress? Why do they hold manœuvres and
parades, distribute rewards to military men, and erect monuments to generals and successful commanders? Why do rich
people of independent position consider it an honour to perform a lackey's duties to crowned personages, humiliating
themselves and flattering them, and pretend to believe in the
special grandeur of these people? Why do people who have
long ceased to believe in the medieval Church superstitions
and who cannot believe in them, seriously and consistently
pretend to be believers, and support those demoralizing and
blasphemous ecclesiastical institutions? Why is the ignorance
of the people safeguarded so zealously not only by the governments but also by private members of the higher classes?
Why do they so passionately oppose any attempt to break
down religious superstitions for the true enlightenment of the
people? Why do historians, novelists, and poets, who can now
gain nothing by their flattery, describe as heroes emperors,
kings, and military leaders, who have long been dead? Why

---

[9] General Skóbelev, who had a prominent part in the capture of
Khiva in 1873 and took part in storming Pleva in 1878, was exceed-
ingly popular. His death in Moscow under particularly shameful
circumstances in 1882 caused a considerable sensation. There is a
reference to him on the last page of *Tales of Army Life.*—A. M.

do men who call themselves learned dedicate their whole lives to composing theories to prove that violence inflicted by a government on its people is not violence at all but some peculiar right?

One often wonders why a society woman or an artist, who would appear not to be interested either in social or military questions, should always condemn a workers' strike and advocate a war, and should always attack the one and defend the other so definitely.

But one ceases to wonder at all this as soon as one realizes that it is only done because people of the ruling classes feel instinctively what it is that supports, and what it is that destroys, the organization under which they can enjoy the privileges they possess.

The society lady does not deliberately argue that if there were no capitalists and no army to defend them, her husband would have no money and she consequently would have no *salon* and no wonderful gowns; and the artist does not reflect that capitalists defended by armies are necessary for him in order that there may be buyers for his pictures. But instinct, which in this case takes the place of reason, guides them unerringly.

And it is precisely the same instinct that, with few exceptions, guides the people who support all those political, religious, and economic institutions which are advantageous to them.

But is it possible that people of the upper classes support this order of things only because it is advantageous for them? They cannot but see that this order of things is in itself irrational, no longer corresponds to men's consciousness or even to public opinion, and is full of danger. People of the governing classes—the honest, good, clever people among them—cannot fail to suffer from those inner contradictions and to see the dangers they are exposed to. And is it possible that all the millions of people of the lower orders can with tranquil minds perform all the evidently evil actions—tortures and murders—they are compelled to do, merely because they fear punishment? It cannot be so, and neither the one nor the other could fail to see the unreasonableness of their conduct if the complexity of the state-structure did not conceal from them the irrationality and unnaturalness of what they are doing.

This irrationality is concealed by the fact that when any such action is committed there are so many instigators, accomplices, and abettors, that not one of those concerned in the affair feels himself morally responsible.

Murderers oblige all those who witness a murder to strike at the body of the man who has been killed, so that the responsibility may rest on as large a number of people as possible. That same principle, in a more definitely organized form, is applied to the perpetration of those crimes without the constant commission of which no governmental organization could exist. Rulers always try to draw as many citizens as possible into as much participation as possible in the crimes they commit and that are necessary for them.

Of late this has found very obvious expression in the drafting of citizens into the courts as jurors,[10] into the army as soldiers, and into local government—in the legislative assemblies—as electors and representatives.[11]

As all the ends of a wicker basket are so hidden that it is difficult to find them, so responsibility for the crimes committed in a State organization is so concealed from men that they do not see their own responsibility for the most atrocious acts.

In ancient times tyrants were accused when evil deeds were committed, but in our day the most atrocious crimes—crimes inconceivable under Nero—are perpetrated and there is no one who can be blamed.

Some people demand the perpetration of a crime, others decide that it shall be done, a third set confirm that decision, a fourth propose its execution, a fifth report on it, a sixth finally decree it, and a seventh carry out the decree. Women,

---

[10] Trial by jury was introduced in Russia as part of the judicial reforms in 1864.—A. M.

[11] The Zémstvos (County Councils on an electoral basis) were also introduced in 1864.—A. M.

old men, and innocent people, are killed, hanged, and flogged, as was done recently in Russia at the Yúsov works,[12] and as is done everywhere in Europe and America in the struggle with anarchists and other infringers of the existing order. Hundreds and thousands of people are shot or hanged, or millions of people are massacred as is done in war, or people's souls are ruined by solitary confinement or by the corruption of a soldier's life, as is constantly done—and no one is responsible.

At the bottom of the social ladder soldiers with rifles, revolvers, and swords, torture and murder men and by those means compel them to become soldiers. And these soldiers are fully convinced that the responsibility for their deed is taken from them by the officers who order those actions. At the top of the ladder the Tsars, presidents, and ministers, decree these tortures and murders and conscriptions. And they are fully convinced that since they are either placed in authority by God, or the society they rule over demands such decrees from them, they cannot be held responsible.

Between these two extremes are the intermediate folk who superintend the acts of violence and the murders and the conscriptions of the soldiers. And these, too, are fully convinced that they are relieved of all responsibility, partly because of orders received by them from their superiors, and partly because such orders are expected from them by those on the lower steps of the ladder.

The authority that commands and the authority that executes, at the two extremes of the State organization, are joined like the two ends of a chain-ring—each conditions and supports the other and all intermediate links.

Without the conviction that there is a person or persons on whom the whole responsibility rests, not one soldier would raise his hand to torture or murder. Without the conviction that it is expected of them by the people, not a single emperor, king, president, or parliament, would decree those murders or acts of violence. Without the conviction that there

---

[12] Large ironworks founded by an Englishman, Hughes, in South Russia.—A. M.

are persons standing below him who have to do such deeds for their welfare, not one of the intermediate people would take part in such deeds.

The State organization is such that on whatever rung of the social ladder a man may be, his lack of responsibility is always the same. The higher his grade the more he is under the influence of demands for instructions from below and the less he is controlled by orders from above, and vice versa.

So it was in the case I had before me. The more each of those taking part in that affair was exposed to demands for directions from below and the less under the influence of orders from above, the higher was his position and vice versa.

But not only do all the men involved in the State organization throw the responsibility for their acts on one another—the soldier on the nobleman or merchant who is his officer, and the officer on the nobleman who occupies the post of Governor, and the Governor on the gentleman or son of an official who holds the post of minister, and the minister on the member of the royal family who occupies the position of Tsar, and the Tsar again on all those officials, nobles, merchants, and peasants—not only do people free themselves in this way from the sense of responsibility for their actions, but they also lose their moral consciousness of responsibility because, being involved in a State organization, they so unceasingly, strenuously, and persistently assure themselves and one another that they are not all equal, but differ among themselves 'as one star differeth from another', that they begin really to believe this. Thus some are persuaded that they are not simple people like other folk but are special beings who ought to be specially honoured. And it is instilled into others by all possible means that they are inferior creatures, and should therefore uncomplainingly submit to what those above them dictate.

This inequality, this exaltation of some and degradation of others, is the chief cause of men's capacity to ignore the irrationality and cruelty and wickedness of the existing order, as well as the deception practised by some and suffered by others.

Those in whom has been instilled the idea that they are invested with a special, supernatural importance and grandeur[13] become so intoxicated with their own imaginary dignity that they cease to see their responsibility for their own actions.

Others on whom it is impressed that they are insignificant creatures bound to submit to their superiors in everything, fall into a strange state of stupefied servility in consequence of this continual humiliation, and so lose consciousness of their responsibility for what they do.

The intermediate people—who on the one hand obey the orders of their superiors and on the other give orders to their inferiors—are intoxicated by both power and servility, and so they, too, lose consciousness of their own responsibility.

One need only attend a review and glance at the commander-in-chief intoxicated with self-importance. He is accompanied by his staff, all on splendidly caparisoned horses and wearing special uniforms and decorations. To the sound of harmonious and triumphant military music the commander-in-chief rides before the ranks of soldiers presenting arms and petrified with servile adoration. One need only see that, to understand that at such moments the commander-in-chief, the soldiers, and all the officers, are in a state of complete intoxication and capable of committing actions they would never dream of committing under other conditions.

The intoxication produced by such spectacles as parades, imperial receptions, Church solemnities and coronations is, however, an acute and merely temporary condition. But there are other forms of intoxication that are chronic and continual, and these are experienced alike by those who have any power (from that of the Tsar to that of a policeman in the street) and by those in subjection to authority and in a condition of stupefied servility.

To justify that condition such people always attribute the greatest possible importance and dignity to those whom they

---

13 The eccentricities of Kaiser Wilhelm II were then already endangering the peace of the world and the stability of the three Eastern European empires.—A. M.

serve—as has been seen and is still seen in the case of all slaves.

It is principally through this false idea of inequality, and the intoxication of power and servility, that men associated in State organizations are enabled to commit without scruple or remorse actions opposed to their conscience.

Under the influence of such intoxication men imagine themselves and represent themselves to others as being not what they really are, men, but as some special conventional beings: noblemen, merchants, governors, judges, officers, Tsars, ministers, or soldiers, not subject to ordinary human duties but to aristocratic, commercial, governatorial, judicial, military, royal, or ministerial, obligations.

Thus the landowner going to law about the wood acted as he did only because he appeared to himself to be not an ordinary man having merely the same human rights as the peasant-folk living beside him, but a great landowner and a member of the gentry, and under the influence of the intoxication of power he felt his dignity offended by the peasants' claim. Only on that account did he send in a claim to be reinstated in his pretended rights without considering the consequences that might result.

In just the same way the judges who wrongfully awarded the wood to the landowner, did so only because they considered themselves to be not ordinary men like everybody else and therefore bound to be guided in everything by truth alone, but, under the intoxication of power, imagined themselves to be guardians of official justice and incapable of error. And while under the intoxicating influence of servility they imagined themselves to be men bound to execute certain rules written down in a certain book, and called laws. And all the other participants in the affair—from the highest representative of authority who signed the report, the marshal of nobility who presided at the recruiting sessions, and the priest who deluded the conscripts, to the lowest of the soldiers now preparing himself to shoot his fellow-men—under the influence of power or of servility considered themselves to be, and represented themselves to others as being, not what they really are but something quite different. They all did what they did, and prepare to do what they still have to do, only because they seem to themselves and to others to be not what they are in reality—men faced by the question whether they ought or ought not to take part in wicked actions which their conscience condemns—but different, conventional characters: one an anointed Tsar, a special being destined to watch over the welfare of a hundred million people; another the representative of the nobility; another a priest who has received special grace by his ordination; another a soldier bound by his oath unreflectingly to do all that he is commanded to do. All these people could only, and can only, act as they do under the influence of intoxication by power or servility, resulting from their imagined positions.

If they were not all firmly convinced that the calling of a tsar, minister, governor, judge, nobleman, landowner, marshal, officer, or soldier, is something real and very important, not one of them could think without horror and aversion of taking part in the things they now take part in.

The conventional positions established hundreds of years ago, recognized for centuries, and now accepted by all around, distinguished by special names and a special dress and confirmed by all kinds of ceremonies which act on the senses, influence men to such a degree that forgetting the normal conditions of life common to all, they regard themselves and everyone else only from this conventional point of view, and estimate their own and other people's actions solely from that conventional view-point.

Thus a man in full mental health and no longer young, suddenly becomes self-assured, proud, and even happy, merely because he is decked out with some gewgaw, or has keys hanging at his backside, or wears a blue ribbon, suitable only for some little girl in costume, and is told that he is a general, a chamberlain, a Chevalier of St. Andrew, or some such nonsense; and on the contrary he grows sad and unhappy and even falls ill, if he is deprived of the expected trinket or nickname, or fails to obtain it. And what is still more striking, a young man quite sane in other respects, in-

dependent and well provided for, will tear an unfortunate
widow from her little children and lock her up or have her imprisoned, leaving her children uncared for, all because the
unhappy woman has secretly trafficked in vódka and so deprived the Crown of twenty-five rubles' revenue. And he does
not feel the least remorse for having done this, because he
has called himself and been called by others, a public prosecutor or district chief. Or what is still more extraordinary, a man
otherwise reasonable and kindly will begin to fire bullets at
people merely because he has been given a badge or a uniform and told that he is an excise or customs officer, and
neither he nor those around him consider him guilty of anything wrong, but on the contrary consider that he is to blame
if he does not fire. And then there are the judges and jurymen who condemn men to death, and the military who kill
thousands without the least remorse, merely because it has
been instilled into them that they are not simply men, but
jurymen, judges, generals, and soldiers.

This strange and unnatural condition of men in political
life is usually expressed by words such as these: 'As a man I
am sorry for him, but as a watchman, judge, general, governor, tsar, or soldier, it is my duty to kill or torture him'—as
if any position given or recognized by men could set aside
the obligations imposed on each of us by our common humanity.

In the case before us, for instance, men are going to murder
and torture others who are famishing. They admit that in the
quarrel with the landowner the peasants are in the right (the
superior officers told me so). They know that the peasants are
wretched, poor, and hungry, and the landowner is rich and
evokes no sympathy. Yet all these men are going to punish
the peasants in order to obtain three thousand rubles for the
landowner, just because at this moment each imagines himself to be not a man, but either a governor, an official, a chief
of gendarmes, an officer, or a soldier, and because they consider as obligatory on them not the eternal demands of man's
conscience but the casual, temporary demands of their positions as officers or soldiers.

Strange as it may sound, the only explanation of this remarkable phenomenon is that these men are in the same state as hypnotized people who feel convinced that they are whatever character is suggested to them. When, for instance, it is suggested to a hypnotized person that he is lame he begins to limp, when it is suggested that he is blind he ceases to see, and when it is suggested that he is an animal he begins to bite. And the men going by this train were in such a state, and so are not only they, but all who fulfil their State and social duties in preference to and to the detriment of their duties as men.

The essence of the hypnotic state is that under the influence of an idea suggested to them, people lose the power of reflecting on their actions and do without thinking whatever is consistent with the suggestion to which they are led by example, precept, or insinuation.

The difference between those hypnotized by artificial means and those under the influence of political suggestion, is this: that in the one case the imaginary condition is suggested suddenly, by one person, in a very brief space of time, and so that hypnotism presents itself to us in a glaring and startling form; while the imaginary position induced by political suggestion takes place by degrees, gradually, imperceptibly, from childhood, sometimes for a period of years or even generations, and is moreover induced not by one person only but by the whole of society.

'But', it will be said, 'in all societies the majority of people —all the children, all the women absorbed in bearing and rearing children, all the immense number of working people under the necessity of intense and incessant physical labour, all those of a naturally weak mind and those whose intellectual capacities have been enfeebled by nicotine, alcohol, opium poisoning, or other intoxicants—are always incapable of independent thought and consequently submit either to those on a higher level of reasonable consciousness, or else to family or State traditions—to what is called public opinion —and in this submission there is nothing unnatural or incongruous.'

And it is true that there is nothing unnatural in it and that it is a usual characteristic of people who think little, to submit to the guidance of those on a higher level of consciousness. It is owing to this that men can live in societies submitting to the same reasonable principles. The minority consciously adopt these reasonable principles because they correspond with their reason, while the majority submit to the same principles unconsciously, merely because those demands have become public opinion.

So long as public opinion is not split in two there is nothing unnatural in this submission to public opinion by people who think but little.

But there are times when a higher consciousness of truth reveals itself, and gradually passing from one to another takes hold of such a number of people that the former public opinion, based on a lower level of consciousness, begins to totter, and the new one is ready to establish itself but has not yet done so. There are times resembling the coming of spring. The old public opinion has not yet been demolished and the new one established, but men already begin to discuss their own and other people's actions on the basis of the new consciousness, though they still by inertia and tradition continue to obey the principles that formed the highest stage of reasonable consciousness at an earlier period but are now already in flagrant contradiction to it. At such times men, feeling the necessity of submitting to the new public opinion and yet unable to break with the former, are in an unnatural and wavering condition. And not only the men in that train, but the majority of men in our time, find themselves in such a condition in their relation to Christian truths.

People of the higher classes holding exceptionally advantageous positions are in that state, as well as people of the lower classes who submit absolutely to the orders given them.

The ruling classes, having no longer any reasonable justification for the advantageous positions they hold, are obliged, in order to keep these positions, to repress their higher rational capacities and love for their fellow-men, and to hypnotize themselves into the belief that their exceptional positions are necessary. And the lower classes, crushed by toil and intentionally stupefied, live in a continual condition of hypnotization, deliberately and incessantly induced by people of the upper classes.

Only in this way can one explain the amazing contradiction that fills our life, and of which a striking example was presented by those kindly and mild acquaintances whom I met on the 9th of September, who with quiet minds were going to commit the most cruel, senseless, and vile crimes. Had conscience not been stifled in some way in those men, not one of them could have done a one-hundredth part of what they were preparing to do, and very likely will do.

It is not that they have no conscience forbidding them to do what they are preparing to do—as those who burnt others at the stake and tortured and mutilated men four hundred, three hundred, two hundred, and even a hundred years ago, had no conscience. Conscience does exist in all these people now, but it has been put to sleep. In the case of those in command and those in exceptionally advantageous positions, it has been put to sleep by what the psychiatrists call autosuggestion. In the case of the soldiers it has been put to sleep by direct intentional suggestion and hypnotization exerted by the higher classes.

But although conscience has been put to sleep in these men, it still exists and may awaken at any moment. Indeed its voice can already be heard in them penetrating the self-suggestion and hypnotization that possess them.

All these men are in a state similar to that of a hypnotized man who under that influence has been ordered to do something contrary to all that he regards as reasonable and right —such as to kill his mother or child. He feels himself bound to carry out the suggestion and it seems to him that he cannot stop, yet the nearer he gets to the time and place of action the more strongly does his benumbed conscience begin to stir, to resist, to writhe, and to try to awake. And one cannot say in advance whether he will or will not do the deed suggested to him. It is impossible to tell which will prevail: his rational consciousness or the irrational suggestion. It all depends on their relative strength.

That is just what is happening to-day, both with the men in that train and with men of our day in general who commit political acts of violence and profit by them.

There was a time when men who set out to torture and murder and make examples, never returned without having accomplished the business they set out to do, and were never troubled by doubts or remorse, but having flogged men to death, quietly returned to their families, petted their children, jested, laughed, and enjoyed the peaceful pleasures of family life. It did not then enter the heads of those who profited by such acts of violence—landowners and wealthy people—that the advantages they enjoyed had any connexion with those cruelties.

But now it is otherwise. People already know, or almost know, what they are doing and why they do it. They can close their eyes and stifle their conscience, but with open eyes and unstifled conscience both those who commit violence and those who profit by it can no longer fail to see its import. Sometimes people understand the significance of an action only after it has already been done, but sometimes they realize it just before its perpetration. The men who arranged the floggings at Nízhni-Nóvgorod, Sarátov, Orël, and at the Yúzov factory, realized what they had done only afterwards, and are now tormented with shame by public opinion and by their own consciences. I have spoken with soldiers who took part in such affairs and they always tried to turn the conversation from that subject, and when they spoke of it did so with perplexity and horror. But there are cases when men recollect themselves just before the commission of the deed. Thus I know of a sergeant who was beaten by two peasants during the suppression of a riot and who reported accordingly, but next day when he saw the tortures inflicted on other peasants, he begged his company commander to tear up the report and to let off the men who had beaten him. I know a case where the soldiers appointed to shoot some

men declined to obey, and I know many cases of officers refusing to take charge of floggings and murders. So that men
engaged in arranging or committing violence sometimes recollect themselves long before the performance of the deed,
sometimes just before its perpetration, and sometimes only
after it.

The men travelling by that train set out to injure and murder their fellow men, but no one knows whether they will or
will not carry out their object. However much his responsibility may be concealed from each of them, and however strong
may be the suggestion instilled into each of them that they
are not men, but governors, police-captains, officers, and
soldiers, and as such may violate their human duties, the
nearer they approach their destination the stronger will be
their doubts as to whether they are going to do what is necessary and right, and this doubt will reach its highest degree
at the moment of execution.

In spite of the intoxicating effect of his surroundings the
Governor cannot help hesitating when he gives the final deci-
sive command to murder and to torture. He knows that the
action of the Governor of Orël evoked indignation from the
best members of society, and he himself, under the influence
of the opinion of the circles in which he lives, has more
than once expressed disapproval of that affair. He knows that
the public prosecutor, who was to have come, has simply refused to take part because he considered it a shameful affair;
and he knows that to-day or to-morrow there may be changes
in the government, and that what procured favour yesterday
may incur disfavour to-morrow. And he knows that there is a
public press, if not in Russia then abroad, which may report
this matter and so disgrace him for life. He already scents a
change in public opinion, which now repudiates what was
formerly demanded. And he cannot feel absolutely sure that
at the last moment the soldiers will obey him. He wavers and
it is impossible to tell what he will do.

The same is felt in a greater or lesser degree by all the
officials and officers with him. They all in the depth of
their hearts know that what they are engaged on is shameful,

and that to take part in it degrades and pollutes them in the eyes of some people whose opinion they value. Each of them knows that after murdering and torturing defenceless people he will be ashamed to face his betrothed or the woman he is wooing. And besides, they too, like the Governor, are in doubt as to whether their soldiers will obey them. And contrary as it is to the assured appearance with which they saunter about the station and along the platform, they all in the depth of their souls both suffer and hesitate. They assume that self-assured appearance to conceal the hesitation within. And that feeling increases as they approach the scene of action.

And however little noticeable it may be, and strange as it seems to say so, all these young fellows who seem so submissive are in the same state of mind.

They are not the soldiers of former days who had renounced a natural and laborious life and devoted their whole existence to debauchery, plunder, and murder—like Roman legionaries, or soldiers of the Thirty Years' War, or even the soldiers of not so long ago who had to serve for twenty-five years. Now they are for the most part men recently taken from their families and still full of recollections of the good, natural, and reasonable life they have left behind them.

For the most part they are peasant lads, who know the business they are engaged on; know that the landlords always take advantage of their brothers, the peasants, and that it is no doubt the same in this case. Moreover more than half of them can now read books, and not all the books they read extol the business of war—there are some that point out its wrongfulness. Among the soldiers there are often free-thinking volunteers, or among the officers young liberals of a similar way of thinking, and seeds of doubt as to the absolute legitimacy and glory of their occupation have been sown.

It is true that they have all passed through that terrible, artificial system of drill, elaborated through centuries and deadly to all initiative in man, and that they are so trained to mechanical obedience that at the command: 'Ready! Present! Fire!' &c., their rifles will be lifted and the habitual movements mechanically performed. But at this moment the word

'Fire!' does not mean amusing themselves by shooting at a target, it means killing their tormented and ill-treated fathers and brothers, whom they see standing huddled together in a crowd in the street with their women and children waving their arms. There they stand, one man with a thin beard and patched coat and plaited bast shoes, just like the father left behind at home in Kazán or Ryazán province; another with a grey beard and bent back, leaning on a big staff, just like grandfather; a third—a young fellow in high boots and a red shirt—just like himself a year ago: he, the soldier who is now going to shoot him down. And there, too, is a woman in a linen skirt and bast shoes, just like the mother left at home. . . . Are they really going to fire on them?

And it is impossible to say what each soldier will do at the final moment. The least indication that it cannot be done, or above all that it is possible not to do it, would be enough to stop him.

All the men travelling by that train, when it comes to doing the thing for which they are going, will be in the position of a hypnotized man to whom it has been suggested that he should chop a log and who, on coming up to what has been pointed out to him as a log and when already swinging his axe, sees that it is not a log at all but the body of his sleeping brother. He may go through with what he has been told to do, or he may come to himself before doing it. In the same way all these men may or may not come to themselves in time.

If they do not come to themselves a terrible crime will be committed, as at Orël, and then the auto-suggestion and hypnotism under which they act will be strengthened in other people. If they do come to themselves, not only will this crime not be perpetrated but many who hear of the turn things have taken will be freed from the hypnotic influence which has held them spellbound, or will at least be nearer to such emancipation.

If even a few come to themselves and refrain from taking part in this affair and boldly point out to others the wickedness of it, the influence of those few may result in all the rest shaking off the influence of the suggestion that oppresses them, and the intended atrocity will not be committed.

If even just a few people who are not taking part in that affair, but are merely present at the preparations for it or have just heard of such things being done in the past, would boldly and plainly express their detestation of those who participate in such affairs and point out to them all the sense-lessness, cruelty, and wickedness of such acts, instead of re-maining indifferent, even that would not pass without some effect.

So it was in the instance before us. It was enough for some participants and non-participants in the affair boldly to ex-press their indignation at the floggings that had been inflicted elsewhere and their repulsion and contempt for those who had taken part in them—it was enough in the present Túla case for some people to express their unwillingness to take part in it, for a lady passenger and a few bystanders at the station to express to those who formed the expedition, their indignation at what they were doing; it was enough for one of the regimental commanders from whom troops were de-manded for the restoration of order, to express his opinion that soldiers cannot be executioners—and thanks to these and some other seemingly insignificant private influences brought to bear on those who were under the hypnotic in-fluence of suggestion, the matter took quite a different turn. The troops when they reached the place did not torture the peasants but only cut down the wood and handed the timber over to the landowner.

Had there not been a few people with a clear perception that they were doing wrong, and had there not been in con-sequence of this an influence exerted in that sense by some people on others, what happened at Orël would have hap-pened in Túla. Had that consciousness been yet stronger and had the influence exerted been greater than it was, the Governor and troops would very likely not have decided to cut down the wood and give it over to the landowner. Had that consciousness been stronger still and those influences yet more numerous, the Governor would very likely not even have decided to go to the scene of the action; and had it been stronger again and the influences still more numerous, the minister would very likely not have made up his mind to prescribe such a decision, or the Emperor to confirm it.

All depends therefore on the strength of the consciousness of Christian truth in each individual man.

And therefore it would seem that the efforts of all men of our time who profess a wish to promote the welfare of mankind, should be directed to strengthening and elucidating in themselves and others a consciousness of Christian truth and its requirements.

4

But strange to say in our day it is just those people who talk most about the betterment of human life and are regarded as intellectual leaders of public opinion, who declare all this to be quite unnecessary, and say that there are other more effective means of improving man's condition. These men affirm that the improvement of human life is effected not by the moral efforts of individual men towards the recognition, elucidation, and profession of truth, but by a gradual alteration of the general external conditions of life. They believe that the efforts of each individual should be directed not to that moral advance but to a general modification of external conditions. Any individual profession of truth incompatible with the existing order is not merely useless but harmful, because it provokes governmental restrictions that hinder individuals from continuing an activity useful to society. According to this doctrine all alterations of human life are governed by the same laws as those of animal life.

So that according to that doctrine all the founders of religions, such as Moses and the prophets, Confucius, Lao-tsze, Buddha, Christ, and others, preached their doctrines, and their followers adopted them, not because they loved truth and sought to elucidate and propagate it, but because the political, social, and above all the economic circumstances of the nations among whom those teachings appeared and spread were favourable to their manifestation and development.

And therefore the chief activity of a man who wishes to serve society and improve the condition of mankind should be directed not to the elucidation and profession of truth, but to the amelioration of external political, social, and, above all else, economic conditions. And the modification of those conditions is, they say, effected partly by serving the government and introducing liberal and progressive principles into it, partly by contributing to the development of industry and the dissemination of socialistic ideas, and most of all by the diffusion of scientific education.

It is not important for a man to profess the truth that has revealed itself to him, and so inevitably be compelled to apply it in his life or at least to refrain from committing actions contrary to that truth—such as serving the government or strengthening its authority if he considers that authority harmful, profiting by the capitalist system if he regards it as wrong, showing reverence for ceremonies he regards as degrading superstitions, taking part in judicial proceedings when he considers their organization false, serving as a soldier, taking oaths, and in general telling lies and acting as a scoundrel. But it is important for a man, without altering the existing forms of life but conforming to them contrary to his convictions, to introduce liberalism into existing institutions, to promote industry, to propagate socialism, the triumphs of what is called science, and the diffusion of education.

According to that theory a man can remain a landowner, a trader, a manufacturer, a judge, an official in government pay, a soldier or an officer, and still be not merely humane but even a socialist and a revolutionary.

Hypocrisy, which had formerly only a religious basis in the doctrine of the fall of man, the redemption, and the Church, has to-day secured a new scientific basis, and has consequently caught in its net all those who at the stage of development they had reached could no longer find support in religious hypocrisy. So that while formerly only a man professing the teachings of the Church could take part in the crimes committed by the State, profit by them, and yet consider himself free from any taint of sin so long as he fulfilled the external observances of his religion, nowadays everyone, without believing in Church Christianity, can have an equally firm scientific ground for regarding himself as blameless and even highly moral, despite his participation in the evil done by the State and in the advantages he derives therefrom.

We see landowners not only in Russia but everywhere—in France, England, Germany, and America—who, for allowing people living on their land to draw subsistence from it, extort from these (generally needy) people all they possibly can. The owner's right of property in the land is based on the fact that at every attempt on the part of the oppressed to avail themselves, without his consent, of the land he considers to be his, troops come and subject them to punishment and murder. It would seem evident that a man living in such a way is an evil and egotistic creature who cannot possibly consider himself a Christian or a liberal. It would seem evident that the first thing such a man should do if he wishes even to approximate to Christianity or liberalism, is to cease to rob and ruin people by means of his claim to the land, which the government supports by murder and violence. And it would be evident, were it not for this hypocritical reasoning which says that from a religious point of view the possession or non-possession of land is immaterial for salvation, and that from a scientific point of view the giving up of the ownership of the land would be a useless personal sacrifice because the welfare of humanity is not promoted in that way but by a gradual change in external forms. And so we see that man, in no way abashed and never doubting that people will believe in his sincerity, organizing an agricultural exhibition or a temperance society, or distributing, through his wife and children, underclothing and soup to three or four old women, and boldly discoursing in his own house, in other people's drawing-rooms, in committees, and in the press, on the duty of Christian and humanitarian love of one's neighbour in general and the labouring agricultural folk (whom he is continually exploiting and oppressing) in particular. And others who are in the same position as he, believe him, and solemnly discuss with him measures for improving the condition of those labouring folk on whose exploitation their whole life is based, and devising every possible means except the one without which no improvement is possible—namely, ceasing to deprive men of the land necessary for their subsistence.

(A most striking example of such hypocrisy was given by the landowners last year in their endeavour to combat the famine which they had produced, and of which they took advantage not only by selling grain at the highest possible price, but even by charging the freezing peasants five rubles a *desyatína* [2¾ acres] for potato bines, before they would allow them to be used as fuel.)

Take a trader whose whole business is, as usual, based on a system of trickery, by means of which, taking advantage of the people's needs and of their ignorance, he buys goods below their value and sells them again above it. It would seem evident that a man whose whole occupation is based on what, were it done under other circumstances, he would himself term swindling, ought to be ashamed of his position, and be quite unable to represent himself as a Christian or a liberal while remaining in it. But there is an hypocritical sophistry that tells him he can be regarded as a virtuous man without abandoning his harmful activity: a religious man need only have faith, and a liberal man need only promote the modification of external conditions—the progress of industry. And so that trader who, besides his nefarious occupation, often commits a series of direct frauds (selling adulterated goods, using false weights and measures, or dealing in things pernicious to health such as spirits and opium) boldly regards himself, and is regarded by others, as a model of probity and conscientiousness so long as he does not defraud his associates in business. And if he spends a thousandth part of his stolen wealth on some public institution—a hospital, museum, or educational establishment—he is even regarded as a benefactor of the people on whose exploitation and corruption his prosperity has been founded. And if he devotes a portion of his ill-gotten gains to a church or to the poor, then he is considered a model Christian.

Or take a manufacturer whose profit comes from fines he imposes on his workmen, and whose whole activity is based on compulsory and unnatural labour that ruins whole generations of men. It would seem obvious that if he professes any Christian or liberal principles he should first of all cease to ruin human lives for his own profit. But according to the existing theory he is promoting industry and ought not to cease his activity. It would even be harmful to society for him to do so. And so this man, the cruel slave-driver of thousands of people, having arranged cottages with five-foot gardens for those broken down by toiling for him, and having founded a savings-bank, a poor-house, and a hospital, proudly continues his activity, fully persuaded that he has more than paid for all the human lives he has ruined physically and morally.

Or take a ruler, or some civil, ecclesiastical, or military employee serving the State either to satisfy his vanity or ambition, or as is most often the case simply to receive a salary collected from exhausted and toil-worn workers (all taxes, from whomsoever collected, always originate from labour, that is, from the working people), and if (which is very seldom the case) he does not also steal State money in irregular ways, he considers himself and is considered by his fellows a most useful and virtuous member of society.

Or take some judge, public prosecutor, or ruler, who knows that by his sentences or decisions hundreds and thousands of poor wretches torn from their families are now lingering in solitary confinement or convict settlements, where they go out of their minds and kill themselves either with pieces of broken glass or by starving. He knows that these thousands of people have thousands of mothers, wives, and children, suffering from their separation, shamed, not allowed interviews, vainly petitioning for pardons or even for an alleviation of their sentences; but he has become so hardened in his hypocrisy that he and those like him, and their wives and households, are fully convinced that in spite of it all he can be a very good and sensitive man. Does not hypocritical sophistry show that he is doing a work of social utility? And this man, having ruined hundreds and thousands of people who curse him and are driven to desperation thanks to his activity, believes in goodness and in God and goes to mass with a beaming and benevolent smile on his smooth face, hears the Gospel, utters liberal speeches, pets his children, inculcates moral principles in them and grows sentimental over imaginary sufferings.

All these people and those who live on them—their wives, tutors, children, cooks, actors, jockeys, and so forth—live on the blood of the working people which in one way or another they suck like leeches, consuming every day for their pleasure hundreds or thousands of the working days of wretched labourers driven to work by threats of murder. They see the sufferings and privations of these workmen and their children, old men, women, and sick people, and they know of the penalties that infringers of that organized spoliation undergo. Yet they not only do not moderate or conceal their luxury, but they insolently display it before these oppressed workmen (who for the most part hate them) as though on purpose to provoke them with their parks and palaces, theatres, hunts, and races. And at the same time they unceasingly assure themselves and one another that they are much concerned about the welfare of those people whom they are always trampling under foot; and on Sundays, in fine clothes, they drive in fine carriages to houses of God specially built for the mockery of Christianity, and there listen to men specially trained in that mockery, and who preach in all sorts of ways (with vestments and without, and wearing or not wearing white ties) the love of man which their daily lives belie. And doing all this, these people so enter into their parts that they seriously believe they really are what they pretend to be.

In general, hypocrisy having entered into the flesh and blood of all classes in our time has reached such proportions that nothing of that kind any longer arouses indignation. Not for nothing was 'hypocrisy' derived from 'acting'. And anyone can act, that is, play a part. Such facts as that the representatives of Christ, at divine service, bless ranks of murderers holding loaded rifles in readiness to shoot their fellow men, that ministers of all the Christian sects take part at executions as inevitably as the executioners, by their presence acknowledging murder to be compatible with Christianity (a clergyman officiated in America at the first experiment of murder by electricity), no longer occasion surprise to anyone.

There was recently an international prison exhibition in Petersburg where instruments of torture—shackles and models of solitary cells—were shown, that is, instruments of torture worse than rods or the knout, and sensitive gentlemen and ladies went to amuse themselves by looking at them.

No one is surprised that liberal science, with its recognition of the principles of liberty, equality, and fraternity, should admit the necessity of armies, executions, custom-houses, the censorship, the legal regulation of prostitution, the exclusion of foreign labourers, the prohibition of emigration, and the necessity and justifiability of colonization based on poisoning with spirits and opium, plundering, and exterminating whole races of men called savages, and so on.

People talk of a time when all men will profess what is called Christianity (that is, various hostile creeds), when everybody will be well fed and clothed, when all will be united from one end of the earth to the other by telegraphs and telephones and flying machines; when all the workmen will be imbued with socialist doctrines, and the trades unions will have so many millions of members and so many millions of rubles and everyone will be educated, and they will all read newspapers and learn all the sciences.

But what that is good or useful can come of all these achievements, if people will not speak or act in accordance with what they consider the truth?

The miseries of men are due to their discord. And their discord results from their not following the truth which is one, but falsehood which is legion. The only means by which men can be united is by union in the truth. And therefore the more sincerely men seek the truth the nearer will they approach to union.

But how can men be united in the truth or even approach to it when they do not even proclaim the truth they know, but consider that they ought not to do so and pretend to believe in the truth of what they know is false?

So long as people pretend, that is, conceal the truth from themselves, no improvement of men's condition is possible. That improvement can only take place when they recognize that their welfare lies solely in the union of all men in the truth, and are therefore ready to put above everything else the recognition and profession of that truth which has revealed itself to them.

Let all those external improvements that religious and scientific people dream of be accomplished; let all men accept Christianity and all the improvements the Bellamys[14] and Richets[15] desire be accomplished with all possible additions and corrections, but if at the same time the hypocrisy remains that now exists, if people do not profess the truth they know but continue to feign belief in what they do not themselves believe and veneration for what they do not respect, the condition of people will not merely remain what it is but will become worse and worse. The better men are materially provided for, the more telegraphs, telephones, books, papers and periodicals they have, the more means will there be of spreading contradictory lies and hypocrisies, and the more disunited and consequently unhappy will men become, as indeed occurs now.

Let all those external alterations be realized and the position of humanity will not be bettered. But let each man according to the strength that is in him profess the truth he knows and practise it in his own life—or at least cease to excuse the falsehood he supports by representing it as truth—and at once, in this very year 1893, such changes would be accomplished towards man's liberation and the establishment of truth on earth, as we dare not hope for in hundreds of years.

Not without reason was Christ's only denunciatory and

---

[14] Edward Bellamy, the author of *Looking Backward.*—A. M.
[15] Perhaps this refers to C. R. Richet, who besides being a physiologist was the editor of the *Revue Scientifique.*—A. M.

harsh speech directed against hypocrites and hypocrisy. Falsehood is what corrupts, embitters, and brutalizes people, and therefore divides them—not theft, robbery, murder, adultery, or forgery, but that special falsehood of hypocrisy which wipes out in men's consciousness the difference between good and evil and thereby debars them from avoiding evil and seeking good, depriving them of the very essence of true human life and therefore blocking the path to all improvement.

Those who do evil through ignorance of the truth arouse sympathy for their victims and aversion to evil; they inflict harm only on their victims. But those who know the truth and conceal the evil they do by hypocrisy, injure both themselves and their victims and thousands and thousands of others who are led astray by the falsehood in which the evil they do is disguised.

Thieves, robbers, murderers and cheats, committing acts that are acknowledged as bad by themselves and by everybody else, serve as an example of what not to do and revolt people. But those who commit similar acts of theft, robbery, murder, and other crimes under cover of religious, scientific, and liberal justifications (as is done by all the landowners, traders, manufacturers, and Government servants of our time) invite others to imitate their conduct and so do evil not only to their direct victims but to thousands and millions of men whose power of distinguishing between good and evil is thus obliterated.

One fortune obtained by exploiting the necessaries of life, or by trading in articles that deprave people, or by speculation on the Stock Exchange, or by acquiring at a low price land the value of which is increased by public needs, or by organizing factories that ruin the life and health of people, or by civil or military service of the State, or by any business pandering to human vices—one fortune acquired by such means, adorned by ostentatious charity, and having not merely the sanction but the approval of leading men of society, corrupts men incomparably more than millions of thefts, frauds, and robberies committed in violation of the recognized forms of law and subject to criminal prosecution.

A single execution carried out dispassionately by prosperous and educated men with the approval and participation of Christian ministers and presented as something necessary and even just, perverts and brutalizes men more than thousands of murders committed by uneducated working people under the influence of passion. An execution such as Zhukóvsky[16] proposed to arrange, which was to arouse in men a sentiment of religious emotion, would have the most depraving influence imaginable.[17]

Every war, even the briefest, with the expenditure usual to war, the destruction of crops, the plundering, the licensed debauchery and murders, the sophistical excuses as to its necessity and justice, the exaltation and glorification of military exploits, patriotism and devotion to the flag, the feigned solicitude for the wounded, and so on, does more to deprave people in a single year than millions of robberies, arsons, and murders committed in hundreds of years by individual men under the influence of passion.

The luxurious life of one opulent, respectable, steady, and so-called honourable family which, however, consumes as many days of labour as would suffice for the maintenance of thousands of people living in privation near by, perverts men's minds more than thousands of outrageous orgies by coarse tradesmen, officers, or workmen, abandoning themselves to debauchery, smashing looking-glasses and crockery for amusement, and so on.

One solemn religious procession or service or lying sermon (in which the preacher does not believe) from the altar-step or pulpit, produces incomparably more evil than thousands of forgeries, adulterations of good, and so forth.

We talk of the hypocrisy of the Pharisees. But the hypocrisy of our society far exceeds the comparatively innocent hypocrisy of the Pharisees. They at least had an external religious law the performance of which hindered their seeing their

---

[16] V. A. Zhukóvsky (1783-1852). Poet and translator of Schiller, Byron, and others; he was Alexander II's tutor.—A. M.
[17] See vol. vi of the Works of Zhukóvsky (Russian edition).—L. T.

duty to their neighbour. Moreover those duties were not then nearly so clearly indicated. But now there is no such religious law to exonerate men from their duty to their neighbour and to every man without distinction. (I am not speaking of those coarse and stupid people who still fancy that they can be released from their sins by receiving the sacrament, or by absolution from the Pope.) On the contrary, that Gospel law which we all profess in one form or other has plainly pointed out that duty. And that same duty, which had then only been vaguely expressed by a few prophets, is now so clearly expressed that it has become a truism repeated by schoolboys and journalists. And so it would seem quite impossible for men of to-day to pretend that they do not know that duty.

Men of our time, availing themselves of the order of things maintained by violence, and at the same time protesting that they love their neighbours very much, and who do not notice that they are doing evil to those neighbours all the time are like a man who, after a life of robbery, when at last caught standing with lifted knife in the act of striking a victim who is frantically crying for help, should declare that he did not know that what he was doing was unpleasant to the man he had robbed and was just about to kill. As that robber and murderer could not deny what was evident to everyone, so it would seem impossible for men of our time, living on the sufferings of the oppressed classes, to persuade themselves and others that they desire the welfare of those whom they unceasingly plunder, and that they do not know how the advantages they enjoy are obtained.

We cannot now assert that we do not know of those hundred thousand men in Russia alone who are always confined in prisons and convict settlements for the security of our tranquillity and property, and that we do not know of those trials in which we ourselves take part, and which at our instigation condemn men who have made attempts on our property or security to prisons, exile, or convict settlements where men, no worse than those who sentence them, perish or become corrupt. Nor can we pretend that we do not know that all that we have has been obtained and is maintained for us by murders and violence. We cannot pretend that we do not see the constable who with a loaded revolver walks in front of our windows defending us while we eat our appetizing dinner or see a new play at the theatre, or that we do not know of those soldiers who set off so promptly with rifles and live cartridges to where our property is in danger of being infringed.

We know that if we are not interrupted at our dinner, at our theatre, at balls, Christmas trees, skating-rinks, races, and hunts, it is only thanks to the bullet in the constable's revolver and the soldier's rifle, which will pierce the hungry stomach of the exploited man round the corner who is licking his lips while he watches our pleasures and is ready to disturb them directly the constable with the revolver goes away or there is no soldier in the barracks ready to come at our first call.

And so, as a man caught in robbery in broad daylight cannot persuade us that he did not raise his hand to take his victim's purse and had no idea of cutting his throat, so we, it would seem, can no longer persuade ourselves or others that the soldiers and armed constables who surround us are not there for our protection but only for defence against foreign foes, to maintain order, and in general for ornament, amusement, and parades. We cannot persuade ourselves that we do not know that men dislike dying of hunger, bereft of the right to gain subsistence from the soil on which they live, and that they do not like labouring underground, in water or in scorching heat, for ten to fourteen hours a day, or at night, in factories and mills, manufacturing articles for our pleasure. It would seem impossible to deny what is so evident. Yet that is just what is denied.

And though among the rich there are some people (whom I am fortunate enough to meet more and more often) who are really alive—especially among the women and young people —who when reminded how and at what cost their pleasures are purchased, do not attempt to hide the truth, but clutch their heads and say: 'Ah, don't speak of that! If it is so, why then it is impossible to live!' But though there are such sincere people, who even though they cannot free themselves from their entanglements recognize their sin, the vast majority of men in our time have so entered into their hypocritical role that they boldly deny the fact that stares everyone in the face.

'What you say is all unjust!' they reply. 'No one forces people to work for the landowners and manufacturers. It is a matter of free agreement. Large properties and capital are necessary in order to organize and provide work for the labouring classes. Work at the mills and factories is not nearly as terrible as you make out. And if there are some abuses in factories, the government and society take measures to abolish them and render the work of the labouring classes still easier and more agreeable. The working classes are accustomed to physical toil and are as yet unfit for anything else. The poverty of the people does not result at all from the landlords or from capitalistic oppression, but from other causes: it is the result of the people's ignorance, brutality, and drunkenness. And we, men in authority, counteract that poverty by wise legislation; we capitalists counteract it by the diffusion of useful inventions, we priests by religious instruction, and we liberals by the organization of trades unions and by diffusing and promoting education. By these means we are increasing the welfare of the people without altering our own position. We do not want everybody to be poor like the poor, we want everybody to be rich like the rich. And it is a sophistry to say that the poor are ill-treated and killed to force them to work for the rich. The troops are called out against the people only when—not understanding their own interests—they riot and disturb the tranquillity necessary for the public welfare. The restraint of malefactors for whom prisons, gallows, and penal settlements, are arranged, is also indispensable at present though we ourselves should like to see those things abolished, and are working in that direction.'

Hypocrisy in our time is supported by two things—pseudo-religion and pseudo-science—and has reached such colossal dimensions that were we not living in the midst of it, it would be impossible to believe that men could reach such a degree of self-deception. They have now reached such a strange condition and their hearts are so hardened that though they have eyes they see not, and having ears they hear not, neither do they understand.

Men have long been living in antagonism with their conscience. If it were not for hypocrisy they could not continue to do so. Their present arrangement of life in opposition to their conscience only exists because it is masked by hypocrisy.

And the more the divergence between reality and men's conscience increases, the more is that hypocrisy extended. But hypocrisy has its limits. And it seems that in our day those limits have been reached.

Every man of our time, with the Christian principles he has involuntarily assimilated, finds himself in a position exactly like that of a sleeper who dreams that he must do something that even in his dream he knows he ought not to do. He knows it in the very depth of his consciousness, and yet feels that he cannot change his position or stop doing what he knows he ought not to do. And as happens in a dream, his position becomes more and more tormenting till at last it reaches such a pitch of intensity that he begins to doubt the reality of what is happening and makes an effort of consciousness to shake off the obsession.

Such is the condition of an average man of our Christian society. He feels that all that is being done by him and around him is absurd, monstrous, impossible, and opposed to his conscience. He feels that this position is becoming more and more unendurable and has already reached a crisis of intensity.

Surely it is impossible that men of our time, with the Christian sense of the dignity of man and the equality of man that has permeated our flesh and blood, and with our need of peaceful intercourse and union among the nations, should really live in such a way that our every joy and every convenience must be purchased by the sufferings and death of our fellow men, and that at the same time we should every instant be within a hair's breadth of flinging ourselves on one another like wild beasts, nation against nation, pitilessly destroying men's lives and labour, merely because some deluded diplomat or ruler says or writes some absurdity to another diplomat or ruler as misguided as himself.

It is impossible! Yet every man of our time sees that this very thing is being done and that he too will be compelled to do it. And the situation becomes more and more tormenting.

And as a man who is dreaming does not believe that what presents itself to him as reality is actually real, and tries to awake to another actual reality, so the average man of our day cannot in the depth of his heart believe that the terrible state in which he finds himself and which is growing ever worse and worse can be true reality, and he tries to wake up to the living reality which already exists in his consciousness.

And as it is only necessary for the dreamer to make an effort of consciousness and ask himself: 'But is not this a dream?' in order instantly to destroy the position that seemed to him so hopeless and to wake up to a peaceful and joyful reality, so also the man of to-day need only make a moral effort to question the reality of what is suggested to him by his own and the surrounding hypocrisy, and ask himself: 'Is not this a deception?' to feel himself instantly transported, like an awakening dreamer, from an imaginary and dreadful world to a true, peaceful, and joyful reality.

And for this a man need not perform any achievement or exploit, he need only make an internal effort of consciousness.

5

But can a man make this effort?

According to the existing theory indispensable to hypocrisy, man is not free and cannot change his life.

'A man cannot change his life because he is not free, and he is not free because all his actions are conditioned by preceding causes. And whatever a man may do there are always such and such causes which oblige him to do such and such actions. Therefore man cannot be free and cannot change his life,' say the defenders of the hypocritical theory. And they would be quite right if man were an unconscious being incapable of growth in relation to truth, that is, if having once recognized some truth he always remained at the same stage of cognition. But man is a conscious being capable of recognizing truth in higher and still higher degrees. And therefore, even if a man is not free to do such and such actions because previous causes exist for every action, those very causes themselves (which for a conscious man consist in the recognition of such and such truths as an adequate cause for an action) are within his power.

So that while a man is not free in regard to the performance of certain actions, he is free as regards the source of his future actions—just as an engine-driver cannot control the past movement of his locomotive and has not complete control of its present movement, but is able to control its future movements.

Whatever a conscious man may do, he does it either because he now considers that it conforms with the truth and that he ought to act so, or because at some previous time he has recognized a truth and now does from inertia or habit what he formerly did from conviction.

In any case the cause of his action is not some external fact, but the consciousness that a certain conception is true and the consequent recognition of this or that fact as a sufficient reason for the action.

Whether a man eats or refrains from eating, works or rests, runs from danger or exposes himself to it, he does so (if he acts consciously) only because he now considers it to be right and in accordance with the truth or because he believed so at some former time.

But the recognition or non-recognition of a certain truth depends not on external causes but on some cause within the man himself. So that sometimes a man with external conditions apparently favourable for the recognition of a truth will not recognize it, while another, with all the conditions apparently most unfavourable, will recognize it without any apparent cause. As is said in the Gospel: 'No man can come to me, except the Father . . . draw him.' (John vi. 44.) That is to say, the recognition of truth which is the cause of all the manifestations of human life, does not depend on external phenomena but on certain inner qualities of a man not subject to his observation.

And so a man, though not free in his actions, always feels himself free in that which serves as the motive of his actions— the recognition or non-recognition of truth. And he feels himself free not only in relation to occurrences external to himself but even in relation to his own actions.

Thus a man, having under the influence of passion committed an action conflicting with his consciousness of truth, remains none the less free to recognize it or not recognize it. That is, he can refuse to recognize the truth, consider his action necessary, and so justify himself for committing it, or he may recognize the truth, consider his action bad, and so condemn himself for it.

A gambler or a drunkard who, instead of resisting temptation, has yielded to his passion, is still free to acknowledge gambling or drunkenness to be wrong or to regard them as harmless amusements. In the first case, even if he does not immediately free himself from his passion, he ultimately gets free from it in proportion to the sincerity with which he admits the truth. In the second case he strengthens his passion and deprives himself of all possibility of freeing himself from it.

In just the same way a man who has not endured the heat and has escaped from a burning house without saving his friend, remains free to consider his action bad and therefore to condemn himself for it (recognizing it to be true that a man should save the life of another even at the risk of his own), or to regard his action as natural and necessary and justify himself for it (not recognizing that truth). In the first case, if he recognizes the truth despite his departure from it, that recognition will result in his preparing himself for a whole series of acts of self-sacrifice. In the second case he will, on the contrary, prepare for a whole series of selfish actions.

Not that a man can always recognize every truth. There

are truths long ago recognized by the man himself or conveyed to him by education and tradition and accepted by him on faith, to follow which has become a habit and a second nature. And there are truths that have only presented themselves to him dimly and from afar. A man lacks freedom alike to reject the former or to confess the latter. But there are truths of a third kind which have not as yet become unconscious motives of action but yet have revealed themselves to him so clearly that he cannot pass them by, but must inevitably adopt some attitude towards them—recognizing or refusing to recognize them. And it is in regard to these truths that man's freedom is manifest. In his relation to truth every man in life finds himself in the position of a traveller who walks in the dark by the light of a lantern carried in front of him. He does not see what is not yet lit up by the lantern nor does he see what he has left behind in the darkness, and he is powerless to change his relation to the one or the other. But wherever he may be he sees what is revealed by the lantern, and it is always in his power to choose one side or the other of the road he is travelling.

There are always truths a man has not yet perceived, there are always others he has already outlived, forgotten, or assimilated, and there are again always others freshly illumined by the light of his reason and demanding recognition. And it is in the recognition or rejection of these truths that the consciousness of our freedom manifests itself.

The whole difficulty and apparent insolubility of the question of man's freedom arises from the fact that when deciding that question people regard themselves as fixed in relation to truth.

Man is certainly not free if we regard him as immovable and if we forget that the life of man and humanity in general is nothing but a continual movement from darkness to light, from a lower stage of truth to a higher, from truth greatly intermixed with error to truth more free from it.

Man would not be free if he knew no truth at all, and he would not be free or even have any idea of freedom, if the whole truth that should guide him in life were revealed to him once for all in complete purity with no admixture of error.

But man is not fixed in relation to truth. As he passes through life, each individual man and humanity in general gains knowledge of a greater and greater degree of truth and frees himself more and more from error.

And therefore men are always in a threefold relation to truth. They have already so assimilated some truths that these have become an unconscious basis for their actions; other truths are only beginning to be perceived by them; and a third group, though not yet assimilated, have revealed themselves with sufficient clearness to compel recognition in one way or other—they must either be acknowledged or rejected.

And it is in the recognition or rejection of such truths that man is free.

His freedom does not consist in being able to act spontaneously, independently of the course of life and of the influence of existing causes, but it means that by recognizing and professing the truth revealed to him he can become a free and joyful participant in the eternal and infinite work performed by God or by the life of the world; or he can, by not recognizing that truth, become its slave and be painfully forced to go where he does not wish to go.

Truth not only points out the path of human life, it also reveals the only path along which it can go. And therefore all men must inevitably follow that path willingly or unwillingly—some voluntarily accomplishing the task life sets before them, others involuntarily submitting to the law of life. Man's freedom lies in having that choice.

Freedom within such narrow limits seems so significant to men that they do not notice it. Some people (the determinists) consider that amount of freedom so small that they do not recognize it at all. Others (advocates of complete free will) having an imaginary freedom in view, despise the degree of freedom they really possess, which seems to them insignificant. Freedom confined between the limits of complete ignorance of the truth and recognition of a certain degree of it, seems to some people not to be freedom at all, especially as man is inevitably compelled to carry out in life the truth that reveals itself to him, whether he is willing to recognize it or not.

A horse harnessed with others to a wagon is not free to refrain from moving in front of the wagon. If he does not pull, the wagon will knock against his legs and force him to go in the direction in which it is moving, and he will have to pull the wagon willingly or to be pushed by it. And so it is with man.

Whether that freedom be great or small in comparison with the imaginary freedom we should like to have, it is the only freedom that indubitably exists, and in it lies the only welfare accessible to man.

And not only does that freedom give welfare to men, it is the sole means of co-operating in the work that is being accomplished by the life of the world.

According to Christ's teaching the man who sees the significance of life in the domain in which it is not free—in the domain of effect, that is of acts—lacks true life. True life, according to the Christian teaching, is only possessed by a man who has transferred his life to the domain in which he is free—the domain of cause, that is, the domain in which lies the knowledge and recognition of the truth that is revealing itself—and who professes that truth and therefore inevitably ensures its fulfilment, as the wagon follows the horse.

If a man's life lies in corporeal affairs, he busies himself with things always dependent on temporal and spatial causes outside himself. He really does nothing himself. His acts are a mere self-deception. Everything he imagines himself to be doing is really done through him by a superior force. He is not a creator of life but its slave. But if a man acknowledges his life to lie in the recognition and confession of the truths that are revealing themselves to him, he identifies himself with the source of universal life and accomplishes acts not personal and dependent on conditions of time and space, but acts unconditioned by external causes, and that themselves constitute the cause of everything else and have an infinite, unlimited significance.

Men of the Pagan conception of life, disregarding the essential of true life which consists in the recognition and profession of truth, and directing all their efforts to strengthening and improving their personal life by external actions—resemble people on a steamer who in order to reach their destination damp down the boiler that hinders them from placing oarsmen, and in a storm, instead of relying on the screw and on the steam already generated, try to propel the ship by oars which do not reach the water.

The Kingdom of God can only be reached by effort, and only those who make such effort reach it. And it is just by this violent effort to rise above external conditions and reach the acknowledgement and announcement of the truth, that the Kingdom of God is taken. And this effort can and should be made in our time.

Men need only understand this, they need only cease to be troubled about general and external affairs in which they are not free, and devote even a one-hundredth part of the energy they now expend on those material affairs, to the affair in which they are free—that is, to the recognition and realization of the truth that is before them and to liberating themselves and others from the lies and hypocrisy which hide that truth —and without violence and conflict there would at once be an end of the false organization of life which makes men miserable and threatens them with still greater calamities. Then the Kingdom of God—or at least that first stage of it for which men are now ready in their consciousness—would be realized.

Just as a single shake may precipitate into crystals a liquid fully saturated with salt, so now a very small effort may be all that is needed to cause the truth that is already disclosed to men, to take hold of hundreds, thousands, and millions of people, and a public opinion corresponding to our consciousness may establish itself and the whole order of life consequently be transformed. And it is for us to make that effort.

If only each one of us tried to understand and acknowledge that Christian truth which in most diverse forms surrounds us on all sides and seeks to enter our souls; if only we ceased from lying and pretending that we do not see this truth, or that we wish to fulfil it but not in the chief demand it makes on us, if only we acknowledged that truth which is calling to us and boldly professed it—we should immediately find that hundreds, thousands, and millions of people were in the same position as ourselves—that they see the truth, and like us are only waiting for others to acknowledge it.

If only people ceased to be hypocrites they would at once see that the whole of this cruel, social organization—which alone binds them and appears to them to be something ordained by God, solid, indispensable, and sacred—is already tottering and is only maintained by that hypocritical lie by which we and others like us support it.

But if that is so, if it is true that it depends on us to destroy the existing order of life, have we a right to destroy it without knowing clearly what to put in its place? What will happen to the world when the existing order of things is at an end?

'What will there be beyond the walls of the world we leave behind?'

'There will be terror—a void, a vast emptiness, freedom . . . How can we advance not knowing whither? How abandon what we have without seeing what we shall obtain? . . .' [18]

Had Columbus reasoned so, he would never have weighed anchor. It is madness to sail the sea without knowing the way, to sail a sea no one has traversed before, and to make for a land the existence of which is doubtful. But by that madness he discovered a new world. Of course if the nations could simply move as it were from one set of furnished rooms to a better one it would be easier, but the trouble is that there is no one to prepare the new quarters. To sail into the future is even worse than to sail the ocean. There is nothing there. The future will be what men and circumstances make it.

'If you are content with the old world try to preserve it, it is very decrepit and will not last long. But if you cannot endure to live in perpetual discord between your convictions and

---

[18] Quoted from Herzen, vol. v, p. 55.—L. T.

your life, thinking one thing and doing another, then leave your medieval whitewashed cloisters at your own risk. I know very well that this is not easy. It is no trifle for a man to part with all he has been accustomed to from the day of his birth and with which he has grown up to maturity. Men are ready for terrible sacrifices, but not for those demanded of them by the new life. Are they ready to sacrifice their existing civilizations, their manner of life, religion, and the accepted conventional morality? Are they prepared to forgo all the fruits raised with such effort—the fruit we have been boasting of for three centuries? Are they prepared to forgo all the conveniences and delights of our existence, to prefer the crudities of youth to cultured decrepitude, to break down their hereditary castle just for the pleasure of helping to lay the foundation of a new house which will certainly not be built till long after they are gone?' (Herzen, vol. v, p. 55.)

That was written nearly half a century ago by a Russian writer whose penetrating mind even then clearly saw what is now seen by all thoughtful men—the impossibility of continuing life on its former foundations, and the necessity of establishing new forms of life.

From the very simplest, lowest, and most worldly point of view it is already clear that it is madness to remain in a building which cannot sustain the weight of its roof. It is obvious that we must leave it. Indeed it is difficult to imagine a position more wretched than that in which the Christian world now is, with its nations armed one against another, with the ever-growing taxes for the maintenance of its ever-increasing armaments, with the growing hatred of the working classes for the rich, and with war hanging over us all like the sword of Damocles, threatening to fall at any moment and certain to do so sooner or later.

A revolution could hardly be more disastrous for the great mass of the people than the existing order or rather disorder of our life, with its habitual sacrifices to unnatural toil, poverty, drunkenness, and debauchery, and with all the horrors of impending war, which will devour in a year more victims than all the revolutions of a century.

What will become of us and of the entire human race if each of us fulfils what God, through the conscience implanted in us, demands of us? Will it not be disastrous if being wholly in the power of a master I carry out what he orders me to do in the establishment arranged and ruled by him, strange though it may seem to me who do not know his ultimate purpose?

But it is not even the question as to what will happen, that troubles people when they hesitate to do the master's will. What distresses them is the question how they are to live without those customary conditions of life known as science, art, civilization, and culture. We ourselves feel all the burden of our present life, we see that this organization of life if it continues will inevitably be our ruin, but at the same time we want the conditions that have grown out of that life (our science, art, civilization, and culture) to remain intact when our life changes.

It is as if a man living in an old house and suffering from cold and other inconveniences in it, knowing too that it will soon collapse, should consent to its being rebuilt, but only on condition that he should not have to move out of it—a condition tantamount to refusing to let it be rebuilt at all. 'What if I leave the house, depriving myself of all its conveniences, and the new house does not get built or is built differently, leaving me without the things I am accustomed to?'

But the materials and the builders being there the probability is that the new house will be built better than the former one. Besides there is not only the likelihood, but the certainty, that the old house will collapse and crush those who remain in it.

Whether the former habitual conditions of life will continue, or whether they will be abolished and quite new and better ones arise, it is in any case inevitably necessary to emerge from the old conditions which have become impossible and fatal, and to move forward to meet the future.

'Civilization and culture, science and art, will disappear!'

But all these are only manifestations of truth, and the coming change is to be made solely for the sake of a closer approximation to the realization of truth. How then can manifestations of the truth disappear through our realization of it? The manifestations will be different, better, and higher, but they will certainly not cease to be. What was false in them will be destroyed but what was true in them will blossom out and be strengthened.

6

Bethink yourselves men, or believe the Gospel, the teaching of welfare. If you do not bethink yourselves you will all perish, like those whom Pilate slew, and like those upon whom the tower of Siloam fell, like millions and millions who have perished, slayers and slain, executioners and executed, torturers and tortured, and like that man who having filled his barns thinking to enjoy a long life, perished stupidly the very night he meant to begin living. 'Bethink yourselves and believe in the glad tidings,' said Christ nineteen hundred years ago, and he says so yet more convincingly now, because the wretchedness and irrationality of our life, which he foretold, has now reached its utmost limits.

Nowadays after so many centuries of fruitless efforts to make our life secure by the Pagan organization of violence, it should be evident to everyone that efforts in that direction merely bring fresh dangers both into our personal and our social life instead of rendering it more secure.

By whatever names we dignify ourselves, in whatever apparel we attire ourselves, by whatever and before whatever priests we may be smeared with oil, however many millions we possess, however many special guards are stationed along our route,[19] however many policemen guard our wealth, however many so-called miscreant-revolutionaries and anarchists we may execute, whatever exploits we ourselves may perform, whatever States we may found, whatever fortresses and towers we may erect—from the Tower of Babel to that of Eiffel

---

[19] These references are evidently to the procedure at the Tsar's coronation.—A. M.

—we are always all of us confronted by two inevitable conditions of life which destroy its whole meaning. There is first
of all death, which may at any moment overtake any of us,
and there is the transitoriness of all that we do and that is
so quickly destroyed leaving no trace. Whatever we may do
—found kingdoms, build palaces and monuments, compose
poems and romances—everything is transitory, and soon
passes leaving no trace. And therefore, however we may conceal it from ourselves, we cannot help seeing that the meaning
of our life can be neither in our personal physical existence
subject to unavoidable sufferings and inevitable death, nor
in any worldly institution or organization.

Whoever you may be who read these lines, consider your
position and your duties—not the position of landowner,
merchant, judge, emperor, president, minister, priest, or
soldier, temporarily attributed to you by men, nor those imaginary duties imposed on you by that position—but your
real position in eternity as a creature who by Someone's will
has been called out of unconsciousness after an eternity of
non-existence, to which by the same will you may at any moment be recalled. Think of your duties—not your imaginary
duties as a landowner to your estate, as a merchant to your
capital, as an emperor, minister, or official to the State—but
those real duties which follow from your real position as a
being called to life and endowed with reason and love.

Are you doing what He demands of you who sent you into
the world and to whom you will soon return? Are you doing
what He wills? Are you doing His will when as landowner
or manufacturer you take the produce of the toil of the poor,
arranging your life on that spoliation, or when as ruler or judge
you do violence, sentencing men to execution, or when as
soldiers you prepare yourselves for war, go to war, plunder
and kill?

You say that the world is so made that this is inevitable,
that you do this not of your own free-will but because you
are compelled. But is it possible that so strong an aversion for
human suffering, for ill-treatment, for the killing of men,
should have been so deeply implanted in you; that you

should be so imbued with the need of loving your fellows and a still stronger need of being loved by them, that you see clearly that only by recognizing the equality of all men and by mutual service one of another can the greatest good that is accessible to man be realized; that the same thing is taught you by your heart, by your reason, by the faith you profess, and the same said by science—is it possible that despite all this you can by some very vague and complicated reasoning be forced to do everything directly opposed to it? Are you really, as landowner or capitalists, obliged to base your whole life on the oppression of the people; as an emperor or president are you really obliged to command armies—that is, to be the head and leader of murders; as a government official are you really forced to take by violence from the poor the money earned by the sweat of their brow, to avail yourself of it or hand it over to rich men; as judge or juryman are you really obliged to sentence erring men to ill-treatment and death because the truth has not been revealed to them; and above all (for on this the whole evil is based) are you—and every young man—really compelled to be a soldier, and renouncing your own will and all human sentiments, compelled to promise to kill all those whom men you do not know may order you to kill?

That cannot be!

If people tell you that all this is necessary for the maintenance of the existing order of life and that this social order, with its destitution, hunger, prisons, executions, armies and wars, is necessary for society, that still more miseries would ensue were that organization infringed; all *that* is said only by those who profit by such an organization. Those who suffer from it—and they are ten times as numerous—all think and say the contrary. And in the depth of your soul you yourself know it is untrue, you know that the existing organization of life has outlived its time and must inevitably be reconstructed on new principles, and that therefore there is no need to sacrifice all human feeling to maintain it.

Even admitting that the existing order is necessary, why do you believe that it is just your business to maintain it at the cost of all your best human feelings? Who has made you a nurse in charge of this sick system? Neither society, nor the State, nor anyone else has ever asked you to support the existing organization by occupying the position (of landowner, trader, emperor, priest, or soldier) that you occupy, and you know very well that you occupy your position not at all with the self-sacrificing aim of maintaining an order of life necessary for the welfare of mankind, but for yourself—for the sake of your covetousness, vanity, ambition, insolence, or cowardice. If you did not want that position you would not have done all that it constantly demands of you in order to retain it. Only try to stop doing those complex, cruel, cunning and contemptible things that you constantly do to retain your position and you will quickly be deprived of it. Only try, as a ruler or an official, to give up lying, acting meanly, and participating in acts of violence and executions; try as a priest to give up deception; try in the army not to kill; as a landlord or manufacturer try to cease protecting your property by violence and by the law-courts; and you will immediately lose the position which you pretend is forced upon you and which you pretend oppresses you.

It is impossible for a man to be placed against his will in a situation repugnant to his conscience.

If you are in such a position it is not because it is necessary for anybody, but because you yourself want it. And therefore knowing that your position is directly opposed to your heart, to your reason, to your religion, and even to science in which you believe, you cannot but reflect on the question as to whether by remaining in that position, and above all by trying to justify it, you are doing right.

It might be possible to risk making a mistake if you had time to see it and to retrieve your error and if you ran the risk for something of any importance. But when you know for certain that you may disappear at any moment without the least possibility of retrieving a mistake either for yourself or for others involved in it, and when you also know that whatever you may do in the external arrangement of the world will soon all disappear as certainly as you yourself and without leaving a trace, it is evident that there is no reason for you to risk making so terrible a mistake.

This would be quite simple and clear if only we did not by hypocrisy befog the truth indubitably revealed to us.

Divide up what you possess with others, do not gather riches, do not exalt yourself, do not steal, do not cause suffering, do not kill anyone, do not do to another what you would not have done to yourself, was said not only nineteen hundred but five thousand years ago. And there can be no doubt of the truth of this law, and but for hypocrisy it would be impossible for men—even if they themselves did not conform to it—to fail to recognize at least its necessity, and that he who does not do these things is doing wrong.

But you say there is a public welfare for the sake of which these rules may and should be infringed: for the public good it is permissible to kill, torture, and rob. You say, as Caiaphas did, that it is better for one man to perish than the whole nation, and you sign the death sentence of a first, a second, and a third man, load your rifle against this man who is to perish for the public welfare, put him in prison, and take his possessions. You say that you do these cruel things because as a member of society and of the State you feel that it is your duty to serve them: as a landowner, judge, emperor, or military man to conform to their laws. But besides belonging to a certain State and having duties arising from that position, you belong also to eternity and to God and have duties arising from that.

And as a man's duty to his family or class is always subordinate to his duty as a citizen of a State, so that duty in its turn is of necessity subordinate to his duty in relation to the universal life and to God.

And as it would be irrational to cut down telegraph posts to obtain fuel for a family or a society to increase their welfare, thus infringing the laws which guard the welfare of the country as a whole, so also is it irrational to torture, execute, and kill a man in order to make the State secure and increase its welfare, thus violating the unquestionable laws which guard the welfare of the world.

The obligations which result from your citizenship of the State must be subordinate to your higher eternal obligations to the infinite life of the world and to God, and cannot contradict these, as Christ's disciples said nineteen hundred years ago: 'Whether it be right to hearken unto you more than unto God, judge ye' (Acts iv. 19), and 'We ought to obey God rather than men' (Acts v. 29).

We are told that in order not to infringe the ever-changing system established yesterday by a few men in one particular corner of the world, we must do acts of violence, commit murder, and oppress men, thus violating the eternal and immutable order of the world established by God and by reason. Is that possible?

And therefore we cannot but reflect that our position as landowner, trader, judge, emperor, president, minister, priest, or soldier, is bound up with oppression, violence, deceptions, and murder, and recognize that it is wrong.

I do not say that if you are a landowner you are bound immediately to give your land to the poor; if you are a capitalist to give your money or your factory to the workpeople; if you are a tsar, minister, official, judge, or general, that you should at once renounce your advantageous position; or if you are a soldier (if, that is to say, you occupy the position on which all violence is based) that you should immediately refuse military service despite all the danger of doing so.

Were you to do this you would be doing the very best thing possible, but it may be, as is most likely, that you have not the strength. You have ties; a family, dependents, and superiors; you are under such powerful influences that you are not strong enough to shake them off. But to recognize the truth as a truth and avoid lying about it is a thing you can always do. It is always in your power to cease asserting that you remain a landowner, a manufacturer, a merchant, an artist, or a writer, because that is useful to mankind; that you are a governor, a public prosecutor, or tsar, not because it is agreeable to you and you are used to it, but for the public good; that you continue to be a soldier not from fear of punishment but because you consider the army necessary for the security of people's lives. It is always in your power to stop lying like that to yourself and to others, and you not only can but should do this, because in this alone—in freeing yourself from falsehood and confessing the truth—lies the sole welfare of your life.

You need only free yourself from falsehood and your situation will inevitably change of itself.

There is one and only one thing in life in which it is granted man to be free and over which he has full control—all else being beyond his power. That one thing is to perceive the truth and profess it.

And yet, just because other wretched, erring creatures like yourself assure you that you are a soldier, an emperor, a landowner, a rich man, a priest, or a general, you do evil deeds obviously contrary to your reason and your heart: you torment, plunder, and kill people, base your existence on their sufferings, and above all instead of fulfilling the one duty of your life—acknowledging and confessing the truth known to you—you carefully pretend not to know it and hide it from yourself and from others, acting thereby in direct opposition to that sole purpose to which you are called.

And in what circumstances do you do that? You who may die at any moment, sign death sentences, declare war, go to war, fleece the labourers, sit in judgement, and punish people; you live in luxury surrounded by the poor, and teach weak men who trust you that these things must be, and that such is the duty of men. And yet it may be that at the very moment you are doing these things a germ or a bullet may come in your direction and you will rattle in your throat and die and forever lose the possibility of repairing the evil you have done to others and above all to yourself. You will have ruined the only life given to you in the whole of eternity, without having accomplished the one thing you unquestionably ought to have done.

However simple and however old it may be and however we may have stupefied ourselves by hypocrisy and the auto-suggestion resulting from it, nothing can destroy the certainty of this clear and simple truth, that no external efforts can safeguard our life which is inevitably attended by unavoidable sufferings and ends in yet more inevitable death, which may come to each of us at any moment, and that consequently our life can have no other meaning than the constant fulfilment of what is demanded of us by that Power that has placed us in this life and given us an indubitable guide—our rational consciousness.

That power cannot want of us what is irrational and impossible—the establishment of our temporary carnal life, the life of society or of the State. It demands of us what alone is certain, rational, and possible—the service of the Kingdom of God, that is, our co-operation in establishing the greatest possible unity among all living beings—a unity possible only in the truth. It therefore demands that we acknowledge and profess the truth revealed to us—the only thing that is always in our power.

'Seek ye first the Kingdom of God and his righteousness, and all these things shall be added unto you.'

The sole meaning of human life in serving the world by promoting the establishment of the Kingdom of God. This service can be accomplished only by the recognition and avowal of the truth by each separate individual.

'The Kingdom of God cometh not with outward show; neither shall they say, Lo here! or, lo there! for, behold, the Kingdom of God is within you.'

[1893.]

'THOU SHALT NOT KILL'

'Thou shalt not kill.' EXOD. xx. 13.

'The disciple is not above his master: but every one when he is perfected shall be as his master.' LUKE vi. 40.

'For all they that take the sword shall perish with the sword.' MATT. xxvi. 52.

'Therefore all things whatsoever ye would that men should do to you, do ye even so to them.' MATT. vii. 12.

When Kings are executed after trial, as in the case of Charles I, Louis XVI, and Maximilian of Mexico; or when they are killed in Court conspiracies, like Peter III, Paul, and various Sultans, Shahs, and Khans—little is said about it. But when they are killed without a trial and without a Court conspiracy—as in the case of Henry IV of France, Alexander II, the Empress of Austria, the late Shah of Persia, and, recently, Humbert—such murders excite the greatest surprise and indignation among Kings and Emperors and their adherents, just as if they themselves never took part in murders, or profited by them, or instigated them. But in fact the mildest of the murdered Kings (Alexander II or Humbert, for instance), were instigators of and accomplices and partakers in the murder of tens of thousands of men who perished on the field of battle, not to speak of executions in their own countries; while more cruel Kings and Emperors have been guilty of hundreds of thousands, and even millions, of murders.

The teaching of Christ repeals the law, 'An eye for an eye, and a tooth for a tooth'; but those who have always clung to that law, and still cling to it, and who apply it to a terrible degree—not only claiming an eye for an eye, but without provocation decreeing the slaughter of thousands, as they do when they declare war—have no right to be indignant at the application of that same law to themselves in so small and insignificant a degree that hardly one King or Emperor is killed for each hundred thousand, or perhaps even for each million, who are killed by the order and with the consent of Kings and Emperors. Kings and Emperors not only should not be indignant at such murders as those of Alexander II and Humbert, but they should be surprised that such murders are so rare, considering the continual and universal example of murder that they give to mankind.

The crowd are so hypnotized that they do not understand the meaning of what is going on before their eyes. They see what constant care Kings, Emperors, and Presidents devote to their disciplined armies; they see the reviews, parades, and manœuvres the rulers hold, about which they boast to one another; and the people crowd to see their own brothers, dressed up in the bright clothes of fools, turned into machines to the sound of drum and trumpet, and all making one and the same movement at one and the same moment at the shout of one man—but they do not understand what it all means. Yet the meaning of this drilling is very clear and simple: it is nothing but a preparation for killing.

It is stupefying men in order to make them fit instruments for murder. And those who do this, who chiefly direct it and are proud of it, are the Kings, Emperors, and Presidents. And it is just these men—who are specially occupied in organizing murder and who have made murder their profession, who wear military uniforms and carry murderous weapons (swords) at their sides—who are horrified and indignant when one of themselves is murdered.

The murder of Kings—the murder of Humbert—is terrible, but not on account of its cruelty. The things done by command of Kings and Emperors—not only past events such as the massacre of St. Bartholomew, religious butcheries, the terrible repressions of peasant rebellions, and Paris *coups d'état*, but the present-day government executions, the doing-to-death of prisoners in solitary confinement, the Disciplinary Battalions, the hangings, the beheadings, the shootings and slaughter in wars—are incomparably more cruel than the murders committed by Anarchists. Nor are these murders terrible because undeserved. If Alexander II and Humbert did not deserve death, still less did the thousands of Russians who perished at Plevna, or of Italians who perished in Abyssinia.[1] Such murders are terrible not because they are cruel or unmerited, but because of the unreasonableness of those who commit them.

If the regicides act under the influence of personal feelings of indignation evoked by the sufferings of an oppressed people for which they hold Alexander or Carnot or Humbert responsible, or if they act from personal feelings of revenge, then however immoral their conduct may be it is at least intelligible. But how is it that a body of men (Anarchists, we are told) such as those by whom Bresci was sent, and who are now threatening another Emperor—how is it that they cannot devise any better means of improving the condition of humanity than by killing people whose destruction can be of no more use than the decapitation of that mythical monster on whose neck a new head appeared as soon as one was cut off? Kings and Emperors have long ago arranged for themselves a system like that of a magazine-rifle: as soon as one bullet has been discharged another takes its place. *Le roi est mort, vive le roi!* So what is the use of killing them?

Only on a most superficial view can the killing of these men seem a means of saving the nations from oppression and from wars destructive of human life.

One only need remember that similar oppressions and similar wars went on no matter who was at the head of the government—Nicholas or Alexander, Frederick or Wilhelm, Napoleon or Louis, Palmerston or Gladstone, McKinley or anyone else—in order to understand that it is not any particular person who causes these oppressions and these wars from which the nations suffer. The misery of nations is caused not

---

[1] In the war of 1896.—A. M.

by particular persons but by the particular order of society under which the people are so tied up together that they find themselves all in the power of a few men, or more often in the power of one single man: a man so perverted by his unnatural position as arbiter of the fate and lives of millions that he is always in an unhealthy state, and always suffers more or less from a mania of self-aggrandizement, which only his exceptional position conceals from general notice.

Apart from the fact that such men are surrounded from earliest childhood to the grave by the most insensate luxury and an atmosphere of falsehood and flattery which always accompanies them, their whole education and all their occupations are centred on one object: learning about former murders, the best present-day ways of murdering, and the best preparations for future murder. From childhood they learn about killing in all its possible forms. They always carry about with them murderous weapons—swords or sabres; they dress themselves in various uniforms; they attend parades, reviews, and manœuvres; they visit one another, presenting one another with Orders and nominating one another to the command of regiments—and not only does no one tell them plainly what they are doing, or say that to busy oneself with preparations for killing is revolting and criminal, but from all sides they hear nothing but approval and enthusiasm for all this activity of theirs. Every time they go out, and at each parade and review, crowds of people flock to greet them with enthusiasm, and it seems to them as if the whole nation approves of their conduct. The only part of the Press that reaches them, and that seems to them the expression of the feelings of the whole people, or at least of its best representatives, most slavishly extols their every word and action, however silly or wicked they may be. Those around them, men and women, clergy and laity—all people who do not prize human dignity—vying with one another in refined flattery, agree with them about anything and deceive them about everything, making it impossible for them to see life as it is. Such rulers might live a hundred years without ever seeing one single really independent man or ever hearing the truth spoken. One is sometimes appalled to hear of the words and deeds of these men; but one need only consider their position in order to understand that anyone in their place would act as they do. If a reasonable man found himself in their place there is only one reasonable action he could perform, and that would be to get away from such a position. Anyone remaining in it would behave as they do.

What indeed must go on in the head of some Wilhelm of Germany—a narrow-minded, ill-educated, vain man, with the ideals of a German Junker—when nothing he can say, however stupid or horrid, will not be met by an enthusiastic 'Hoch!' and be commented on by the Press of the entire world as though it were something highly important. When he says that at his word soldiers should be ready to kill their own fathers, people shout 'Hurrah!' When he says that the Gospel must be introduced with an iron fist—'Hurrah!' When he says the army is to take no prisoners in China but to slaughter everybody, he is not put into a lunatic asylum but people shout 'Hurrah!' and set sail for China to execute his commands. Or Nicholas II (a man naturally modest) begins his reign by announcing to venerable old men who had expressed a wish to be allowed to discuss their own affairs that such ideas of self-government were 'insensate dreams'—and the organs of the Press he sees and the people he meets praise him for it. He proposes a childish, silly, and hypocritical project of universal peace while at the same time ordering an increase in the army—and there are no limits to the laudations of his wisdom and virtue. Without any need, he foolishly and mercilessly insults and oppresses a whole nation, the Finns, and again he hears nothing but praise. Finally, he arranges the Chinese slaughter—terrible in its injustice, cruelty, and incompatibility with his peace projects—and people applaud him from all sides, both as a victor and as a continuer of his father's peace policy.

What indeed must be going on in the heads and hearts of these men?

So it is not the Alexanders and Humberts, nor the Wilhelms, Nicholases, and Chamberlains[2]—though they decree these oppressions of the nations and these wars—who are really most guilty of these sins; it is rather those who place and support them in the position of arbiters over the lives of their fellow men. And therefore the thing to do is not to kill the Alexanders, Nicholases, Wilhelms, and Humberts, but to cease to support the arrangement of society of which they are a result. And the present order of society is supported by the selfishness and stupefaction of the people, who sell their freedom and honour for insignificant material advantages.

People who stand on the lowest rung of the ladder—partly as a result of being stupefied by a patriotic and pseudo-religious education and partly for the sake of personal advantages—cede their freedom and sense of human dignity at the bidding of those who stand above them and offer them material advantages. In the same way—in consequence of stupefaction, but chiefly for the sake of advantages—those who are a little higher up the ladder cede their freedom and manly dignity, and the same thing repeats itself with those standing yet higher, and so on to the topmost rung—to those who, or to him who, standing at the apex of the social cone have nothing more to obtain, for whom the only motives of action are love of power and vanity, and who are generally so perverted and stupefied by the power of life and death which they hold over their fellow men, and by the consequent servility and flattery of those who surround them, that without ceasing to do evil they feel quite assured that they are benefactors to the human race.

It is the people who sacrifice their dignity as men for material profit who produce these men who cannot act otherwise than as they do act, and with whom it is useless to be angry for their stupid and wicked actions. To kill such men is like whipping children whom one has first spoilt.

That nations should not be oppressed, and that there

---

[2] In Russia and indeed generally throughout Europe Chamberlain was considered responsible for the Boer War.—A. M.

should be none of these useless wars, and that men should not be indignant with those who seem to cause these evils and should not kill them—it seems that only a very small thing is necessary. It is necessary that men should understand things as they are, should call them by their right names, and should know that an army is an instrument for killing, and that the enrolment and management of an army—the very things which Kings, Emperors, and Presidents occupy themselves with so self-confidently—is a preparation for murder.

If only each King, Emperor, and President understood that his work of directing armies is not an honourable and important duty, as his flatterers persuade him it is, but a bad and shameful act of preparation for murder—and if each private individual understood that the payment of taxes wherewith to hire and equip soldiers, and above all army service itself, are not matters of indifference, but are bad and shameful actions by which he not only permits but participates in murder—then this power of Emperors, Kings, and Presidents, which now arouses our indignation and which causes them to be murdered, would disappear of itself.

So the Alexanders, Carnots, Humberts, and others should not be murdered, but it should be explained to them that they are themselves murderers, and above all they should not be allowed to kill people: men should refuse to murder at their command.

If people do not yet act in this way it is only because governments, to maintain themselves, diligently exercise an hypnotic influence upon the people. And therefore we may help to prevent people killing either Kings or one another, not by killing—murder only increases the hypnotism—but by arousing people from their hypnotic condition.

And it is this I have tried to do by these remarks.

[August 8, o.s., 1900.]

Prohibited in Russia, an attempt was made to print this article in the Russian language in Germany; but the edition was seized in July, 1903, and after a trial in the Provincial Court of Leipzig (August, 1903) it was pronounced to be insulting to the German Kaiser, and all copies were ordered to be destroyed.—A. M.

WHAT'S TO BE DONE?

About a month ago I had a visit from two young men, one of whom was wearing a cap and peasant bast shoes, and the other a once fashionable black hat and torn boots.

I asked them who they were, and with unconcealed pride they informed me that they were workmen expelled from Moscow for taking part in the armed rising. Passing our village they had found employment as watchmen on an estate, but had lived there less than a month. The day before they came to see me they had been dismissed, the owner charging them with attempting to persuade the peasants to lay waste the estate. They denied the charge with a smile, saying they had attempted no persuasion but had merely gone into the village of an evening and chatted with their fellows.

They had both read revolutionary literature, particularly the bolder of the two, who had sparkling black eyes and white teeth and smiled a great deal, and they both used foreign words such as 'orator',[1] 'proletariat', 'Social-Democrat', 'exploitation', and so on, in and out of place.

I asked them what they had read, and the darker one replied with a smile that he had read various pamphlets.

'Which?' I asked.

'All sorts. "Land and Liberty" for instance.'

I then asked them what they thought of such pamphlets.

'They tell the real truth,' replied the dark one.

'What is it you find so true in them?' I asked.

---

[1] Meaning a stump orator for one of the political parties.—A. M.

'Why, that it has become impossible to go on living as we do.'

'Why is it impossible?'

'Why? Because we have neither land nor work, and the government throttles the people without sense or reason.'

And interrupting one another, they began to tell how people who had done nothing wrong were flogged by Cossacks with their heavy whips, seized haphazard by the police, and even shot in their own houses.

On my saying that an armed rebellion was a bad and irrational affair, the dark one smiled and replied quietly: 'We are of a different opinion.'

When I spoke of the sin of murder and the law of God they exchanged glances, and the darker one shrugged his shoulders.

'Does the law of God say the proletariat is to be exploited?' he asked. 'People used to think so, but now they know better, and it can't go on. . . .'

I brought them out some booklets, chiefly on religious subjects. They glanced at the titles and were evidently not pleased.

'Perhaps you don't care for them? If so, don't take them.'

'Why not?' said the darker one, and putting the booklets into their blouses they took their leave.

Though I had not been reading the papers, I knew what had been going on in Russia recently from the talk of my family, from letters I had received, and from accounts given by visitors; and just because I had not read the papers I knew particularly well of the amazing change that had latterly taken place in the views held by our society and by the people, a change amounting to this, that whereas people formerly considered the government to be necessary, now all except a very few looked upon its activity as criminal and wrong and blamed the government alone for all the disturbances. That opinion was shared by professors, postal officials, authors, shopkeepers, doctors, and workmen alike, and the feeling was strengthened by the dissolution of the first Duma and had reached its highest point as a result of the cruel measures lately adopted by the government.

I knew this. But my talk with these two men had a great effect on me. Like the shock which suddenly turns freezing liquid into ice, it suddenly turned a whole series of similar impressions I had previously received into a definite and indubitable conviction.

After my talk with them I saw clearly that all the crimes the government is now committing in order to crush the revolution not only fail to crush it but inflame it all the more, and that if the revolutionary movement appears for a time to die down under the cruelties of the government, it is not destroyed but merely temporarily hidden, and will inevitably spring up again with new and increased strength. The fire is now in such a state that any contact with it can only increase its fierceness. And it became clear to me that the only thing that could help would be for the government to cease any and every attempt to enforce its will, to cease not only executing and arresting, but all banishing, persecuting, and proscribing. Only in that way could this horrible strife between brutalized men be brought to an end.

It became perfectly clear to me that the only means of stopping the horrors that are being committed, and the perversion of the people, was the resignation by the government of its power. I was convinced that that was the best thing the government could do, but I was equally firmly convinced that were I to make any such proposal it would be received merely as an indication that I was quite insane. And therefore, though it was perfectly clear to me that the continuance of governmental cruelty could only make things worse and not better, I did not attempt to write or even to speak about it.

Nearly a month has passed, and unfortunately my supposition finds more and more confirmation. There are more and more executions and more and more murders and robberies. I know this both from conversation and from chance glances at the papers, and I know that the mood of the people and of

'But *what's to be done?* They can't be allowed to rob and kill and go unpunished,' said one of those present.

Those words: *What's to be done?* were the very words the two vagabonds from the estate and to-day's peasant revolutionary had used.

'It is impossible to endure these insensate horrors committed by a corrupt government which is ruining both the country and the people. We hate the means we have to employ, but *What's to be done?*' say the revolutionists on the one side.

'One cannot allow some self-appointed pretenders to seize power and rule Russia as they like, perverting and ruining it. Of course, the temporary measures now employed are lamentable, but *What's to be done?*' say the others, the conservatives.

And I thought of people near to me—revolutionists and conservatives—and of to-day's peasant and of those unfortunate revolutionists who import and prepare bombs and murder and rob, and of the equally pitiable, lost men who decree and organize the courts martial, take part in them, and shoot and hang, all alike assuring themselves that they are doing what is necessary and all alike repeating the same words: *What's to be done?*

What's to be done? they all ask, but they do not put it as a question: 'What ought I to do?' They put it as an assertion that it will be much worse for everyone if we cease to do what we are doing.

And everyone is so accustomed to these words which hide an explanation and justification of the most horrible and immoral actions, that it enters no one's head to ask: 'Who are you who ask *What's to be done?* Who are you that you consider yourselves called on to decide other people's fate by actions which all men—even you yourselves—know to be odious and wicked? How do you know that what you wish to alter should be altered in the way that seems to you to be good? Do you not know that there are many men such as you who consider bad and harmful what you consider good and useful? And how do you know that what you are doing will produce the results you expect, for you cannot but be aware that the results attained are generally contrary to those aimed at—especially in affairs relating to the life of a whole nation? And above all, what right have you to do what is contrary to the law of God (if you acknowledge a God), or to the most generally accepted laws of morality (if you acknowledge nothing but the generally accepted laws of morality)? By what right do you consider yourselves freed from those most simple and indubitable human obligations which are irreconcilable with your revolutionary or governmental actions?

If your question *What's to be done?* is really a question and not a justification, and if you put it as you should do to yourselves, a quite clear and simple answer naturally suggests itself. The answer is that you must do not what the Tsar, Governor, police-officers, Duma, or some political party demands of you, but what is natural to you as a man, what is demanded of you by that Power which sent you into the world—the Power most people are accustomed to call God.

And as soon as this reply is given to the question *What's to be done?* it immediately dispels the stupid, crime-begetting fog under whose influence men imagine, for some reason, that they, alone of all men—they who are perhaps the most entangled and the most astray from the true path of life—are called on to decide the fate of millions and for the questionable benefit of these millions to commit deeds which unquestionably and evidently bring disaster to them.

There exists a general law acknowledged by all reasonable men and confirmed by tradition, by all the religions of all the nations, and by true science. This law is that men, to fulfil their destiny and attain their greatest welfare, should help one another, love one another, and in any case not attack each other's liberty and life. Yet strange to say, there are people who assure us that it is quite needless to obey this law, that there are cases in which one may and should act contrary to it, and that such deviations from the eternal law will bring more welfare both to individuals and to societies than the fulfilment of the reasonable, supreme law common to all mankind.

The workmen in a vast complex factory have received and accepted clear instructions from the master as to what they should and should not do, both that the works may go well and for their own welfare. But people turn up who have no idea of what the works produce or of how they produce it, and they assure the workmen that they should cease to do what the master has ordered and should do just the contrary, in order that the works may go properly and the workers obtain the greatest benefit.

Is not that just what these people are doing—unable as they are to grasp all the consequences flowing from the general activity of humanity? They not only do not obey the eternal laws (common to all mankind and confirmed by the human intellect) framed for the success of that complex human activity as well as for the benefit of its individual members, but they break them directly and consciously for the sake of some small one-sided casual aims set up by some of themselves (generally the most erring) under the impression that they will thereby attain results more beneficial than those obtainable by fulfilling the eternal law common to all men and consonant with man's nature—forgetting that others imagine quite the contrary.

I know that to men suffering from that spiritual disease, political obsession, a plain and clear answer to the question *What's to be done?*, an answer telling them to obey the highest law common to all mankind—the law of love to one's neighbour—will appear abstract and unpractical. An answer that would seem to them practical would be one telling them that men, who cannot know the consequences of their actions and cannot know whether they will be alive an hour hence, but who know very well that every murder and act of violence is bad, should nevertheless—under the fanciful pretext that they are establishing other people's future welfare—continually act as if they knew infallibly what consequences their actions will produce, and as if they did not know that to kill and torment people is bad, but only knew that such or such a monarchy or constitution is desirable.

That will be the case with many who are suffering from

the spiritual disease of political obsession, but I think the great majority of people suffering from the horrors and crimes committed by men who are so diseased will at last understand the terrible deception under which those lie who regard coercive power used by man to man to be rightful and beneficent, and having understood this will free themselves for ever from the madness and wickedness of either participating in force-using power or submitting to it, and will understand that each man must do one thing—that is, fulfil what is demanded of him by the reasonable and beneficent Source which men call 'God', of whose demands no man possessed of reason can fail to be conscious.

I cannot but think that if all men, forgetting their various positions as ministers, policemen, presidents, and members of various combative or non-combative parties, would only do what is natural to each of them as a human being—not only would those horrors and sufferings cease of which the life of man (and especially of the Russian people) is now full, but the Kingdom of God would have come upon earth.

If only some people would act so, the more of them there were the less evil would there be and the more good order and general welfare.

[October, 1906.]

I CANNOT BE SILENT

'Seven death sentences: two in Petersburg, one in Moscow, two in Pénza, and two in Riga. Four executions: two in Khersón, one in Vílna, one in Odessa.'

This, repeated daily in every newspaper and continued not for weeks, not for months, not for a year, but for years. And this in Russia, that Russia where the people regard every criminal as a man to be pitied and where till quite recently capital punishment was not recognized by law! I remember how proud I used to be of that when talking to Western Europeans. But now for a second and even a third year we have executions, executions, executions, unceasingly!

I take up to-day's paper.

To-day, May 9th, the paper contains these few words: 'To-day in Khersón on the Strelbítsky Field, twenty peasants[1] were hung for an attack, made with intent to rob, on a landed proprietor's estate in the Elisabetgrad district.'

Twelve of those by whose labour we live, the very men whom we have depraved and are still depraving by every means in our power—from the poison of vódka to the terrible falsehood of a creed we impose on them with all our might, but do not ourselves believe in—twelve of these men stran-

---

[1] The papers have since contradicted the statement that twenty peasants were hung. I can only be glad of the mistake, glad not only that eight less have been strangled than was stated at first, but glad also that the awful figure moved me to express in these pages a feeling that has long tormented me. I leave the rest unchanged, therefore, merely substituting the word twelve for the word twenty, since what I said refers not only to the twelve who were hung but to all the thousands who have lately been crushed and killed.—L. T.

gled with cords by those whom they feed and clothe and house, and who have depraved and still continue to deprave them. Twelve husbands, fathers, and sons, from among those upon whose kindness, industry, and simplicity alone rests the whole of Russian life, are seized, imprisoned, and shackled. Then their hands are tied behind their backs lest they should seize the ropes by which they are to be hung, and they are led to the gallows. Several peasants similar to those about to be hung, but armed, dressed in clean soldiers' uniforms with good boots on their feet and with guns in their hands, accompany the condemned men. Beside them walks a long-haired man wearing a stole and vestments of gold or silver cloth, and bearing a cross. The procession stops. The man in command of the whole business says something, the secretary reads a paper; and when the paper has been read the long-haired man, addressing those whom other people are about to strangle with cords, says something about God and Christ. Immediately after these words the hangmen (there are several, for one man could not manage so complicated a business) dissolve some soap, and, having soaped the loops in the cords that they may tighten better, seize the shackled men, put shrouds on them, lead them to a scaffold, and place the well-soaped nooses round their necks.

And then, one after another, living men are pushed off the benches which are drawn from under their feet, and by their own weight suddenly tighten the nooses round their necks and are painfully strangled. Men, alive a minute before, become corpses dangling from a rope, at first swinging slowly and then resting motionless.

All this is carefully arranged and planned by learned and enlightened people of the upper class. They arrange to do these things secretly at daybreak so that no one shall see them done, and they arrange that the responsibility for these iniquities shall be so subdivided among those who commit them that each may think and say that it is not he who is responsible for them. They arrange to seek out the most depraved and unfortunate of men, and, while obliging them to do this business planned and approved by themselves, still keep

up an appearance of abhorring those who do it. They even
plan such a subtle device as this: sentences are pronounced
by a military tribunal, yet it is not military people but civilians
who have to be present at the execution. And the business is
performed by unhappy, deluded, perverted, and despised
men who have nothing left them but to soap the cords well
that they may grip the necks without fail, and then to get
well drunk on poison sold them by these same enlightened
upper-class people in order the more quickly and fully to forget their souls and their quality as men. A doctor makes his
round of the bodies, feels them, and reports to those in authority that the business has been done properly—all twelve
are certainly dead. And those in authority depart to their
ordinary occupations with the consciousness of a necessary
though painful task performed. The bodies, now grown cold,
are taken down and buried.

The thing is awful!

And this is done not once, and not only to these twelve unhappy, misguided men from among the best class of the Russian people; it is done unceasingly for years, to hundreds
and thousands of similar misguided men, misguided by the
very people who do these terrible things to them.

And it is not this dreadful thing alone that is being done.
All sorts of other tortures and violence are being perpetrated
in prisons, fortresses, and convict settlements, on the same
plea and with the same cold-blooded cruelty.

This is dreadful, but most dreadful of all is the fact that it
is not done impulsively under the sway of feelings that
silence reason, as occurs in fights, war, or even burglary, but
on the contrary it is done at the demand of reason and calculation that silence feeling. That is what makes these deeds
so particularly dreadful. Dreadful because these acts—committed by men who, from the judge to the hangman, do not
wish to do them—prove more vividly than anything else
how pernicious to human souls is despotism; the power of
man over man.

It is revolting that one man can take from another his
labour, his money, his cow, his horse, nay, even his son or his

daughter—but how much more revolting it is that one man can take another's soul by forcing him to do what destroys his spiritual ego and deprives him of spiritual welfare. And that is just what is done by these men who arrange executions, and who by bribes, threats, and deceptions calmly force men—from the judge to the hangman—to commit deeds that certainly deprive them of their true welfare though they are committed in the name of the welfare of mankind.

And while this goes on for years all over Russia, the chief culprits—those by whose order these things are done, those who could put a stop to them—fully convinced that such deeds are useful and even absolutely necessary, either compose speeches and devise methods to prevent the Finns from living as they want to live, and to compel them to live as certain Russian personages wish them to live, or else publish orders to the effect that: 'In Hussar regiments the cuffs and collars of the men's jackets are to be of the same colour as the latter, while those entitled to wear pelisses are not to have braid round the cuffs over the fur.'

What is most dreadful in the whole matter is that all this inhuman violence and killing, besides the direct evil done to the victims and their families, brings a yet more enormous evil on the whole people by spreading depravity—as fire spread amid dry straw—among every class of Russians. This depravity grows with special rapidity among the simple working folk because all these iniquities—exceeding as they do a hundredfold all that is or has been done by thieves, robbers, and all the revolutionaries put together—are done as though they were something necessary, good, and unavoidable; and are not merely excused but supported by different institutions inseparably connected in the people's minds with justice, and even with sanctity—namely, the Senate, the Synod, the Duma, the Church, and the Tsar.

And this depravity spreads with remarkable rapidity.

A short time ago there were not two executioners to be found in all Russia. In the eighties there was only one. I remember how joyfully Vladímir Solovëv then told me that no second executioner could be found in all Russia and so the one was taken from place to place. Not so now.

A small shopkeeper in Moscow whose affairs were in a bad way offered his services to perform the murders arranged by the government, and, receiving a hundred rubles (£ 10) for each person hung, soon mended his affairs so well that he no longer required this additional business and has now reverted to his former trade.

In Orël last month, as elsewhere, an executioner was wanted, and a man was immediately found who agreed with the organizers of governmental murders to do the business for fifty rubles per head. But this volunteer hangman, after making the agreement, heard that more was paid in other towns, and at the time of the execution, having put the shroud sack on the victim, instead of leading him to the scaffold, stopped, and, approaching the superintendent, said: "You must add another twenty-five rubles, your Excellency, or I won't do it!' And he got the increase and did the job.

A little later five people were to be hanged, and the day before the execution a stranger came to see the organizer of governmental murders on a private matter. The organizer went out to him, and the stranger said:

'The other day so-and-so charged you seventy-five rubles a man. I hear five are to be done to-morrow. Let me have the whole job and I'll do it at fifteen rubles a head, and you can rely on its being done properly!'

I do not know whether the offer was accepted or not, but I know it was made.

That is how the crimes committed by the government act on the worst, the least moral, of the people, and these terrible deeds must also have an influence on the majority of men of average morality. Continually hearing and reading about the most terrible inhuman brutality committed by the authorities —that is, by persons whom the people are accustomed to honour as the best of men—the majority of average people, especially the young, preoccupied with their own affairs, instead of realizing that those who do such horrible deeds are unworthy of honour, involuntarily come to the opposite conclusion and argue that if men generally honoured do things that seem to us horrible, these things cannot be as horrible as we suppose.

Of executions, hangings, murders, and bombs, people now write and speak as they used to speak about the weather. Children play at hangings. Lads from the high schools who are almost children go out on expropriating expeditions, ready to kill, just as they used to go out hunting. To kill off the large landed proprietors in order to seize their estates appears now to many people to be the very best solution of the land question.

In general, thanks to the activity of the government which has allowed killing as a means of obtaining its ends, all crimes, robbery, theft, lies, tortures, and murders are now considered by miserable people who have been perverted by that example to be most natural deeds, proper to a man.

Yes! Terrible as are the deeds themselves, the moral, spiritual, unseen evil they produce is incomparably more terrible.

You say you commit all these horrors to restore peace and order.

You restore peace and order!

By what means do you restore them? By destroying the last vestige of faith and morality in men—you, representatives of a Christian authority, leaders and teachers approved and encouraged by the servants of the Church! By committing the greatest crimes: lies, perfidy, torture of all sorts, and this last and most terrible of crimes, the one most abhorrent to every human heart that is not utterly depraved—not just a single murder but murders innumerable, which you think to justify by stupid references to such and such statutes written by yourselves in those stupid and lying books of yours which you blasphemously call 'the laws'.

You say that this is the only means of pacifying the people and quelling the revolution; but that is evidently false! It is plain that you cannot pacify the people unless you satisfy the demand of most elementary justice advanced by Russia's whole agricultural population (that is, the demand for the

abolition of private property in land) and refrain from confirming it and in various ways irritating the peasants, as well
as those unbalanced and envenomed people who have begun
a violent struggle with you. You cannot pacify people by
tormenting them and worrying, exiling, imprisoning, and
hanging women and children! However hard you may try to
stifle in yourselves the reason and love natural to human beings, you still have them within you, and need only come to
your senses and think, in order to see that by acting as you
do—that is, by taking part in such terrible crimes—you not
only fail to cure the disease, but by driving it inwards make it
worse.

That is only too evident.

The cause of what is happening does not lie in physical
events, but depends entirely on the spiritual mood of the people, which has changed and which no efforts can bring back
to its former condition, just as no efforts can turn a grown-up
man into a child again. Social irritation or tranquillity cannot
depend on whether Peter is hanged or allowed to live, or on
whether John lives in Tambóv or in penal servitude at Ner-
chínsk. Social irritation or tranquillity must depend not on
Peter or John alone but on how the great majority of the nation regard their position, and on the attitude of this majority
to the government, to landed property, to the religion taught
them, and on what this majority consider to be good or bad.
The power of events does not lie in the material conditions of
life at all, but in the spiritual condition of the people. Even if
you were to kill and torture a tenth of the Russian nation, the
spiritual condition of the rest would not become what you
desire.

So that all you are now doing, with all your searchings,
spyings, exiling, prisons, penal settlements, and gallows, does
not bring the people to the state you desire, but on the contrary increases the irritation and destroys all possibility of
peace and order.

'But what is to be done?' you say. 'What is to be done?
How are the iniquities that are now perpetrated to be
stopped?'

The answer is very simple: 'Cease to do what you are doing.'

Even if no one knew what ought to be done to pacify 'the people'—the whole people (many people know very well that what is most wanted to pacify the Russian people is the freeing of the land from private ownership, just as fifty years ago what was wanted was to free the peasants from serfdom) —if no one knew this, it would still be evident that to pacify the people one ought not to do what only increases its irritation. Yet that is just what you are doing!

What you are doing, you do not for the people but for yourselves, to retain the position you occupy, a position you consider advantageous but which is really a most pitiful and abominable one. So do not say that you do it for the people; that is not true! All the abominations you do are done for yourselves, for your own covetous, ambitious, vain, vindictive, personal ends, in order to continue for a little longer in the depravity in which you live and which seems to you desirable.

However much you may declare that all you do is done for the good of the people, men are beginning to understand you and despise you more and more, and to regard your measures of restraint and suppression not as you wish them to be regarded—as the action of some kind of higher collective Being, the government—but as the personal evil deeds of individual and evil self-seekers.

Then again you say: 'The revolutionaries began all this, not we, and their terrible crimes can only be suppressed by firm measures' (so you call your crimes) 'on the part of the government.'

You say the atrocities committed by the revolutionaries are terrible.

I do not dispute it. I will add that besides being terrible they are stupid, and—like your own actions—fall beside the mark. Yet however terrible and stupid may be their actions— all those bombs and tunnellings, those revolting murders and thefts of money—still all these deeds do not come anywhere near the criminality and stupidity of the deeds you commit.

They are doing just the same as you and for the same motives. They are in the same (I would say 'comic' were its consequences not so terrible) delusion, that men having formed for themselves a plan of what in their opinion is the desirable and proper arrangement of society, have the right and possibility of arranging other people's lives according to that plan. The delusion is the same. These methods are violence of all kinds—including taking life. And the excuse is that an evil deed committed for the benefit of many, ceases to be immoral; and that therefore without offending against the moral law, one may lie, rob, and kill whenever this tends to the realization of that supposed good condition for the many which we imagine that we know and can foresee, and which we wish to establish.

You government people call the acts of the revolutionaries 'atrocities' and 'great crimes'; but the revolutionaries have done and are doing nothing that you have not done, and done to an incomparably greater extent. They only do what you do; you keep spies, practise deception, and spread printed lies, and so do they. You take people's property by all sorts of violent means and use it as you consider best, and they do the same. You execute those whom you think dangerous, and so do they.

So you certainly cannot blame the revolutionaries while you employ the same immoral means as they do for the attainment of your aim. All that you can adduce for your own justification, they can equally adduce for theirs; not to mention that you do much evil that they do not commit, such as squandering the wealth of the nation, preparing for war, making war, subduing and oppressing foreign nationalities, and much else.

You say you have the traditions of the past to guard and the actions of the great men of the past as examples. They, too, have their traditions, also arising from the past—even before the French Revolution. And as to great men, models to copy, martyrs that perished for truth and freedom—they have no fewer of these than you.

So that if there is any difference between you it is only that you wish everything to remain as it has been and is, while they wish for a change. And in thinking that everything cannot always remain as it has been they would be more right than you, had they not adopted from you that curious, destructive delusion that one set of men can know the form of life suitable for all men in the future, and that this form can be established by force. For the rest they only do what you do, using the same means. They are altogether your disciples. They have, as the saying is, picked up all your little dodges. They are not only your disciples, they are your products, your children. If you did not exist neither would they; so that when you try to suppress them by force you behave like a man who presses with his whole weight against a door that opens towards him.

If there be any difference between you and them, it is certainly not in your favour but in theirs. The mitigating circumstances on their side are, firstly, that their crimes are committed under conditions of greater personal danger than you are exposed to, and risks and danger excuse much in the eyes of impressionable youth. Secondly, the immense majority of them are quite young people to whom it is natural to go astray, while you for the most part are men of mature age— old men to whom reasoned calm and leniency towards the deluded should be natural. A third mitigating circumstance in their favour is that however odious their murders may be, they are still not so coldly, systematically cruel as are your Schlüsselburgs, transportations, gallows, and shootings. And a fourth mitigating circumstance for the revolutionaries is that they all quite categorically repudiate all religious teaching and consider that the end justifies the means. Therefore when they kill one or more men for the sake of the imaginary welfare of the majority, they act quite consistently; whereas you government men—from the lowest hangman to the highest official—all support religion and Christianity, which is altogether incompatible with the deeds you commit.

And it is you elderly men, leaders of other men, professing Christianity, it is you who say, like children who have been fighting, 'We didn't begin—they did!' That is the best you can say—you who have taken on yourselves the role of rulers of the people. And what sort of men are you? Men who acknowledge as God one who most definitely forbade not only judgement and punishment, but even condemnation of others; one who in clearest terms repudiated all punishment, and affirmed the necessity of continual forgiveness however often a crime may be repeated; one who commanded us to turn the other cheek to the smiter, and not return evil for evil; one who in the case of the woman sentenced to be stoned, showed so simply and clearly the impossibility of judgement and punishment between man and man. And you, acknowledging that teacher to be God, can find nothing better to say in your defence than: 'They began it! They kill people, so let us kill them!'

An artist of my acquaintance thought of painting a picture of an execution, and he wanted a model for the executioner. He heard that the duty of executioner in Moscow was at that time performed by a watchman, so he went to the watchman's house. It was Easter-time. The family were sitting in their best clothes at the tea-table, but the master of the house was not there. It turned out afterwards that on catching sight of a stranger he had hidden himself. His wife also seemed abashed, and said that her husband was not at home; but his little girl betrayed him by saying: 'Daddy's in the garret.' She did not know that her father was aware that what he did was evil and therefore could not help being afraid of everybody. The artist explained to the wife that he wanted her husband as a model because his face suited the picture he had planned (of course he did not say what the picture was). Having got into conversation with the wife, the artist, in order to conciliate her, offered to take her little son as a pupil, an offer which evidently tempted her. She went out and after a time the husband entered, morose, rest-less, frightened, and looking askance. For a long time he tried to get the artist to say why he required just him. When the artist told him he had met him in the street and his face seemed suitable to the projected picture, the watchman asked where had he met him? At what time? In what clothes? And he would not come to terms, evidently fearing and suspecting something bad.

Yes, this executioner at first-hand knows that he is an executioner, he knows that he does wrong and is therefore hated, and he is afraid of men: and I think that this consciousness and this fear before men atone for at least a part of his guilt. But none of you—from the Secretary of the Court to the Premier and the Tsar—who are indirect participators in the iniquities perpetrated every day, seem to feel your guilt or the shame that your participation in these horrors ought to evoke. It is true that like the executioner you fear men, and the greater your responsibility for the crimes the more your fear: the Public Prosecutor feels more fear than the Secretary; the President of the Court more than the Public Prosecutor; the General Governor more than the President; the President of the Council of Ministers more still, and the Tsar most of all. You are all afraid, but unlike the executioner you are afraid not because you know you are doing evil, but because you think other people do evil.

Therefore I think that, low as that unfortunate watchman has fallen, he is morally immeasurably higher than you participators and part authors of these awful crimes: you who condemn others instead of yourselves and carry your heads so high.

I know that men are but human, that we are all weak, that we all err, and that one cannot judge another. I have long struggled against the feeling that was and is aroused in me by those responsible for these awful crimes, and aroused the more the higher they stand on the social ladder. But I cannot and will not struggle against that feeling any longer.

I cannot and will not. First, because an exposure of these people who do not see the full criminality of their actions is necessary for them as well as for the multitude which, influenced by the external honour and laudation accorded to these people, approves their terrible deeds and even tries to imitate them. And secondly because (I frankly confess it) I hope my exposure of those men will in one way or other evoke the expulsion I desire from the set in which I am now living, and in which I cannot but feel myself a participant in the crimes committed around me.

Everything now being done in Russia is done in the name of the general welfare, in the name of the protection and tranquillity of the people of Russia. And if this be so, then it is also done for me who live in Russia. For me, therefore, exists the destitution of the people deprived of the first and most natural right of man—the right to use the land on which he is born; for me those half-million men torn away from wholesome peasant life and dressed in uniforms and taught to kill; for me that false so-called priesthood whose chief duty it is to pervert and conceal true Christianity; for me all these transportations of men from place to place; for me these hundreds of thousands of hungry migratory workmen; for me these hundreds of thousands of unfortunates dying of typhus and scurvy in the fortresses and prisons which are insufficient for such a multitude; for me the mothers, wives, and fathers of the exiles, the prisoners, and those who are hanged, are suffering; for me are these spies and this bribery; for me the interment of these dozens and hundreds of men who have been shot; for me the horrible work of these hangmen goes on—who were at first enlisted with difficulty but now no longer so loathe their work; for me exist these gallows with well-soaped cords from which hang women, children, and peasants; and for me exists this terrible embitterment of man against his fellow man.

Strange as it seems to say that all this is done for me, and that I am a participator in these terrible deeds, I cannot but feel that there is an indubitable interdependence between my spacious room, my dinner, my clothing, my leisure, and the terrible crimes committed to get rid of those who would like to take from me what I have. And though I know that these homeless, embittered, depraved people—who but for the government's threats would deprive me of all I am using—are products of that same government's actions, still I cannot help feeling that at present my peace really is dependent on all the horrors that are now being perpetrated by the government.

And being conscious of this I can no longer endure it, but must free myself from this intolerable position!

It is impossible to live so! I, at any rate, cannot and will not live so.

That is why I write this and will circulate it by all means in my power both in Russia and abroad—that one of two things may happen: either that these inhuman deeds may be stopped, or that my connexion with them may be snapped and I put in prison, where I may be clearly conscious that these horrors are not committed on my behalf; or still better (so good that I dare not even dream of such happiness) that they may put on me, as on those twelve or twenty peasants, a shroud and a cap and may push me also off a bench, so that by my own weight I may tighten the well-soaped noose round my old throat.

To attain one of these two aims I address myself to all participators in these terrible deeds, beginning with those who put on their brother men and women and children those caps and nooses—from the prison warders up to you, chief organizers and authorizers of these terrible crimes.

Brother men! Come to your senses, stop and think, consider what you are doing! Remember who you are!

Before being hangmen, generals, public prosecutors, judges, premier or Tsar, are you not men—to-day allowed a peep into God's world, to-morrow ceasing to be? (You hangmen of all grades in particular, who have evoked and are evoking special hatred, should remember this.) Is it possible that you who have had this brief glimpse of God's world (for even if you be not murdered, death is always close behind us all), is it possible that in your lucid moments you do not see that your vocation in life cannot be to torment and kill men; your-selves trembling with fear of being killed, lying to yourselves, to others, and to God, assuring yourselves and others that by participating in these things you are doing an important and grand work for the welfare of millions? Is it possible that—when not intoxicated by your surroundings, by flattery, and by the customary sophistries—you do not each one of you know that this is all mere talk, only invented that, while doing most evil deeds, you may still consider yourself a good man? You cannot but know that you, like each of us, have but one real duty which includes all others—the duty of living the short space granted us in accord with the Will that sent you into this world, and of leaving it in accord with that Will. And that Will desires only one thing: love from man to man.

But what are you doing? To what are you devoting your spiritual strength? Whom do you love? Who loves you? Your wife? Your child? But that is not love. The love of wife and children is not human love. Animals love in that way even more strongly. Human love is the love of man for man—for every man as a son of God and therefore a brother. Whom do you love in that way? No one. Who loves you in that way? No one.

You are feared as a hangman or a wild animal is feared. People flatter you because at heart they despise and hate you—and how they hate you! And you know it and are afraid of men.

Yes, consider it—all you accomplices in murder from the highest to the lowest, consider who you are and cease to do what you are doing. Cease, not for your own sakes, not for the sake of your own personality, not for the sake of men, not that you may cease to be blamed, but for your soul's sake and for the God who lives within you!

[1908.]

The Best of the World's Best Books
COMPLETE LIST OF TITLES IN
THE MODERN LIBRARY

76 ADAMS, HENRY: *The Education of Henry Adams*
310 AESCHYLUS: *The Complete Greek Tragedies*, Vol. I
311 AESCHYLUS: *The Complete Greek Tragedies*, Vol. II
101 AIKEN, CONRAD (Editor): *A Comprehensive Anthology of American Poetry*
127 AIKEN, CONRAD (Editor): *20th-Century American Poetry*
145 ALEICHEM, SHOLOM: *Selected Stories*
104 ANDERSON, SHERWOOD: *Winesburg, Ohio*
259 AQUINAS, ST. THOMAS: *Introduction to St. Thomas Aquinas*
248 ARISTOTLE: *Introduction to Aristotle*
228 ARISTOTLE: *Politics*
246 ARISTOTLE: *Rhetoric and Poetics*
160 AUDEN, W. H.: *Selected Poetry*
263 AUGUSTINE, ST.: *Confessions*
264 AUSTEN, JANE: *Pride and Prejudice* and *Sense and Sensibility*

256 BACON, FRANCIS: *Selected Writings*
299 BALZAC: *Cousin Bette*
193 BALZAC: *Droll Stories*
245 BALZAC: *Père Goriot* and *Eugénie Grandet*
116 BEERBOHM, MAX: *Zuleika Dobson*
22 BELLAMY, EDWARD: *Looking Backward*
184 BENNETT, ARNOLD: *The Old Wives' Tale*
231 BERGSON, HENRI: *Creative Evolution*
285 BLAKE, WILLIAM: *Selected Poetry and Prose*
71 BOCCACCIO: *The Decameron*
282 BOSWELL, JAMES: *The Life of Samuel Johnson*
64 BRONTË, CHARLOTTE: *Jane Eyre*
106 BRONTË, EMILY: *Wuthering Heights*
198 BROWNING, ROBERT: *Selected Poetry*
15 BUCK, PEARL: *The Good Earth*
32 BURCKHARDT, JACOB: *The Civilization of the Renaissance in [Italy*
241 BURK, JOHN N.: *The Life and Works of Beethoven*
289 BURKE, EDMUND: *Selected Writings*
136 BUTLER, SAMUEL: *Erewhon* and *Erewhon Revisited*
13 BUTLER, SAMUEL: *The Way of All Flesh*
195 BYRON, LORD: *Selected Poetry*
24 BYRON, LORD: *Don Juan*

295 CAESAR, JULIUS: *The Gallic War and Other Writings*
51 CALDWELL, ERSKINE· *God's Little Acre*

249 CALDWELL, ERSKINE: *Tobacco Road*
352 CAMUS, ALBERT: *The Fall & Exile and the Kingdom*
109 CAMUS, ALBERT: *The Plague*
339 CAMUS, ALBERT: *Resistance, Rebellion and Death*
 79 CARROLL, LEWIS: *Alice in Wonderland*, etc.
165 CASANOVA, JACQUES: *Memoirs of Casanova*
150 CELLINI, BENVENUTO: *Autobiography of Cellini*
174 CERVANTES: *Don Quixote*
161 CHAUCER: *The Canterbury Tales*
171 CHEKHOV, ANTON: *Best Plays*
 50 CHEKHOV, ANTON: *Short Stories*
272 CICERO: *Basic Works*
279 COLERIDGE: *Selected Poetry and Prose*
251 COLETTE: *Six Novels*
235 COMMAGER, HENRY STEELE & NEVINS, ALLAN: *A Short History of the United States*
306 CONFUCIUS: *The Wisdom of Confucius*
186 CONRAD, JOSEPH: *Lord Jim*
275 CONRAD, JOSEPH: *Nostromo*
 34 CONRAD, JOSEPH: *Victory*
105 COOPER, JAMES FENIMORE: *The Pathfinder*
194 CORNEILLE & RACINE: *Six Plays by Corneille and Racine*
130 CRANE, STEPHEN: *The Red Badge of Courage*
214 CUMMINGS, E. E.: *The Enormous Room*

236 DANA, RICHARD HENRY: *Two Years Before the Mast*
208 DANTE: *The Divine Comedy*
122 DEFOE, DANIEL: *Moll Flanders*
 92 DEFOE, DANIEL: *Robinson Crusoe* and *A Journal of the Plague Year*
 43 DESCARTES, RENÉ: *Philosophical Writings*
173 DEWEY, JOHN: *Human Nature and Conduct*
348 DEWEY, JOHN: *John Dewey on Education*
110 DICKENS, CHARLES: *David Copperfield*
204 DICKENS, CHARLES: *Pickwick Papers*
308 DICKENS, CHARLES: *Our Mutual Friend*
189 DICKENS, CHARLES: *A Tale of Two Cities*
 25 DICKINSON, EMILY: *Selected Poems*
 23 DINESEN, ISAK: *Out of Africa*
 54 DINESEN, ISAK: *Seven Gothic Tales*
 12 DONNE, JOHN: *Complete Poetry and Selected Prose*
205 DOS PASSOS, JOHN: *Three Soldiers*
293 DOSTOYEVSKY, FYODOR: *Best Short Stories*
151 DOSTOYEVSKY, FYODOR: *The Brothers Karamazov*
199 DOSTOYEVSKY, FYODOR: *Crime and Punishment*
 55 DOSTOYEVSKY, FYODOR: *The Possessed*
  5 DOUGLAS, NORMAN: *South Wind*
206 DOYLE, SIR ARTHUR CONAN: *The Adventure and Memoirs of Sherlock Holmes*
  8 DREISER, THEODORE: *Sister Carrie*
 69 DUMAS, ALEXANDRE: *Camille*
143 DUMAS, ALEXANDRE: *The Three Musketeers*
227 DU MAURIER, DAPHNE: *Rebecca*

338 ELLISON, RALPH: *Invisible Man*
192 EMERSON, RALPH WALDO: *The Journals*

91   EMERSON, RALPH WALDO: *Essays and Other Writings*
331   ERASMUS, DESIDERIUS: *The Praise of Folly*
314   EURIPIDES: *The Complete Greek Tragedies*, Vol. V
315   EURIPIDES: *The Complete Greek Tragedies*, Vol. VI
316   EURIPIDES: *The Complete Greek Tragedies*, Vol. VII

271   FAULKNER, WILLIAM: *Absalom, Absalom!*
175   FAULKNER, WILLIAM: *Go Down, Moses*
351   FAULKNER, WILLIAM: *Intruder in the Dust*
88   FAULKNER, WILLIAM: *Light in August*
61   FAULKNER, WILLIAM: *Sanctuary*   [*Dying*
187   FAULKNER, WILLIAM: *The Sound and the Fury* and *As I Lay*
324   FAULKNER, WILLIAM: *Selected Short Stories*
117   FIELDING, HENRY: *Joseph Andrews*
185   FIELDING, HENRY: *Tom Jones*
28   FLAUBERT, GUSTAVE: *Madame Bovary*
102   FORESTER, C. S.: *The African Queen*
210   FRANCE, ANATOLE: *Penguin Island*
298   FRANK, ANNE: *Diary of a Young Girl*
39   FRANKLIN, BENJAMIN: *Autobiography*, etc.
96   FREUD, SIGMUND: *The Interpretation of Dreams*

36   GEORGE, HENRY: *Progress and Poverty*
327   GIDE, ANDRÉ: *The Counterfeiters*
177   GOETHE: *Faust*
40   GOGOL, NIKOLAI: *Dead Souls*
291   GOLDSMITH, OLIVER: *The Vicar of Wakefield and Other*
20   GRAVES, ROBERT: *I, Claudius*   [*Writings*
286   GUNTHER, JOHN: *Death Be Not Proud*

265   HACKETT, FRANCIS: *The Personal History of Henry the Eighth*
163   HAGGARD, H. RIDER: *She* and *King Solomon's Mines*
320   HAMILTON, EDITH: *The Greek Way*
135   HARDY, THOMAS: *Jude the Obscure*
17   HARDY, THOMAS: *The Mayor of Casterbridge*
121   HARDY, THOMAS: *The Return of the Native*
72   HARDY, THOMAS: *Tess of the D'Urbervilles*
233   HART & KAUFMAN: *Six Plays*
329   HART, MOSS: *Act One*
250   HARTE, BRET: *Best Stories*
93   HAWTHORNE, NATHANIEL: *The Scarlet Letter*
239   HEGEL: *The Philosophy of Hegel*
223   HELLMAN, LILLIAN: *Six Plays*
26   HENRY, O.: *Best Short Stories*
255   HERODOTUS: *The Persian Wars*
328   HERSEY, JOHN: *Hiroshima*
334   HESSE, HERMAN: *Steppenwolf*
166   HOMER: *The Iliad*
167   HOMER: *The Odyssey*
141   HORACE: *Complete Works*
302   HOWARD, JOHN TASKER: *World's Great Operas*
277   HOWELLS, WILLIAM DEAN: *The Rise of Silas Lapham*
89   HUDSON, W. H.: *Green Mansions*
35   HUGO, VICTOR: *The Hunchback of Notre Dame*
340   HUME, DAVID: *Philosophy*
209   HUXLEY, ALDOUS: *Antic Hay*

 48 HUXLEY, ALDOUS: *Brave New World*
180 HUXLEY, ALDOUS: *Point Counter Point*

305 IBSEN, HENRIK: *Six Plays*
307 IBSEN, HENRIK: *The Wild Duck and Other Plays*
240 IRVING, WASHINGTON: *Selected Writings*

 16 JAMES, HENRY: *The Bostonians*
107 JAMES, HENRY: *The Portrait of a Lady*
169 JAMES, HENRY: *The Turn of the Screw*
269 JAMES, HENRY: *Washington Square*
244 JAMES, HENRY: *The Wings of the Dove*
114 JAMES, WILLIAM: *The Philosophy of William James*
 70 JAMES, WILLIAM: *The Varieties of Religious Experience*
234 JEFFERSON, THOMAS: *The Life and Selected Writings*
124 JOYCE, JAMES: *Dubliners*
300 JUNG, C. G.: *Basic Writings*

318 KAFKA, FRANZ: *The Trial*
283 KAFKA, FRANZ: *Selected Stories*
297 KANT: *Critique of Pure Reason*
266 KANT: *The Philosophy of Kant*
233 KAUFMAN & HART: *Six Plays*
273 KEATS: *Complete Poetry and Selected Prose*
303 KIERKEGAARD, SØREN: *A Kierkegaard Anthology*
 99 KIPLING, RUDYARD: *Kim*
 74 KOESTLER, ARTHUR: *Darkness at Noon*

262 LAOTSE: *The Wisdom of Laotse*
148 LAWRENCE, D. H.: *Lady Chatterley's Lover*
128 LAWRENCE, D. H.: *The Rainbow*
333 LAWRENCE, D. H.: *Sons and Lovers*
 68 LAWRENCE, D. H.: *Women in Love*
252 LEWIS, SINCLAIR: *Dodsworth*
221 LEWIS, SINCLAIR: *Cass Timberlane*
325 LIVY: *A History of Rome*
 56 LONGFELLOW, HENRY W.: *Poems*
 77 LOUYS, PIERRE: *Aphrodite*
 95 LUDWIG, EMIL: *Napoleon*

 65 MACHIAVELLI: *The Prince and The Discourses*
321 MAILER, NORMAN: *The Naked and the Dead*
317 MALAMUD, BERNARD: *Two Novels*
 33 MALRAUX, ANDRÉ: *Man's Fate*
309 MALTHUS, THOMAS ROBERT: *On Population*
182 MARQUAND, JOHN P.: *The Late George Apley*
202 MARX, KARL: *Capital and Other Writings*
 14 MAUGHAM, W. SOMERSET: *Best Short Stories*
270 MAUGHAM, W. SOMERSET: *Cakes and Ale*
 27 MAUGHAM, W. SOMERSET: *The Moon and Sixpence*
176 MAUGHAM, W. SOMERSET: *Of Human Bondage*
 98 MAUPASSANT, GUY DE: *Best Short Stories*
 46 MAUROIS, ANDRÉ: *Disraeli*
119 MELVILLE, HERMAN: *Moby Dick*
253 MEREDITH, GEORGE: *The Egoist*
134 MEREDITH, GEORGE: *The Ordeal of Richard Feverel*
138 MEREJKOWSKI, DMITRI: *The Romance of Leonardo da Vinci*
296 MICHENER, JAMES A.: *Selected Writings*